ANDREW ORDOVER

THE CAT
CAME
BACK

Crafting-a-Life Books

2016

ISBN: 0-98989 69-4-3
ISBN-13: 978-0-9898969-4-8

For my Mona Lisas and Mad Hatters

For my Mona Lisas and Mad Hatters

Drop your jack in the old juke box,
Play your favorite disc.
When you dance with the bobby socks,
You dance at your own risk.

Alec Wilder/Benny Goodman

Keep away from the little deaths.

Carl Sandburg

Part One

1

Tits McGraw, I'm calling you out. I know it's been a few years, and maybe you think it's unfair to dredge the whole thing up—but if you hadn't brought me to that god-awful play, I never would have met the kid. And if I hadn't met the kid, the rest of it wouldn't have happened.

I don't know—maybe you don't see it that way. Maybe you don't even think about it. But I do. A lot. If he hadn't come to me—if I hadn't pushed him away—if I hadn't been there, in the middle of it...

But what's the use? He did, and I did, and I *was* there, in the middle of it. And that's just how the music played out for that particular song. Minor-key blues. I can't change what it was. But I sure wouldn't mind if the tune stopped playing on endless rotation in my head. I wouldn't mind that at all.

It started like this: I was on my way to La Fonda Latina for my usual Friday lunch. I had spent the whole morning watching a redneck cop grill a poor, old woman who thought someone had broken into her house. It was almost Thanksgiving, and the weather was gross. Not kind-of-hot or sort-of-humid, but seriously gross.

Yeah. I know. I'm talking about the weather. *Again.* I can't help it. I've lived in the South for years now, but somehow, being a Yankee at heart, I still get pissed off and moody when Halloween rolls around and it's 90 degrees and I'm having to change my shirt halfway through the day and it still doesn't help.

Anyway. We were having lunch. Kate was telling us about these love notes that some girl named Michelle had been leaving on her windshield. Kate had never met this girl or caught her in the act. She had no idea who the girl was, or how the girl had found her, or why the girl was fixated on her. We were all fascinated by the mystery, which, thankfully, nobody asked me to solve.

Porkchop, whose imagination runs in the straightest and most direct line to porn, was enthralled. He had some predictable suggestions about how Kate could take the story to "the next level," which led Kate to smack him in the arm. Kate being angular and bony, her punch should have been painful. But Porkchop being round and doughy after nearly a decade of not playing rugby, it didn't seem to have any effect. He just smiled. Porkchop is the kind of guy who sees getting punched by a woman as an act of flirtation, even when it comes from a close friend who has made it very clear that she's never, ever going to sleep with him. It's hopeless, but you've got to admire the guy's optimism.

Porkchop's comment and Kate's punch stopped the conversation cold, which is a capital offense in this crowd. After about four seconds, Kitty yelled, "Lull!" at the top of her lungs, which made everybody laugh. Any time Kitty yells, it's funny, because Kitty is about five feet tall, and most of that is hair.

To fill the gap before Kitty could yell again, Patty started telling us about a show she had been working on at Candler College, which was opening that very night and which we Absolutely Had To See. As usual, everyone made some lame excuse and begged off, and, as usual, I had no excuse, lame or otherwise, which left me as the sucker. I could have made something up, but Patty has always been a good friend. She comes out to see my band whenever we have a gig, so when she works on a show, I try to go see it. I call it Social Obligation Theatre.

Patty is a beautiful, buxom redhead who we used to call Tits McGraw back in college, which we thought was really funny, because McGraw isn't even close to her name. Nowadays, she works as a stage manager at every theatre around town. This is also amusing, because stage managers dress in black and hide in the dark, wearing headphones—things most beautiful, buxom redheads don't do. Some people say Patty went into stage management to avoid the spotlight and stop having people call her Tits, but that's ridiculous, because we all still call her that.

No, the truth is that Patty is a geek, and she doesn't care who knows it. She turns heads wherever she goes, but she loves doing the dirty, grungy, backstage work. And she's really good at it. Patty once found a chamber pot someone needed for a play—a chamber pot, just lying around somewhere in modern-day Atlanta. I know this because she brought it to lunch that week. She plopped it right down on the table in the midst of our food, causing all of us to stare dumbly at it until Kitty yelled, "Lull!"

Patty doesn't ask me to see every awful show she works on, any more than I beg her to see every shitty gig I play. So when she asks, I try to go, even when it's a student production, like this atrocity was going to be.

If you think I'm being unfair, you haven't seen college theatre. I have. There's always a lot of shouting, a lot of crying, and, sometimes, a little nudity. Unless it's a more avant-garde kind of play, in which case there's less crying and more nudity. You'd think at least the nudity would be entertaining, but it never is. It's just uncomfortable. Especially if you're in the front row. But Patty was my friend, so I said I'd go.

First, though, I headed downtown to my little office. There wasn't much going on, but I had some client reports to finish, and it seemed like a reasonably virtuous way to round out the workweek. I called Susannah and informed her that we were going to Candler to see some play whose name I had already forgotten. She groaned and told me that I owed her, big time, which I already knew. And we made plans to meet near campus for dinner.

I accuse Susannah of being a philistine, but it's just part of our New York Jew vs. Southern Tomboy comedy routine. She actually has a lot more patience for Arty Art than I have. Deep down, I'm still a suburban schmo from Long Island who once played in an all-bass band called Fuck Guitars…which we thought was a classy name.

But that night, I was vindicated. The play was every bit as terrible as I thought it was going to be, and maybe even a little worse. First of all, it had all this *chanting*—from a chorus of women sitting on one side of the stage, rocking back and forth and looking really unhappy. All night long, chanting, with occasional breaks for moaning.

Here's a free tip for you, by the way: if you ever find yourself at a play that isn't a musical, but the program says there's a bunch of people called the Chorus, *run*.

There were also masks. What I just said about choruses goes double for masks. Even if it *is* a musical, if you see them putting on masks, head for the exit. Because a play like that, if you don't make your move soon, they might lock you inside for the duration. They might even throw stuff at you. You never know, when it's Art.

The only interesting thing about this play was that it was written by a guy. And this was interesting because the play was a total diatribe against men, and dicks, and men who acted like dicks, and the "male gaze," which is something I dimly remembered from a Women's Lit class I took back in college, when everything seemed profound.

The play was about a beauty pageant winner and swimsuit model, and how she got pissed off and radicalized to the point that she started parading around in bikinis made of steak. According to the program, it was a true story. Anyway, it was *based* on a true story. The actual events did not involve masks or chanting, I'm pretty sure. But they did involve a steak bikini, which, if you ask me, would have been arty enough all by itself.

Anyway, it was terrible, and it was long, and when it was over, we had to hang around to tell Patty how great it had been, because that's what you do at Social Obligation Theatre.

"Cool, right?" she said, when she emerged from backstage in her stage manager ninja outfit.

"Sure," I agreed.

"It totally changed my outlook," Susannah said, one-upping me.

"Me, too!" said Patty, nodding her head vigorously.

"And a guy wrote it?" I said.

"Yeah. A sophomore. Scary smart. You want to meet him?" And before I could say Please God No, she reached out to grab the author, dragging him over to us.

"Chris Tremaine," she announced. "Chris, these are my friends, Jordan and Susannah."

The kid was a couple of inches shorter than me, but he looked even smaller. He was painfully skinny, and either his head was too big for his body or his body was too scrawny for his head. Either way, he was all out of proportion. His face was a little zitty and a little babyish, but he had an intense and serious look on his face. He shook our hands and thanked us for coming. He was painfully sincere.

"Jordan's a detective," Patty said, for no particular reason.

"Seriously?" said the kid, leaning forward a little bit, like he was trying to sniff me. "That's intense."

"Actually, it's pretty boring most of the time," I said.

"Are you a cop, or are you like a PI or something?"

"I'm exactly like a PI," I said.

"But lazier," added my wife.

The kid nodded for too many seconds and then said, "So…did you like the play?"

I hate that question. Because, first of all, how rude is it to put someone on the spot like that? You've got to say Yes, no matter what, just to be polite, and whoever is asking knows this, so why bother asking? There's no way for him to know whether he's hearing the truth or not, so the whole thing is just an act. More theatre.

But I must have been in a surly mood or something, because instead of just saying Yes, I said, "I don't know, man. Was it supposed to be likable?"

And apparently, this was the perfect thing to say. Because scrawny Chris broke out in a zitty, shit-eating grin, and said, "Exactly!"

"He wrote a play about Charles Manson last semester," Patty said proudly, rubbing his stringy hair like he was a puppy or something.

"Well, Brecht said art should be a hammer, not a mirror," the kid said, trying to escape Patty's mothering.

We all nodded, saying nothing, pretending to understand what the fuck he had just said.

Without Kitty on hand to yell "Lull!" Susannah and I had to navigate our own way out of the silence and make a polite exit, which we did as quickly as we could. But just as we were exiting the lobby, I felt a tug on my sleeve. It was my new best friend.

"Hey," he said, looking nervous.

"Hey yourself," I replied.

"Can I ask you something?" He looked nervously over my shoulder at Susannah.

I got the hint. "Sure," I said, steering him a few feet away, to something like privacy. "What's up?"

"Well," he said, studying his sneakers, "I was just wondering if…I mean, the kind of stuff you do…"

"Yeah?"

"Well, is it for…I mean, could just anybody…you know…"

I knew, but I left him hanging. It was cruel, but he deserved it after the torture he had put me through all evening.

He finally met my eyes. "I mean, if *I* had a question…something I needed advice about…something in your…area…could I…like…talk to you about it?"

"Sure," I said, letting him off the hook. "I always give a free consult for artists."

"Oh. Great. Okay. That's good to know."

He nodded and said nothing.

"So what's the problem?" I prompted.

"Oh! Nothing. I mean…I shouldn't. Not here. You know? Maybe…maybe some other time?"

"Okay. Well…you give me a call if you want. I didn't bring my card with me, but you can look me up. Barnes Investigations."

"Wait…what?"

"Barnes. Billy Barnes. It's my nom de plume. Nom de…guerre. Whatever. It's the name of the company."

"Okay." He nodded two or three times, more to reassure himself than to communicate anything to me. Then he said, "Thanks," and trotted back into the theatre.

"What was that all about?" Susannah asked, when I rejoined her.

"Hell if I know," I said. "He wants to talk to me about something."

"Interesting."

"Not really. Ten bucks says I never hear from him."

She looked back at his skinny, retreating form and said, "I'll cover all of it."

It was a nice night (the temperature had plummeted to 80), so we decided to walk across campus and get a drink before heading home. We strolled quietly, holding hands, listening to the chirps of birds and undergrads.

"Well," I said, "I don't know about you, but I feel about a thousand years old."

She leaned into me. "They get younger all the time, don't they?"

"Seriously. And look at this place—you can barely recognize it, all the new stuff they keep building."

"If you say so."

"Oh. Right," I said. I've known her for so long, I sometimes forget Susannah didn't go to school with me, Patty, and the rest. "Thank God," I said.

"For what?"

I stared at her, confused for a moment, until I realized I had been responding to my own interior monologue. Typical.

"Never mind," I said. "I was just thinking about those days. It's good you didn't know me then."

"Kate and Kitty knew you then. They still put up with you."

"Yeah, but I didn't go out with them."

Susannah laughed. "And what makes you think you could have gone out with *me*, mister man?"

"I didn't say I could have," I said. "But I sure would have tried."

"I'll bet," she said.

We walked in silence for a while, the campus wrapping itself around me a little too tightly. Susannah said nothing to break the spell, so I grasped at whatever small talk I could come up with.

"So," I said. "The play changed your whole outlook, huh?"

"Absolutely," she said.

"You're so full of shit."

"No, it's true. I came to an important realization. Like an epiphany, almost."

"Epiphany. Get you. All right, Bobby Sue, what was this great epiphany you had?"

"I realized that, since Patty was your friend first, you can go to her goddamn shows by yourself from now on."

"No…" I groaned. "You can't do that to me."

"Sorry. I'm done. I already do Social Obligation Music for you."

"Yeah, but you get drinks at *my* gigs."

"Even so," she said. "I'm drawing the line."

I stumbled along behind her, wounded, and then fell to the ground. She stopped, turned around, and stood over me.

"Jordan Greenblatt," she said sternly, "if you insist on making me spend a whole evening in the dark with you, there's better things we could be doing."

I looked up at her quickly. "No masks, though, right?"

"No masks," she said. "Maybe some moaning, if you're lucky."

She smiled sweetly, turned on her heel, and headed for the car.

I followed happily until a grand piano of realization dropped on my head. Susannah turned back to me. "What's the matter?"

"I can't," I said.

"Can't what?"

"Any of it. I can't. I have to work."

She cocked her head to one side and put her hands on her hips, in that adorably southern way of hers. And she said,

"What the fuck, Jordan? It's Friday night. We were going to get a drink, at least."

"I know, I know," I said, uselessly. "I forgot. I promised Carter I'd do a thing for him."

"What kind of a thing?" she asked.

"A stakeout thing," I said. "It's stupid. But I said I'd do it as a favor."

In my line of work, it's important to do favors for cops when you get the chance. She knew that. Not that it made things any better.

She sidled up to me and purred, "Poor baby. You want some company?" She traced a sharp fingernail up my leg, and breathed into my ear. "Those stakeouts can be so long…and hard…"

That's my wife—always with the helping hand.

2

I dropped Susannah at her car and headed down to Grant Park, where I had been with my friend Carter Wiggins earlier that morning. It was a quiet area near the zoo, where a couple of houses had allegedly had break-ins. When Carter, a sergeant at the midtown precinct, had first briefed me over the phone, he had used the word "allegedly" at least five times. The story had holes all over it, and he was suspicious. The victim he interviewed was an ancient southern belle, living alone, who couldn't quite remember which items had been taken. She just had a vague sense that things had gone missing in the night, and that the harmony of her home had been violated. I accused Carter of being a heartless bastard for refusing to believe the old lady, but he swore that her testimony came pre-impeached, as she kept confusing him with one of her grandsons who lived down in Valdosta and was apparently dating a stripper.

Since the second victim threatened to be just as old and daft as the first, Carter had begged me to tag along with him to let him know if he was just too jaded to protect and serve. I drove out with him early in the morning and stood in the living room while he spoke with the woman, keeping quiet to watch and listen. On the way back to his car, I gave him my learned opinion.

"She's a nice old lady," I offered.

"Crazy as a Claxton fruitcake," he said with a growl.

"She could be your grandmother," I said.

"Damn straight," he said. "That's why I know what I'm talking about."

We climbed into his car and he sighed, looking back up at the ramshackle, old house.

"So what do you think, J?" he said. "Could be something going on?"

"Could be," I said. "It *is* two different houses, two different nights."

"Yeah, two houses, same loony-as-shit story," he said. "That's the problem. They get together, these old ladies. They sit around the porch, drinking sweet tea. Chatter all day about this and that. One of them gets an idea in her head, they all got the same idea by sundown."

"Could be," I said.

"Could be she took her TV to the pawnshop and forgot about it."

"Could be. Or could be somebody took it."

"Who? Some international fucking cat burglar? You see any sign of forced entry?"

"I saw what you saw."

He nodded.

"Maybe the stripper-dating grandson took it," I offered.

He sucked his teeth. He didn't look happy.

"Aaah, you like her," I said, poking him in the ribs.

He batted my hand away. "Course I like her. I liked the first one, too. What the fuck am I supposed to do about it, though? Cap's never gonna let me put a cruiser on the street all night. Not for this."

I thought about the old woman for a moment, and then said, "You could put an old VW on the street."

"You?"

"Why not? Look, if the guy hits two houses on the same street, two nights in a row, chances are he's coming back for a third."

"If he exists," Carter sighed. He thought about it for a second, then said, "Man, I hate to waste your time like that."

I shrugged. "You'll make it up to me, someday."

"All right," he said. "But just tonight. Nobody shows, we file and forget. All right?"

I nodded. "Sounds good."

And that is why, instead of frolicking in bed with my lovely wife on a Friday night, I found myself sitting alone in my car, parked at the end of a sleepy street, keeping an eye on a whole lot of nothing. Obviously, I would have preferred keeping my eye on Susannah, but having her along for the ride was not a good idea. You've got to stay focused and sharp when you're on a stakeout so you can catch the one, tiny flash of movement you've been waiting for—the one, tiny flash that might be all you ever get. And that's hard to do when you're busy pulling off somebody's clothes.

Better by yourself. Work is work.

The problem is, it's hard to stay awake on night jobs like this when you're out in a public place. You can't read or watch a movie. First of all, you don't want to be shining any lights, and second, you'll end up missing what you've been waiting for. But you also don't want to daydream too much and get lost in your head. So I listened to music on my iPod and imagined intricate bass-lines, fingering them on my steering wheel and trying not to think about where else my hands could have been. And I watched the street.

Fortunately, I didn't have to watch all night. At about two in the morning, a car turned onto the far end of the street and turned off its headlights. It glided to a stop and a figure in dark clothes stepped out, closing the door behind him very quietly.

Guess the old ladies weren't crazy after all.

The figure walked silently toward one of the houses, avoiding streetlights and porch lights and anything else that would have illuminated him (I could see just enough to guess that it was a guy, but that's all). He stood in front of a large, first-story window for about five seconds, then opened the window effortlessly and slipped inside like an eel. The guy was good.

I grabbed my cell phone and called Carter's precinct. He had let the night shift know I was going to be watching the street, to be ready to move if something happened. A cop named Lewis picked up the phone, but before I could get a whole sentence out, the burglar was already slipping out the window with an armload of loot. I cursed into the phone and told Lewis to get on the road as fast as he could. But it was too late. The man was already in his car and heading back down the street. He made the turn, flicked on his headlights, and picked up speed. I nudged my car to life and raced to catch up with the guy, keeping my own headlights off for the time being, with the cell tucked between my cheek and shoulder.

"Where's he heading?" asked Lewis, out of breath. I hoped he was running for his car, and wasn't just asthmatic or overweight.

"Boulevard, looks like."

"Okay. I'm coming. Stay on him if you can, and stay on the phone."

Tailing someone isn't as hard as they make it seem in the movies—especially if the guy doesn't know he's being followed. But at two in the morning it can be tricky. It's hard to keep yourself unseen when there aren't many cars on the road. The guy sees one pair of headlights in his rear-view mirror, on him wherever he goes, he starts to get suspicious. But if you stay too far back, the taillights ahead of you all look the same, and you can lose your mark.

Fortunately, tonight there were just enough cars on the street to give me cover, but not so many that I lost my man. I turned on my headlights and got right behind him. I read the license number into the cell phone for Officer Lewis, along with the street-by-street narration, so he would know where we were.

"Okay, I'm just north of you," he said, finally.

"No, you're not," I groaned, seeing a police cruiser sail past me.

"Oh. Shit. Sorry. Hold on. I better put this down." And he hung up.

I was losing confidence in Officer Lewis.

It took only a few seconds for him to turn around and come tearing up the street next to me. I held back and let him get between the burglar and me. He inserted himself in the gap and blasted the siren and lights. And—since this wasn't a movie—the guy pulled over the way he was supposed to, with Lewis parking right behind him.

I pulled up far behind them and sat there to watch the proceedings. Officer Lewis turned out to be a middle-aged, red-faced, good-old-boy with a prominent gut—a portrait of my friend Carter in about fifteen years. He hauled the burglar out of his car and walked him into the beam of the cruiser's headlights, just for my benefit. It was, indeed, a guy—and a scrawny, sad-sack of a guy, too, with a bad haircut and a wispy moustache. I flashed my lights in acknowledgment, and Lewis hauled the guy away. A job well done.

Monday morning, I stopped by Carter's precinct to hear the end of the story.

"Kenny Bansky," he told me, dropping the sad sack's record in front of me. "Professional loser. Breaking and entering a specialty."

"Well, he is good at it," I said, flipping through the pages.

"Not good enough," said Carter. He nodded toward the door, behind which were the holding cells. "He's in with his publicly appointed lawyer now. Can't wait to see what kind of defense they dream up."

"Who'd he get?" I asked.

"Your buddy," he said. "The albino guy."

I laughed. Only one attorney in Atlanta fit Carter's description. "He's not an albino. He's just Norwegian."

Carter shrugged. "He any good?"

"He's good," I said. "But I don't know if anyone's good enough to un-fuck this guy."

Carter nodded wisely, and said, "Stranger shit has happened."

This was true.

"Mind if I go on back?" I asked.

"Sure," he said. "Just try not to get the animals riled up."

I trotted back to the holding cells and glanced into one after another, looking for my friend. There he was, in the third cell on the right, sitting across from a miserable-looking Kenny Bansky and hunched over, strategizing. He was talking; Bansky was nodding.

I banged on the bars and yelled, "Torvik, you fat, Viking shyster! When'd you get your license back?"

The doughy and, to be honest, nearly albino attorney whipped his head around angrily. I blew him a kiss and said, "Morning, Porkchop."

"God damn it, Greenblatt, don't call me that in public."

I laughed. "Sorry if I'm messing with your rep."

"For your information, I do a lot of my best advertising in places like this."

"Uh-huh. Well. Unless you can work some kind of alien abduction angle, this particular client of yours is going down."

"Hey!" the suspect said, jumping up off his bench.

"Give it a rest, Bansky," I said. "I'm the one who saw you do the break-in."

"Oh," he said, sitting back down.

Porkchop patted him on the knee and got up to speak with me privately. "Am I gonna have to recuse myself?" he asked. "Are you testifying?"

"Probably," I said. "Eyewitness and all that. But don't let that stop you. I kind of want to see what you can pull off."

He sighed and shook his head. Then he turned back to his client. "Kenneth, come meet my old friend, Jordan Greenblatt."

Bansky got up, wiped his hands on his clothes, and came over to shake my hand.

"Pretty impressive work," I said. "Except for getting caught and all."

"Thanks," he said in a reedy voice.

"Those old ladies couldn't even figure out what you took."

"Yeah, it's a art," he said proudly. "I ain't like them meth-heads with their goddamn home invasions and shit. I ain't never hurt nobody."

"Yeah," I said, "you're a regular Cary Grant."

He just stared at me.

"Never mind," I said. "I'm glad you're a gentleman. Maybe they'll go easy on you."

Bansky looked at Porkchop hopefully, but got nothing in response.

"I've got to run," I said. "You want to have lunch later?"

My friend thought for a moment, then said, "Probably best if we wait till this thing wraps."

"Fair enough," I said. I waved, wished the cat burglar luck, and headed home for rehearsal.

3

Oticha held his horn up to the sky, closed his eyes as if testing the wind, and said, "I feel the need for reed." Oticha can get away with oracular pronouncements like this because he stands over six feet tall, has a distinguished, greying beard, and is the oldest and wisest member of our little group. He's also the only Genuine Black Man in our little jazz combo, which allows him to get away with tremendous amounts of bullshit.

Pete, Ray, and I had been tuning our instruments or noodling around between songs when Oticha decided to pontificate.

"Reed who?" said Pete, switching his keyboards back and forth between piano mode and something Star Wars-ish.

"Reed as in woodwinds, child," Oticha said. "We got to expand our horizons."

We'd been saying this for years, but none of us had ever acted on it. It's hard enough getting four people together on a semi-regular basis, even with the drummer being a rotating position. Why drummers are in such demand, I have no idea, but we can't ever seem to get one to commit to us. Which I guess is better than having your drummer die of an overdose—or explode, like in Spinal Tap.

"Why woodwinds?" I asked. "Why not a trombone? We're always saying we could use more brass."

"I say we get a reed before we start doubling up," said Oticha. "Clarinet. Maybe sax."

"Maybe both," said Ray, the drummer du jour. "*Some* people can play more than one instrument."

"Very subtle, Raymond," said Oticha. "I tell you what. You buy me a trombone for my birthday, and I will learn said bone. Otherwise, hush up. I got mouths to feed."

It was half true. Oticha wasn't just the oldest member of the group; he was also the only one who had a family. On the other hand, his wife was the one who made all the money, while he stayed home with the kids, so his line to Ray was total crap.

"Fine, let's put the word out," I said. "But let's do it now so we can be ready with some new material for spring."

"I was thinking the same thing. We've got to up our game for the festival."

There was going to be a big music and arts festival in April to coincide with the blooming of the dogwoods and azaleas, and we had already applied for a slot on the main stage. Signing up for the festival was one of the few decisions we had ever made unanimously and instantly—mostly because there was a money prize for the best band.

The problem was, we'd been playing together for years, but we hadn't ever bothered to give ourselves a name. So our application just listed the three main players, with "Drummer TBD."

Susannah came out on the porch with a tray of beers and shots of tequila—her usual refreshments for band practice. We took a break from all the not-playing we were doing and downed our drinks. A MARTA train rattled by in the distance.

"Susannah's Tequila," Pete said, raising his shot glass. We all raised our glasses in a toast. He stared at us, confused. "No, I meant as a name. For us. Susannah's Tequila."

We lowered our shot glasses. "That's the stupidest thing I ever heard," said Ray.

"It's not as stupid as your haircut," said Pete, hurt.

"Dude," said Ray. "Mullets are coming back. I seen it somewhere."

"It's true," I said. "I saw one on a very fashionable guy in jail this morning."

"Too obscure," said Oticha. "Everybody'd be asking which of us is Susannah."

"We could put Pete in a dress," I offered.

"Might finally get a date that way," said Ray.

"Aw, screw y'all," said Pete. "I was just trying to help."

And he was. Every time we met, he came armed with another ridiculous idea for a name. He was the only one who was still trying. Last week it had been "The Morning Paper."

"Just naming whatever's in your hands isn't being a help," I said.

"Seriously," said Ray. "Next week he'll be calling us Limp Dick."

Yes, sadly, jazz musicians can be just as crass and stupid as everyone else.

Susannah tapped me on the shoulder as she went back inside. "Your cell was buzzing," she said.

I got up to fetch my phone. The only friends who ever called me were already assembled on the porch, and the only other people who might have been calling me were clients. I usually forward my office phone to my cell when I quit for the day, since I can't seem to remember to call in and check voice mail.

Sure enough, there was a work message.

"It's the kid," I called out to Susannah, while listening to the message. "Looks like I owe you ten bucks."

"I'll take it in trade," she called back.

"Jesus," I said. "He actually wants, like, an appointment. What do you think—he's doing a play about detectives?"

"Even if it's your life story, I'm not going," she said.

"Unbelievable," I muttered, jotting down the number. "I don't have time for this shit."

But who was I fooling? Of course I had time.

4

The kid poked around my office like he was scouting for a film location—touching things, looking from weird angles, making notes in his head. I sat at my desk and waited for him to get bored. I had no other appointments and nothing but grunt work for the rest of the day.

He picked up an ancient, framed picture of my old boss in full detective regalia—pinstripe suit, fedora, cigarette—and said, "Billy Barnes?"

"That's the man," I said. "This was his company. I used to work for him."

"Oh," he said. "But he's gone now?"

"Dead and gone. The nicotine fairies took him away to tobaccy heaven, and now his kingdom is mine."

He nodded sagely, not even cracking a smile. Hopeless.

He pointed to a couple of newspaper articles I had up on the wall, from the one case that had ever gotten me a bit of notoriety, and said, "Why 'Bulldog'?"

"Why Bulldog," I said with the air of someone who had been asked about his professional nickname a hundred times.

Which I hadn't, really, but I can play the part. "Because my friends are assholes, that's why."

"Your friends are assholes, and that's why you're called Bulldog Barnes?"

"Yes," I said, with conviction and, I hoped, finality. "Now, what can I do for you, Mr. Tremaine?"

He nodded, getting the message, and sat down in the chair facing my desk. "Well. First of all, thank you for making time to see me," he said, in that stilted formality teenagers can have when they put on a tie and talk to grown-ups. Which made me the grown-up in the scene—a fact I found hilarious.

"Not a problem," I said. "So, what's up?"

He looked down at his hands, which were anxiously mangling each other in his lap.

"Come on, kid...Chris. Whatever it is that's bugging you, you can tell me. I barely know you. You got nothing at stake with me."

He nodded and looked up at me. "There's just some...stuff going on, on campus, and...it's bad."

"Okay," I said. "What kind of stuff?"

"You're probably going to think I'm a prude or something. Or a nerd. Or whatever. But it's worse than it sounds."

"Well, you haven't told me anything yet," I pointed out. "So I don't know how it sounds."

"It's drugs," he said. "Hard stuff, like meth, or heroin, or something. I don't know. People say it's bad, and it's everywhere all of a sudden."

"Define everywhere," I said.

He sagged a little bit. "Okay, I don't know about everywhere. But it's all over the theatre department, and it never used to be."

"Seriously?" I said. "The theatre department just discovered drugs?"

"No, that's not…this isn't like pot, or beer, or whatever. It's something new. And, I mean, it's really screwing with people's heads."

"That's kind of the point, isn't it?"

"I mean in a bad way."

This was going nowhere.

"And I think there's something weird going on."

"All right, that sounds promising. What kind of weird?"

He grasped for words, but couldn't seem to find any.

"Look. Chris. Drugs are…you know…they're part of college. I mean, it's something you have to find your way through." Jesus. Listen to me. Papa Bear, all of a sudden.

"It's not *me*," he said defensively. "That's not what I'm saying. I don't do that stuff."

"All right," I said, probably more patronizingly than I meant.

"I don't," he insisted.

"Not even a drink?"

He shrugged. "I got drunk once, in high school. It was…bad. I don't like losing control like that."

I nodded. "I know what you mean. But sometimes it's nice to shut the voice up and just *be*, you know? In the moment?"

"Yeah," he said. "My dad did a lot of that Being in the Moment. Every night, practically. But somebody always had to clean him up and put him to bed *after* the moment. That was my job. So…I guess it's never really been all that interesting to me."

I winced a little and said, "Got it."

"Whatever," he said, noncommittally. "It's just not something I do. I don't care—people can do whatever. That's not what I was trying to say. The thing is…whatever they've been using, the last month or so, it's just…I don't know. It's different. There's something really…intense about it. Scary, you know? They get these crazy highs and then these really bad lows—like miss-class-for-two-days lows. Moody, psycho stuff."

"And you're sure it's not just…you know, basic stress? Midterms or whatever?"

"I had a bunch of pre-meds on my floor last year, and even *they* never got this bad. It's not stress. I mean, doing shows while you're keeping up with classes is hard, and all-night tech rehearsals can make you crazy, but…I've never seen it like this."

"All right. So…weird behavior. Missing class. What else?"

"Staying up for days on end. Not eating anything. Being kind of not-there—lost in their heads. Then crashing and not getting out of bed for days."

"Anything else?"

He looked down at the floor, embarrassed.

"Chris, I can't help you if I don't know what you know. So…what is it?"

"It's like…it makes some people really…" he gestured, trying to find a word. "Sexual. If you know what I mean."

"Uninhibited?"

"Yeah. I mean, to start with."

"All right," I said. "Look. I can think of a couple of things it might be. Coke, ecstasy, maybe some other stuff. Maybe some new mixture I've never heard of. I'm hardly an expert. But Candler's been dealing with drugs forever, like any school. I'm not sure what kind of help you want from me."

"You think I should mind my own business," he said—more a statement than a question.

"Well, yeah, as a general rule," I said.

"I just think it's gonna hurt some people I care about," he said. "More than it's done already."

"You're probably right," I said. "And you should probably go talk to somebody about it."

He nodded that serious nod of his, which I was starting to recognize. "You think I should go to the Dean?"

"Maybe. I mean, that is what they're there for."

He was quiet for a moment. Then he said, "They never do anything, though. They're like a million miles away." He looked back down at his hands. "It's like sixth grade, all over again."

"A lot of life is," I said.

He nodded, but didn't say anything.

"Look, Chris, if what you're saying is true…I mean, if it's going down like you say it is, I'm sure the deans would want to know about it. And they're in a better position to help your friends than I am."

"But I called *you*," he said.

I sighed, frustrated. "Yeah, I know. And I appreciate that. But I'm not the guy for the job."

He sat with that for a while. Then he said, "I had this friend, when I was little. In sixth grade, I found out he was stealing things. Like, shoplifting and stuff. It started out small, like candy and comic books and stuff. But it kept getting bigger. And we all knew about it—all of us. But nobody wanted to say anything because…I don't know. Because we were kids, and we figured it wasn't our job. Or we thought it was mean to tattle on him, or whatever. But I told my parents, and they said yeah, they could call his parents about it, but if I really wanted to be a friend, *I* had to say something. To him, face to face. Tell him it was wrong, he was going to get caught, and he'd better stop. I guess they thought it would be some big life lesson for me.

"So, I talked to two other guys, and we had, like, an intervention. We got together at my house, and we sat around in my basement, and it was just…silent. The other two guys wouldn't say anything. So, I spoke up—I told him what he was doing was wrong, and…all the rest of it. And even then, the other two didn't say anything. They just kind of rolled their eyes. And the whole time I was talking, I could see them looking over at the kid who was shoplifting, and they were smiling at each other like they were…I don't know. I just felt totally alone and stupid."

"And? Did your friend stop shoplifting?"

"I don't know. Maybe. We didn't really spend time together after that. We weren't friends anymore."

"And the other two?"

"They thought I was just a…dork…for talking about it. Which I was. I shouldn't have listened to my parents. They were…"

"A million miles away?"

"Yeah."

I sat with the story for a moment.

"And from this story, we don't learn to mind our own business?" I asked.

He shrugged.

"So...what? You're afraid of looking like a dork again?"

He shook his head. "I'm a dork already," he said quietly. "If I thought it would do any good to say anything, I would. But I don't even drink, you know? They're not going to listen to me."

"Well, they're sure as hell not going to listen to *me*," I said.

He nodded.

"Go see a dean," I said. "They'll listen to you. They have to. It's their job."

"But what'll they *do*? They'll ask a couple of questions, or force us all to go to a workshop or something. That's all they ever do." He stopped for a moment. "I just thought maybe if *you* went and talked to them...I mean, you probably know people over there, and they might take it more seriously if it came from a..."

"Please don't say grown-up," I said.

He smiled. Finally.

"Look," I said. "I do know a few people over there, and I'd be happy to tell them what you told me, if you think it would do any good. But trust me, Chris; they already know this kind of shit goes on—I mean, generally."

"Not dangerous shit like this."

"Like *what*?" I said, getting exasperated. "That's my point. This could be, like, diet pills, for all I can tell. What are they supposed to do with the vague information you're giving me?"

He nodded for a minute or two, thinking.

"What if you *did* know what it was?" he asked. "I mean, what if I could get you more information?"

He stared at me with that teenaged earnestness, waiting for an answer.

"What are you going to do, score some dope for me? Please don't."

"I'm serious," he said.

This was giving me a headache. "Is it that important to you?" I asked.

"Tell me what you need," he said. "I'll get it."

I leaned back in my chair and studied him for a couple of minutes.

"You try to get some better information about what's going on, I'll see what I can do for you. But information only, all right? Do not buy me drugs. I'm serious."

"Got it," he said, smiling again.

I studied him for a moment. "It's not 'people' you're worried about, is it? It's person. One person."

He looked embarrassed again, suddenly, and nodded.

"What's her name?"

He looked back down at his hands again.

"Maddy," he said softly.

5

"Maddy Taylor," Patty said, as soon as I asked. "You saw her—she was in Chris's play." There was a sound of scuffling and heavy breathing on the other end of the line.

"What the hell are you doing, Tits?" I asked.

"Moving boxes and stuff," she grunted. "I've got tech rehearsal at the Puppetry Arts Center, and I've got a ton of shit to bring over."

"Well, could you stop for five minutes and talk to me? It sounds like someone's trying to kill you over there, and I'm off duty."

"It's just a ten-foot puppet of Sarah Palin," she said, panting.

"Which is an image I seriously don't need in my head."

"Okay, okay," she said. "I'll take a break." The noise died down, and I heard a dramatic *oof* as she sat down.

"Thank you," I said. "So…Maddy Taylor?"

"Yeah. She was in the chorus."

"Lovely," I said. "Unfortunately, I've repressed all memories of that evening."

She called me an asshole. I ignored it.

"So what do you know about her?"

"Not much," she said. "You know me. I job-in during the last week or two. I get to know the director more than anyone. The actors are just whiny little chess pieces to me."

"Nice."

"She's Chris's girlfriend, I guess. She's pretty. I don't know."

"Did you notice anything weird about her, or any of the other kids in the play?"

"Weird how?"

"Missing rehearsals? Strung out?"

"Drugs? Is that what you're asking? I didn't notice anything. But those kids wouldn't come to rehearsal stoned. They care about what they're doing."

"I thought you said they were whiny chess pieces."

"They're just like us. Don't you remember? We never let our shit screw up a show."

"Speak for yourself. I was wasted every time I got on stage."

"Yeah, well...you were a rock star. We were just actors."

I smiled but said nothing.

"What's going on, Jordan? Why are you worried about this girl you don't even know?"

"*He's* worried. Your little friend, Chris. He came to my office."

"For real? To tell you Maddy was on drugs?"

"To tell me the whole department was."

"Huh."

I couldn't tell if she was surprised, impressed, or upset. "You think that's crazy?" I asked.

"Well," she said. "He *is* a strange kid."

"Strange how?"

"I don't know. Just strange. I mean, even for a drama geek. He keeps to himself."

"Meaning he wouldn't know?"

"Meaning *I* don't know."

"You said it. You must have meant something."

She was quiet for a moment, then said, "I guess I just mean…if you're not in with the in crowd *or* the out crowd, how does the world look to you?"

Good question.

"So you think he's overreacting."

She sighed. "I don't know. Maybe. Just a gut feeling."

I thought about it. How *does* the world look? Like a party you're not invited to? Or like an anthill you're studying through a magnifying glass? I could see him going either way.

"Thanks, McGraw," I said vaguely, my mind already wandering away from the conversation and down other hallways. She said something like goodbye, and I hung up.

They're all a million miles away, he said. And I could feel it happening with Patty. She worked with them, but she had no idea what was going on with them. Couldn't even see them, really. Had Chris felt the same way, talking to me?

I put my feet up on the edge of a desk drawer and leaned back, staring at the stained ceiling of my office. It was weird to imagine how this kid had seen me. I wasn't used to dealing with people so much younger than me. Most of my friends were my age. Most of my clients were older. So how did I look to a 19-year-old?

I tried to remember how old my professors had been back in college. Probably mid-to-late thirties, like I was now. Not all of them, but the young, hip ones—the ones I would have gone to with a problem, if I had been smart enough to go to anyone. They were my age—my age now. Which was strange, because I didn't feel like the way I remembered them looking. Not that I spent hours staring at myself in the mirror, but, you know, I had a picture of myself in my mind. And I had a memory of those professors in my mind. And those pictures should have matched up, but they didn't. The way I remembered those professors, they looked *different*, in that way you see things when you're a kid: there's us kids, and there's *them*—the not-kids.

However old they are, kids didn't know and didn't care. The grown-ups are just old. Not Us.

And yet he came to me for help.

Why?

Fuck it; it didn't matter why. There was nothing I could do for him. I couldn't go talk to anyone without knowing what was going on. And I couldn't go snooping around campus without permission. Even *with* permission, I'd be a weird grown-up prowling around. Maybe if he brought me something like evidence, I could help him. Maybe.

But not today. Today, I had other work to attend to. Paying work.

For most of the week, I'd been on the payroll of a man in Ohio who had looked me up online and asked me to tail his son, a single guy who lived somewhere in midtown, to find out if the son was gay. So far, it had been a lot of tedious observation, with no big payoff. It was kind of like tailing suspected adulterers, the traditional mainstay of my business…but far more boring.

Why did my client want to know if his son was gay? I had no idea. I had tried a few artful questions when I talked to the guy on the phone, but he had carefully evaded all of them, so I let it alone. The man wants information? The man is willing to pay? That's all I need to know. What he does with the information is his business. Same with suspicious housewives.

Would they be better off not knowing who their husband is screwing? Maybe yes, maybe no.

My mark was an average-looking guy in his late twenties. He didn't give off any of the things a straight guy would take to be gay signifiers—at least, not from a distance. I'd been tailing him for a few days already, picking him up after work (so to speak) and following him to the gym (alone), to an AA meeting (alone), and to the movies (alone). If he was gay, he was either totally closeted or just lonely. Either way, he didn't seem to be bothering anybody.

After hanging up with Patty and finishing my meditation on aging, I drove over to where my mark worked, caught him going out to his car, and followed him some more. He went to the gym like he had done every day since I'd picked up his trail. He went in alone and worked out alone. Again. He met no one, spoke with no one. Again. Afterward he went home to a little apartment complex a few minutes from Piedmont Park. Just like he always did.

A few minutes later, though, he left his house. Apparently, he had decided to go for a stroll. This was a new behavior, so I snapped out of autopilot and started paying attention.

I got out of my car and walked behind him, keeping my distance but keeping him in sight. It was a mild afternoon, closing in on evening. The Maybe-Gay-Son walked along the outside of the park on 10th Street for a while, and then cut inside toward the lake. And there, at last, near the stone gazebo, he made human contact. More than contact, if the shaking of the branches, once they walked down off the bridge and out of sight, was any clue. Why he didn't bring his new friend back to his apartment, I don't know. Hiding in the bushes seemed kind of old-school to me. But what do I know?

When he came out of the shadows, he had a huge smile on his face, and it was the first smile I had seen on his face all week. So…good for him. And good for me, because I finally had something to report. I called the old man in Ohio and told him his son might, in fact, be gay. Not particularly Out, but not living in monk-like celibacy, either.

"Did you get any pictures?" he asked.

"No, sir, I did not," I said, as politely as I could. "I didn't know you wanted to see pictures."

"I didn't," he replied, a little too loudly and defensively. "I don't. I just…never mind. So…you're sure?"

"A hundred percent, take-it-to-court sure? No, sir. But pretty damned sure."

"Huh. All right then."

I was tempted to ask him what he intended to do with this information, now that he had it, but I resisted. Knowing would have made it worse. It would have made it my problem— my responsibility. I would have had to have a real opinion, which is something I didn't want to have. Because when you start judging, you start having to turn down jobs, and, to be honest, I wasn't in a position to turn down jobs.

Like I said—the man pays for information; the man gets his information. I'm like a bartender. The man pays for a drink; he gets a drink. It's not my job to tell him the shit isn't good for him. I'm not his mother.

This is why I don't spend too much time looking in the mirror.

6

Thanksgiving was closing in, and calls for my services were starting to dry up and blow away. Homophobic Dad had paid his bill, Cat Burglar was sitting in lockup, my intense little college student had never called back, and the rest of Metro Atlanta was settling down into its annual ritual of pretending to be nice little Whos down in Whoville, filled with roast beast and goodwill toward men. Time for this private investigator to close out his books for the year.

Which made it a perfect time to focus on music. We didn't have any gigs coming up, so we decided to do that thing we always talked about doing but never actually did: finding another musician. Oticha wanted a reed, and Oticha was the boss, so we started asking some clarinet and sax players to hang out with us and play, to see if there was a happy fit.

I hated every minute of it.

I can't help it; I hate shopping for new friends. I like the little circle I've got. I know them. I know their quirks. I know how they play. We fit together. I had put up with so much stupid drama back when I was trying to be a rock star—all those prima donnas, all that hair. It had seemed worth it at the time, but once the rock-star dream died for good, I didn't want to have any more diva-fits in my life. All I wanted was a few cool cats to hang out with and a few good tunes to play. The simple joys of a simple life.

I met Oticha at a summer concert up in Chastain Park, just a year or two after I had given up the electric bass. Susannah and I were on one blanket; he and Mel were on the blanket next door. They had brought wine; we hadn't. They had forgotten a corkscrew; the ever-resourceful Susannah happened to have one in her bag. Thus, a friendship was born. And more than a friendship. As a newbie to jazz, I had a lot to learn from a pro like Oticha.

Pete I've known even longer, though we'd never been really close. In addition to playing keyboards, he did sound design for theatres around town. Patty introduced us at some cast party she dragged me to, back when I was single and she thought I needed new friends.

As for drummers, we always had a short list of guys who rotated in and out—guys we'd met at various gigs here and there. Somehow, none of them ever settled in as permanent members of the group. I liked a couple of them, like Ray, although he was a total redneck meathead. Others, not so much. But either way, they were never part of the A-Team, and they didn't seem to want to be.

Our little group had always had an improvisational, hang-out-with-friends vibe to it, and the idea of bringing in someone new rubbed me the wrong way. It turned out to be as lousy in practice as I had thought it would be in theory.

First of all, everyone who sat in with us was a sax player, which got irritating really quickly. It was just *way* too much David Sanborn for my taste. Way too much "smooth jazz." I mean, I can deal with a *little* Stan Getz, a little mellow, mid-sixties, cocktail-era music. I can handle that. It doesn't have to be hard bop all the time. But man, this was just a steady stream of Kenny G., air pudding *mush*.

When you're playing with other people, you've got to be able to read each other, follow each other's impulses. You've got to be in synch. And if my partner's impulses tell him there's no difference between Bird, 'Trane, and Sonny on the one hand, and "Romancing the Stone" on the other, then *my* impulse is to drive him from my village and curse his name. Susannah says that's a very judgmental, Old Testament attitude, which is fine by me. God may be love, but jazz is jazz.

So the week dribbled by, with occasional applications of Saxophone Torture, and I set my sights on Turkey Day.

I used to love Thanksgiving. When I was a kid on Long Island, we'd go to my cousin's house and have a daylong orgy of food, basketball, and noise. Once we moved down to Atlanta, though, the holiday got quieter. And after my mother died, it got downright silent.

These days, with me married and my dad in some weird, older person's post-marriage, quasi-serious, hyper-intellectual, and possibly-sexual-but-please-don't-tell-me-about-it relationship with a Political Science professor from India, Thanksgiving has become just another obligatory dinner party. Very tasteful, very reserved, very catered. Lots of stimulating discussion about American foreign policy and independent cinema. In other words, Not Thanksgiving. Plus, being self-employed and all, I take no special joy in the idea of taking a day off work. I can take a day off whenever I want to. All it means is I'm not getting paid.

To make up for that, Susannah and I usually have a Second Thanksgiving at Oticha and Melanie's house to help them eat their leftovers. They always have a huge group in for the holiday—mostly Mel's family, up from Dublin, Georgia, with a rotating cast of characters from Oticha's clan from Detroit. Mel always tries to get people to take leftovers home with them, but they all have to get on planes or drive too many hours. Which is why we're usually called in to help with clean-up. It's a smaller gig than the Thanksgivings of my youth, with a lot more pork on the menu than I ever had—but at least there are kids running around making noise, and regular breaks for drinking, singing, and laughing.

Late in the evening, while Mel and Susannah put the girls to bed, Oticha and I stood side by side in the kitchen, washing and drying dishes. How this household managed to host massive feasts year after year without a dishwasher, I had no idea.

"You know," I said, handing my friend a soapy plate, "I do have very sensitive hands."

"You're a bass player," he said, receiving the plate and drying it. "You got calluses on your calluses."

"True," I admitted, cleaning the next plate. "Maybe I should rent myself out to some restaurants. I could use the cash."

"No work?" he asked.

"Nothing for miles."

"Not even that kid you told me about?"

It took me a minute to figure out who he was referring to. "Nah," I said finally. "I didn't think he was for real, anyway."

"Just imagining things?"

"Just needed to get laid, probably."

Oticha sucked his teeth dramatically and said, "Callused goddamned heart, too."

I laughed. "You ever have one of your kids come to you with something like that? Worried about friends taking drugs, or shoplifting, or whatnot?"

"*My* kids, or at school?" he asked. Oticha had been a high-school teacher for years, which is where he transitioned

from Mr. Dutton to Mr. Teacher, and then to Yo Teacher, and finally Oticha.

"Either."

"My girls, no. Too young for that shit. I hope."

"What about your students?"

"Nah," he said. "School I was at, we had five, six thousand kids. They had their own kid nation going on—kid territories, kid tribes, kid laws. You think you got any clue what's going on in a place like that, you're delusional. You think you got any *control*, you're worse than delusional."

"What's worse than delusional?" I asked, happy to serve up a straight line.

"Tenured," he said, happy to deliver.

"Thanks, folks," I said, waving a sudsy arm at an imaginary audience outside the kitchen window. "We'll be here all weekend."

We returned to the quiet back and forth of cleaning, but Oticha was in the mood for conversation. "So that's it?" Oticha asked.

"I told you, I got nothing," I said. "It's a good thing Susannah gets paid every two weeks."

"Thank God for working wives," he agreed.

"You ever think about going back to teaching? Like when Eva starts school?" I asked.

"Shit, I hope not," he said. Then he shrugged "I might give music lessons. Probably decent money there."

"Could be," I said, "but you'd have to schlep out to Norcross or Roswell to really cash in. All those snooty suburban moms."

"Oticha don't be schlepping nowhere, son," he said grandly. "Oticha be proceeding in a stately manner, head held high, like his Ethiopian ancestors."

"Right," I said, dumping the clean silverware on his side of the sink. "Head held high in a used Hyundai."

"I speak metaphorically," he said.

"You speak bullshit," I said.

"Tomayto, tomahto."

Apparently, it was his turn to give me the straight line. I obliged and sang, "Let's call the whole thing off," in my worst Louis Armstrong voice.

We entertain each other.

But our conversation nagged at me for the next few days. I had pretty much written off Chris Tremaine. I figured the ball was in his court; it was up to him to make the next move. And when he didn't make it, I figured that was his problem. But the more I thought about it, the more it bothered me. He *was* just a kid, after all, and he *had* reached out to me for help.

So, Monday morning, I called my father over at the law school. He was surprised to hear from me since we had just seen each other and our relationship wasn't what you'd call chatty. I told him about Chris and asked him if there was anyone in administration he thought I should get in touch with.

"Well," he said heavily, and I could almost hear his woolly-caterpillar brows furrowing. "I'm sure you're right that the deans already suspect things like this are going on. But I suppose it can't hurt to pass on the information."

"Except it isn't really information," I said. "It's just gossip."

"True," he said. "But you should probably allow *them* the opportunity to assess its truth value. It's their campus, after all."

"I guess so," I said.

"You're hesitating. Why?"

"Just something he said. How it's two different worlds over there. College students don't usually open up to professors about personal stuff. Definitely not deans or whatever. God knows, I didn't."

"You didn't, that's true. But others do. I have law students who come in at least once a week to cry at me about their relationship woes. And I hardly invite such confessions."

"Either way, if the grown-ups start snooping around, chances are most of the kids will clam up and say nothing. Even if it's, you know…something."

"Which, again, isn't your business?"

"Well," I said, my own brow furrowing. "It isn't and it is. That's the whole reason he came to me. If I just pass the buck to the administration and walk away, he's right back where he started, right? Or maybe worse, if the thing goes underground."

He was quiet for a moment. Then I heard his tongue clicking, making a lost-in-thought noise I was more than familiar with. I gave him some time.

"Why don't you split the difference?" he said, finally. "Take it privately to someone you trust. Give them the information and offer to help. That way you're not simply passing the buck, as it were. But you're also not sticking your nose where it doesn't belong, so to speak. Stay in the game, but let them take the lead. Or…stay in the *hunt,* but let them take the lead."

So to speak. As it were. That's my father all over—never one to utter a cliché or a bad metaphor without qualifying and editing himself. That's what years of training in parsing other people's language on the witness stand does to you.

But it was a good idea—a smart idea—and I knew exactly where to go.

7

Lenore Whitman was a dean of something-or-other in the Campus Life office at Candler. When I first knew her, she was a Biology professor and my advisor. I spent a lot of my freshman year in her office, refusing to answer questions about why I was failing my exams. I must have been a total pain in the ass to the woman, but somehow she never wrote me off—even when I failed Bio and dropped pre-med. I gave back my undissected fetal pig like a defeated general handing over his sword, but she never took it personally—and she kept in touch with me all through college to make sure I was doing all right. I guess she felt responsible for me, which was ridiculous but sweet. And it didn't end once I graduated. She still comes to see me play music once in a while, and we talk or email once or twice a year. So…if I was going to reach out to anyone in the administration, Dr. Whitman was the perfect candidate.

Perfect, except she wasn't in when I called. I left a message and went back to writing up some end-of-year invoices, which was all the Actual Work I could think to do. I sat around for the rest of the morning, hearing nothing from her or anybody else. And then, of course, as soon as I stepped out of my office to pick up a crappy sandwich for lunch, she called back and left me a message:

"Jordan! Sorry I missed you. I'm working from home today, which is code for 'I'm planting bulbs in my garden.' I'm going to be up to my elbows in mud most of the afternoon, so if you want to talk about something, why don't you just come on by?"

So I went on by.

Dr. Whitman lived alone in an optical illusion of a house in Salisbury Hills, the neighborhood near Candler where a lot of professors lived. She was only a mile or two from the campus, and she usually rode her bike to and from and around the place. Her house was an optical illusion because from the street it looked like a one-story cottage. When you got inside, though, you discovered the place had been built into a hill that descended into a ravine you couldn't see from the street, and was actually three stories tall, with an enormous, cathedral-ceilinged living room that you looked down into from the front door. The back side of the house was all glass, and looked out into the ravine and what appeared to be a primeval rain forest hidden right in the middle of town. It was a perfect place for her.

Dr. Whitman's mission in life was to love all of God's creatures, but humans were way at the bottom of her list. Not *off* the list; just hanging on by a thread. I think that's why she refused to give up on me, back when I was a freshman. I think I was her pet human.

She didn't live *exactly* alone. There were a lot of others sharing her house—just none from our species. When my car rattled up her street, the sound unleashed a hellish chorus from inside the house: dogs woofing out a bass line, a big bird or two screeching soprano, and a couple of alto animals I couldn't identify, filling in the middle.

Fortunately, Dr. Whitman was working in her front garden, so I didn't have to wade through the beasts to find her. She was, as advertised, up to her elbows in mud, planting spring bulbs all along the walkway to her front door. I saw her look up from beneath an enormous hat as I crossed the street, and she beamed at me and struggled to stand up without muddying her shirt. She pulled off her gardening gloves and stood there, hands on hips, to welcome me.

"Jordan!" she said. "You look good."

"Thanks, Doc," I said. "You, too."

She made a rude noise and waved away the compliment. Dr. Whitman was one of the most unvain women I had ever met. It wasn't that she was ugly, or plain, or dressed funny. She just didn't seem to care how she looked. When I first met her, I hadn't known how to process that. All my teachers in high school had dressed like teachers. Prim dresses, long skirts, or those pant-suit things I've never understood. And those crazy ugly red sweaters at Christmas, with Santas and snowmen on them.

But the first day of college, here comes Dr. Whitman into this enormous, overstuffed Bio class in front of hundreds of kids, dressed like a guy. I mean, she was wearing jeans, a faded T-shirt with some band logo on it, and an old blazer. Her hair was straight, flat, parted in the middle. Coming from Long Island, where the air we breathe is at least ten parts hair spray, this was all new to me.

But at some point during my freshman year, as part of my larger education about life, it occurred to me that I had never thought twice about how any of my *male* teachers dressed, or whether what they chose to wear was appropriately teacher-ly. I moved pretty quickly from that revelation to the more enlightened position of "who-gives-a-shit?"

Say this for me—when I finally figure out I'm being stupid, I *do* try to move on.

"Here," said Dr. Whitman, pushing a small shovel and a dirty mound of vegetation at me. "Dig while you talk."

I dug, and I planted, and I gave her a quick rundown of the Chris Tremaine story, omitting his name. I wanted to test the waters before I sold the kid down the river.

"So," I said, patting the soil on top of the bulb I had just planted. "News? Not news?"

Dr. Whitman sat back on her haunches and pushed her big hat up with the back of her hand, leaving a slight smudge of dirt on her forehead. "Both," she said. "You know, we always try to use the FAME sessions to bring up issues about substance abuse—partly to help kids talk about this kind of stuff, and partly to find out, for ourselves, what's going on out there. But some kids never open up."

"Fame sessions? What is that, some kind of talent show?"

She looked at me quizzically, and I remembered that she was often immune to sarcasm. "No, it's the freshman advising program."

"Huh. I don't remember it ever having a name."

She looked up and to the left for a moment, like wisdom was perched somewhere above her shoulder, whispering in her ear. Then she closed her eyes and nodded. "That's right," she said. "You graduated before we did all that work on it. We have one-on-one and small group sessions now, with faculty advisors, peer advising groups, seminars and discussions all through the year. The first two years, actually. It's a much richer and broader program than we had when you were there."

Now it was my turn to look quizzically at her. "Doc," I said, "I don't need the brochure. How come you're talking to me in official-speak?"

She wiped some sweat off her brow with her sleeve, transforming the smudge into a streak. "Because, Jordan, you're talking about drugs on campus, and it's not something I can treat lightly."

"Or honestly?" I asked.

She glared at me. Guess I had crossed a line there.

"Look," I said. "All I'm asking is whether you've heard about something new and crazily addictive this year. I'm just trying to figure out whether this kid is delusional or has something to worry about. And, you know...I figured you might want to know what I was hearing."

"Of course I do, Jordan, and I thank you for bringing it to me," she said, relaxing. "But you need to know how hard my office works to reach out to students, to give them a safe place to talk about all kinds of issues like this, and get them the help they need."

Again with the party line.

"Yeah, of course, Doc. I mean, I wouldn't have come to you otherwise."

She nodded.

"I can tell you a little bit more, if you want to hear it," I said. "There's one particular department it seems to be hitting hard."

"Then tell me," she said. "I'll take care of it."

It was an early Christmas present. There's nothing sweeter than hearing another person say, "I'll take care of it."

8

My redneck, mullet-haired cat burglar, Kenny Bansky, had been sitting in a holding cell downtown for weeks because of the Thanksgiving holiday, so it was December by the time he got hauled up in front of a judge. For some reason, the poor bastard had been denied bail. I guess "cat burglar" and "flight risk" went hand-in-hand in the mind of the judge.

Porkchop called me the day before the hearing to give me a head's up. Bansky was pleading guilty in exchange for a lighter sentence, so it didn't look like I was going to have to testify. But I rode down to the courthouse anyway, just for the low-rent spectacle and to see my friend.

The courtroom had a restless feel to it, with people moving in and out of the spectator section as different cases were called, dealt with, and dismissed. Loser X: possession of marijuana. Loser Z: drunken assault. I pushed my way through the ooze of people and found a seat behind the defense table, where Porkchop and Bansky had just sat down to wait their turn. I smacked Attorney Torvik on the back of his bald head, and shook Bansky's hand. He was remarkably pleasant, considering I was the guy who had nailed him.

"What are you asking for?" I said, sitting down behind their table.

"One month, plus time served," said Porkchop. "He gave back the stolen property. And the ladies seem to have forgiven him." He pointed across the room to where Bansky's two elderly victims were sitting. They smiled and waved excitedly.

"You pick your marks well, Bansky. I'll give you that," I said.

"Thank you, sir," he said. "I don't like nobody hating me. It's just business, you know what I mean? It's just stuff."

"Other people's stuff," I reminded him.

He shrugged. "They got the insurance," he said. "But I gave it back, anyways."

The judge banged his gavel and called the case. Porkchop and Bansky rose, but not before the judge spied me sitting behind them and gave me the evil eye.

There were two kinds of judges in Atlanta, back when this was all happening: ones who hated me for bringing down one of their most respected colleagues, a year earlier, and ones who thanked me for pursuing justice. The first group was a lot larger.

"People v. Kenneth Bansky," the judge intoned. "How do you plead?"

"Guilty," said Porkchop happily.

The judge looked over at the assistant district attorney who had drawn the short straw on this case. She was a woman in her late twenties—skinny, intense, probably more dedicated than this piece of work required. "What are the people looking for?" asked the judge.

The lawyer jumped to her feet and said, "Judge, we think at least six months is appropriate, given the nature of the crime."

The judge looked at some papers in front of him—probably the arrest report from Officer Lewis. "Six, huh?" he asked.

"Judge," Porkchop chimed in, "Mr. Bansky has already served nearly a month awaiting this hearing because of the holiday."

The judge looked up and studied Bansky more closely. "I denied you bail, didn't I, Mr. Bansky?"

"You did that, Your Honor. Yes, sir."

"Hmph," the judge said, going back to his papers.

"Also, Your Honor, the two victims in the case have asked for leniency to be shown," said Porkchop.

The judge looked up again, and saw the two grandmothers waving at him. I'm not sure he knew what to make of them. He thought for another moment, then checked his watch, sighed, and said. "Time served plus one more month. I think that's plenty." He whacked his gavel and yelled, "Next."

The assistant D.A. huffed, pulled her papers together, and marched out of the room. Bansky shook Porkchop's hand and thanked him profusely before being led out by the bailiff.

"Nice work, counselor," I said. "Now how about you buy me lunch?"

He sighed. "You realize," he said, "that lunch with you is going to cost me more than I made on this case." He stood up, gathered his own papers together, and headed up the aisle with me.

"Jeez, all right," I said. "I don't want to break you. I promise I'll just have one beer."

He nodded. "That's nice of you," he said. "But I'm planning on having five."

As usual, he was true to his word. We went straight to Manuel's Tavern and ended up spending most of the afternoon there. He had no pressing business that day, post-Bansky, and I had no pressing business at all.

After about the fourth beer, I mentioned something about our ability—and willingness—to spend an entire afternoon in a bar. I wondered whether it was unseemly, given our advancing years.

"I don't know about you," he said, "but I'm celebrating an important victory for American justice."

"Yeah," I said, "you look downright festive."

"Fine," he said. "Then I'm mourning a travesty of American justice. Take your pick."

"Well, either way, I'm glad I could be here to help," I said, raising my glass.

"You? You're a goddamned parasite," he said. "You barely have a job."

"I barely have *two* jobs," I corrected him.

"And the one that actually pays, you just fobbed off on some hapless dean."

I cleared the glasses and bar coasters away from the area in front of me, as though I needed room to make a demonstration. "Okay," I said, "first of all, it wasn't an *actual* job; nobody was paying me. I was just trying to do this kid a favor. Second of all, I didn't *fob* anything off, whatever the fuck that means."

"Fob something off," he said. "It's a perfectly normal expression."

"For Montgomery Burns, maybe. For Porkchop J. Rugbyplayer, it's weird as shit."

"See, this is your problem," he said, gearing himself up for a monologue but then stopping himself when the next beer arrived. "Ah, thank you, my good man," he said to the waiter, who had already turned his back and started walking away. He looked with great pleasure at the frosted glass and then quickly drained half of it.

"What's my problem, exactly?" I prompted him.

"God knows," he said, and then belched. "Oh, yes. This Porkchop J. Rugbyplayer crap. You realize I haven't played rugby since we left college?"

"I wasn't keeping track."

"And it's been fifteen years since we graduated?"

"Don't remind me."

"The number of people in my life who think of me as either a rugby player or a guy named Porkchop gets smaller and smaller every year."

"You want me to investigate what happened? It sounds very Agatha Christie."

He stared at me for a moment, then shook his head and drank the rest of his beer. "Never change, Jordy." He thumped the glass down on the table. "Never ever change."

I raised my glass in thanks, and did my best to catch up with him.

"Speaking of which…" he said.

I finished the beer and put it down. "Speaking of what?"

"College," he said. "Fifteen years."

"Right."

"We've got a reunion in the fall."

"Seriously?"

"So I hear. We've never attended one. Anyway, I haven't."

"Me too. Neither."

"I'm thinking it might be time. Fifteen years. Now that we're established members of the establishment, with valuable life lessons to pass along to the undergraduates. What do you say?"

Now it was my turn to stare at him.

"Or not," he said, with a shrug.

I raised my glass to him and said, "I'll drink to that."

9

Back in band world, we had just about given up hope of ever finding new talent when a girl none of us knew showed up, uninvited, at my front porch one Saturday afternoon. She was young—mid-twenties—about 5'2, with short black hair, goth-pale skin, and black eyeliner. Her clothes were black and white to match her hair and skin, and she had tattoos running up and down her arms, the only real color on her. This was a very normal look for my neighborhood, but a very odd look for a jazz musician…which she claimed to be.

"I'm Lydia Sinclair?" she said, more as a question than a statement. "Ray Lovett said you were looking for musicians?"

"You're a friend of Ray's?" I asked, trying to figure out where the mathematical sets of Stone Mountain Redneck and Little Five Points Freak intersected. It was a shame Ray wasn't there to explain.

"I know him," she said with a shrug. "I live next door to him, actually. My mother does, I mean. Which means, you know, I do. For now." She sighed, exhausted by the explanation. "Are you looking for someone or what?"

I glanced over at Oticha, our leader, and he gave me a "why not?" look. "Yeah," I said, "we're looking. So far, we haven't found anything worth seeing. Can you blow?"

She shrugged and said, "Try me."

I waved her onto the porch. She stepped up while Oticha and I grabbed our instruments and Pete shambled over to his electric keyboard.

"What's your pleasure?" asked Oticha.

She shrugged again and said, "It's your gig. Ray said you were letting folks sit in."

Oticha looked over at me and Pete, but we gave him nothing. "Your call, Chief," I said.

"Little Brown Jug?" he said. "E flat?"

"I can handle that," she said, sitting down to unpack. I was thrilled to see a clarinet for a change.

"I'm Oticha. That's Jordy G. and Pete."

"'Kay." She blew a few notes to warm up.

"I'll take the melody. You solo first."

"'Kay," she said again. "Who sings?"

That stopped us.

"Nobody?" she said, looking at each of us in turn. She gave another of her already famous shrugs and said, "I can sing if you want."

Oticha smiled and said, "You got it, little sister. Let's do it this way: all together twice, then you sing us a few verses, then once around again, then it's all you on the wood."

And we launched into it.

You may know this tune, even if you don't know it by name. You probably know the Glenn Miller, big band version, but it's actually an old folk song dating back to the Civil War. I've heard it done folk, I've heard it done swing. When we do it, since there's so few of us, it's pretty spare and spiky. But the melody is simple and sweet, and it's wide open for infinite riffing.

I'm not sure why Oticha latched on to that particular tune for Lydia. Maybe it's just that we'd played it a thousand times, and he figured he could go on autopilot and listen to the clarinet instead of worrying about what he was doing. Whatever the reason, it was perfect—because while we had played the song a thousand times, it had never sounded like this. Right away, in the first run, the clarinet lifted up the song and took it to a whole new place. I could tell Oticha was feeling it, because he didn't stay on autopilot for long. We ran through the melody once, trumpet and clarinet in unison. But the second time through, he was intensely aware of Lydia standing next to him, weaving her woodwind around his horn as he went through the melody. Her notes danced around him, playing with him and then darting away to riff above him, below him, and wrap around him like a snake. It was all the big man could do to keep from cracking a smile and ruining his embouchure. Playing off to the side, *I* could smile without messing up my technique. And that was a good thing, because I was grinning like an idiot.

I don't know when I first heard jazz. Probably long before I was aware of it or knew what to call it. But it wasn't played much in my house. My mother was a Pete Seeger and Kingston Trio fan, with a little Simon and Garfunkel thrown in. My father was strictly classical, though I always suspected it was a post-law-school pose. I've seen pictures of my dad from high school, with his big Jew-fro hairdo and his muttonchop sideburns. I'm betting he wasn't listening to Schubert back then, but who knows?

My musical tastes were totally obvious as a kid. I listened to what everyone else listened to; shitty 1980s rock, with some Springsteen and Bon Jovi thrown in for local spirit. When I moved on to college and my life kind of fell apart, I got into an angry metal phase. It sounded like the way I felt inside, and that's pretty much what teenagers want out of music. After college, it didn't change much, except that I allowed some Pete Seeger and Schubert into my life, on the pretense that I was now a grown-up.

It stayed that way for a long time. And then, when Susannah and I got married, we honeymooned in New Orleans, which was one of her favorite cities but a place I'd never been. And New Orleans changed my life.

I remember the day and the place and the time. It was late morning on our second day, and Susannah wanted to go clothes shopping with some cousin who lived in the French Quarter. I had zero interest in being a part of that excursion, so I went for a walk while they shopped. The quarter was getting ready for a music festival, and a lot of musicians were milling around, jamming informally for fun or to make some spare change. As I walked down Royal Street, I saw little bands set up at every corner, spaced just far enough apart to keep the music from overlapping. They were not like any bands I had ever seen. Trumpet, trombone, bass fiddle. Violin sometimes. Clarinet sometimes. Somebody standing in the back with an old washboard around his neck and two or three tin cans nailed to the bottom board, his fingers covered in thimbles to beat percussion on the metal strips. The instruments were old and beaten-up. The people looked ragged and funky. And the music…

I said I got into metal because it matched the way I felt inside, and that was true. It hit all the anger, all the frustration, and it felt good. But there was something about this new music I was hearing that matched a whole different feeling, a feeling I couldn't name and didn't understand. It wasn't happiness, because the music wasn't always happy. And anyway, "happiness"—I knew what that was, and it was a little enough thing. This wasn't a little thing, or a surface thing. This was something that hit me in a deep-down place I couldn't pinpoint. It made this fluttering feeling in my stomach, and it made my head feel lighter. There was something in the beat, something in the interplay of the instruments—something in the whole spirit of the music that just gave me a feeling of...joy, I guess you'd have to call it. I couldn't identify it for a long time. I don't know if I had ever really felt it before.

I'm not saying I was a glum, depressed kid. I wasn't. I was happy most of the time. Even in college, when I was struggling to deal with shit that had happened back in high school—things I had done, things I couldn't come to grips with—I still had happy moments. Plenty of happy moments. Happy was easy.

But joy? Maybe when I was five or something, playing in a sandbox or running around the backyard. But not since then. It wasn't something I ever expected. Grown-ups didn't do joy.

But standing on that street corner, I felt...lifted, somehow—literally lifted up off my feet. There was joyfulness inside me somewhere, and this music was reaching down and tickling it and bringing it up to the surface. The music made me feel lighter than I had ever felt before. And as I walked down that street from band to band, the goofy smile on my face just grew bigger, and my feet grew lighter, and I was in heaven. I was more than in heaven. I felt like I was home in my own skin for the first time in years.

Every once in a while, when things click with our little group, I still get that feeling. It's why I don't care that I'm not making a gazillion dollars or living in a fancy house—or even a house that has a paint job more recent than the Reagan administration. Feeling that joy in the music, being a part of *making* that music—that's plenty for me.

All of which is just to say this: the day Lydia Sinclair sat in with us, it *clicked*. And all of us knew it. The girl could play.

We went through the song twice, and then Lydia lowered her clarinet to sing. Oticha took a break and let Pete and me accompany her. And this was the second revelation, because all of a sudden, the goth-girl disappeared. She closed her eyes, swayed to the beat, and sang in this lovely, smoky voice:

> *Me and my wife live all alone*
> *In a little log hut we call our own;*
> *She loves gin and I love rum,*
> *And don't we have a lot of fun!*
>
> *Ha, ha, ha, you and me,*
> *Little brown jug, don't I love thee!*
> *Ha, ha, ha, you and me,*
> *Little brown jug, don't I love thee!*

She sang one verse and one chorus, and then put the reed to her lips again. Oticha stayed out of the picture and let her blow. And man, did she blow, as the old-timers would say. She hopped around the porch as the clarinet played variations on the melody. She skipped over toward me, but my basic bass line wasn't interesting enough for her, so she moved on to where Pete was banging out some stride accompaniment for her. She listened to what he was doing, and then matched him. And he listened to her and tried to match her. And back and forth they went, until Oticha came back in with the melody. Lydia let him take it, and sang another verse along with his horn:

> *If all the folks in Adam's race*
> *Were gathered together in one place,*
> *I'd let them go without a tear*
> *Before I'd part from you, my dear.*

She looked over at Pete and me and gestured for us to join her in the chorus. Croaky as our voices were, we couldn't resist.

> *Ha, ha, ha, you and me,*
> *Little brown jug, don't I love thee!*
> *Ha, ha, ha, you and me,*
> *Little brown jug, don't I love thee!*

It was love at first sight.

10

"She's weird," Susannah said, later that night while we were watching TV and letting the day wind down.

"She's a little weird," I admitted, wondering how long she had been stewing about it.

"Did you see Pete looking at her? It was embarrassing."

"Yeah, well. Pete has no filter." It was true—from the moment Lydia had danced over to the piano to jam with Pete, he had been unable to take his eyes off her.

"And what's with the tattoos?" Susannah said.

"She has tattoos," I said. "Half the people we know have ink."

She harrumphed.

"You just don't like the idea of having another girl around. You're being all territorial."

"Mel hangs around all the time."

"Mel's a band wife. Mel's not *in* the band."

Susannah considered this for a minute, and then said, "Fuck you."

"Ha!" I yelled. "I knew it."

"You don't know anything."

I took her hand and looked meaningfully into her eyes. "Honey," I said, super-sincerely, "You'll always be our best girl. Nobody can take your place."

She yanked her hand away and said, "Seriously. Fuck you."

I studied her for a moment, trying to figure out if she was actually upset. It's hard to tell, sometimes.

"What—you want to be in the band?"

"No."

"You want to be in the band, you can be in the band. You can play tambourine or something."

"I don't want to play the fucking tambourine."

"All right, all right."

The phone rang. I pulled myself up off the couch to get it. "She's just weird, that's all," Susannah said, as I walked toward the kitchen.

"Okay."

Louder: "And I don't want Pete to get hurt."

"Okay. So we'll look out for Pete."

"You'd better," she yelled at my back.

"Yeah, yeah."

"Don't be an asshole about this."

I picked up the phone while yelling over my shoulder, "I'm not being an asshole!" I put the receiver to my ear and said, "Sorry."

"Jordan?" a ragged woman's voice said. "Oh God..."

I couldn't place the voice for a second. She was crying. She sounded like she had been crying for a long time.

"Who is this?" I asked.

"It's me—it's Patty," she sobbed.

"What's the matter?" I said, my heart starting to beat faster. "What's going on?"

Susannah was up now, standing next to me, making some confusing sign language gestures at me. I gave her a shrug of "No Idea" in response.

Patty kept crying. Howling, actually. I had never heard a person howl. It was unnerving. "Okay...okay," I said, trying to be soothing, trying to make her stop. "It's all right."

"It's not, it's not," she said.

I took a deep breath. "I'm here, Patty. What's going on? What happened?"

"It's Chris," she said.

"Who?"

"Chris," she sobbed. "Chris Tremaine."

I didn't say anything for a moment. Knowing it, somehow. Dreading it.

Then Patty said, "He's dead."

Part Two

1

Chris Tremaine was dead.

Chris Tremaine was dead, and I hadn't even recognized his name. Not at first.

I hung up the phone, and instantly there were two voices in my head. One said I had blood on my hands; the other told me it was none of my business.

I sat down and tried to figure out which voice to listen to. Susannah lifted my face, kissed me, leaned her forehead against mine, and said, "It's not your fault."

"That's what *he* says," I groaned.

"Who?"

"That asshole in my head who thinks it's not my fault."

She smiled and kissed me again. "He might be right."

Yeah, he might be. And then again...

I sighed. "Only one way to find out."

"Which is?"

"Find out."

2

Atlanta's police zone 6 covers a large and unruly swath of town, from the upscale condos and big homes of Lenox and Morningside through midtown, including the Woodruff Arts Center and the museum, then down through the yuppie havens of Virginia Highlands and Atkins Park, into more mixed neighborhoods like Little Five Points and Candler Park, where I live, and then even farther south, into Grant Park, Cabbagetown, and East Atlanta. It stretches all the way from I-85 in the north to just short of the perimeter, I-285, to the south. It's a lot of territory to cover, and a lot of very different people to deal with, with a weird and wide range of problems. I don't envy my friend Carter, who works the precinct.

Right on the eastern edge of his territory is the neighborhood of Salisbury Hill and the campus of Candler University. Carter's team has jurisdiction over Salisbury Hill, but beyond the college's entrance gate, the Candler Police Department is the Big Dog to deal with, and it deals with everything from parking tickets and underage drunks to underage drunks and parking tickets. When I was at school, we used to call them the Baby Cops, which was unfair, because they were actual police officers. It wasn't their fault that their main job was to babysit over-privileged, out-of-control children. Even though their regular beat tended toward the lamer end of law enforcement, they did have an actual detective unit, and they were responsible for bigger crimes, if any occurred. So if I wanted to find out what happened to Chris Tremaine, I would have to talk to the Baby Cops.

The problem was, I didn't have any friends at the CPD, and I wasn't in what you'd call a position of strength. After all, who was I? A member of the family? No. A close friend? Hardly. Even as a PI, I wasn't in a position to demand anything. The kid had never actually hired me. So what was I? Just an annoying schmuck who wanted to ask questions. And you've got to figure, when a student dies on campus, nobody wants to answer questions if they don't have to.

So I called Carter instead, because he was my friend, and he *could* get questions answered. Carter said he'd call over to the detective unit, where he knew a few people, and see if he could get any details for me. Maybe even get me in to meet with someone.

He rang back within half an hour. "Well," he said in his best, Southern drawl (the kind that can pull three or four syllables out of a simple word), "I got some answers, but I sure as shit can't get you in to see nobody. They're on DEFCON five or something over there."

"I'm not surprised," I said. I was sitting in my office, watching the day dribble away, listening to my friend over the speakerphone. "What do you know?"

"Kid died in his dorm room. Drug overdose, most likely, but they're waiting on the tox report. Time of death, afternoon or evening. Family don't want no autopsy, no press, no trouble—so that's about all you're gonna get. His roommate found him. Totally freaked out—kid came in late from a party, didn't realize he had a corpse in the lower bunk till the next morning. Either your boy was dead when the roommate walked in, or he died in the night. When the roommate figured it out, he kind of went bat-shit."

"Jesus Christ," I muttered. "That would do it to me, too."

"Yeah, I don't think roomie's gonna be finishing out the semester. Anyway...what else?" I heard him ruffling through some papers, looking for his notes. "They interviewed kids on the hall, friends, the usual shit. They all said the kid was kind of down, kind of distracted. Profs say his grades had been bottoming out. Pretty classic, you ask me."

"Classic what?"

"You know—depression, drugs, the usual college thing."

"Yeah," I said, distantly.

"What?"

"Nothing."

"Bullshit. I can tell you got something rattling around your head."

"I don't know. It's probably nothing. But you know that tingly feeling you get, when something's wrong, but you're not sure what?"

"Yeah, I know it. I ain't feeling it here, though. Baby Cops, neither."

"No." I thought for a minute. "Are they holding his personal effects?"

"Naw, I don't think so. They already met with the family, and I think they turned everything over. Why?"

I shook my head, forgetting he couldn't see me. "I don't know." I tried to reach the tingling place, but I couldn't get anything. "Nothing, I guess."

"Well, I asked them give me a call if anything new comes up, so…I'll keep you posted."

"Thanks, Carter."

"No problem."

But there was a problem. I could tell there was a problem. I just couldn't figure out what it was.

I hung up and looked out my window, trying to think. I don't have much of a view—just the side of another old office building. It's not ideal for contemplation, but it's something. Or it would have been something if I could have seen past the grime on the glass.

Whatever my mind was reaching for, it couldn't get any tendrils around it, so I gave up and called Dean Whitman's office. It was a call I'd been putting off, because I wasn't sure how to approach it. Was I supposed to feel angry? Was I supposed to feel guilty? I seemed to be feeling both.

"Jordan," she said, when she heard my voice. It sounded like a confirmation—like she had been expecting the call.

"Yeah," I said. "It's me."

"I'm so sorry," she said.

I sat with that for a moment, and I let her sit with the silence.

"Sorry for what?" I asked, eventually. "Did you do something?"

"Not enough, obviously," she said.

"I told you where the problem was. I told you where to look."

"Yes, dear, but you didn't tell me the boy's name."

That stopped me for a second—but only a second.

"He wasn't the problem," I said. Then I stopped again. "I didn't *think* he was the problem. *He* didn't think he was the problem."

She sighed. "As is so often the case."

A knot in my stomach that I had barely noticed started tightening.

"Do you think it would have...I mean...if I had told you it was Chris who came to see me..."

"I don't know, Jordan. We have excellent programs in place, procedures to deal with children who are in trouble. We really do. Better than most schools. And they get better every year. But can I promise we would have caught him in time? I don't know."

"Even if I had told you?"

"Even then. Some students, just knowing someone's on to them, worried about them, it makes all the difference. Some students, it pushes them away. Look at you."

"Me?"

"Well, we caught you, didn't we? And you did a hell of a job pushing us away."

"What do you mean, you 'caught' me?"

"Jordan, you were textbook depression. You were right on the edge, your whole freshman year."

I felt dizzy all of a sudden. "You thought I was going to...what, kill myself?"

"Jordan. I would never say that. But we were worried, certainly. Your parents were worried. And you wouldn't say a word to anyone. You were a sphinx."

She and I didn't seem to be remembering the same life. I'm the first to admit I had a shitty freshman year, but...textbook depression? Suicidal? That wasn't me.

She cleared her throat. "Anyway, you managed to muddle through, thank God. Most students do, even when they resist help. Children are very resilient. But once in a while, even when we're watching, holding on to them, doing all we can, someone just… slips through our fingers. It's awful."

Her voice sent a chill up my spine.

"Well, I'm sorry," I said quietly. "I guess I should have told you more."

"You were just a child, Jordan."

I winced. "No, I mean…now. About the kid, Chris. I was just trying to protect his privacy."

"I know," she said. "It's a hard line to navigate, especially with this age group. A very hard line. They have a right to their own lives, but you still want to stay close and keep your eyes open."

"Like you stayed close to me?" I asked quietly. "All these years?"

I could hear her smiling on the other end of the phone. "Yes, Jordan. Like that."

The conversation drifted into small talk, and we hung up, promising to see each other soon. I sat in silence for a moment or two, and then an email flashed on my computer screen. It was from Patty. Information on the funeral…in case I wanted to come.

3

The funeral for Chris Tremaine was held at Candler right after finals week. It was a strange time to do it, with kids packing up and heading home, frazzled after exams and just wanting to get the hell out of there. But the family had insisted. They didn't want the thing to stay hanging, unresolved, over the holidays—for his friends or for themselves. They wanted to close the book and take the body home.

They held the service in Dobbs Chapel, a weird, angular, modern arty building smack in the middle of what was otherwise a very traditional looking, marble-walled and slate-roofed campus. The main part of the building crouched next to the Humanities building, with one section vaulting overhead, up and over a brick walkway. I couldn't remember ever having been inside it, though I had walked past it a million times. But, then, there had never been any reason for me to go inside. It's got this huge, flat, concrete tongue depressor sticking straight up into the air, with a big cross cut into it—not exactly a welcome sign for people like Jordan Greenblatt from Long Island, NY.

Patty met me outside, and we exchanged silent hugs before going in. She looked tired and wrung out. Inside, the chapel was tall, grey, and hollow. There were rows of chairs set up on a square, wooden floor where the family seemed to be sitting. Students, friends, and onlookers like me were directed up a flight of stairs to rows of hard, cement pews that wound around the entire square of the chapel. The interior walls were concrete slabs, stretching straight up into the open ceiling. Way up, where the walls connected with the ceiling, were the only windows. Somehow, it felt more like a theatre than a church, and I wasn't surprised to find out, later, that Chris had been planning some kind of production in the chapel for the following semester. Which is why the family had wanted to hold the service there.

I looked around the hall. Sitting directly across from me was a knot of students who all looked vaguely familiar from Chris's play. I tried to figure out which one might be Maddy Taylor, Chris's girlfriend, but none of the females looked any more distraught than the others. Most just looked shell-shocked. One or two looked bored.

It's a strange thing to go to a funeral for somebody you don't know. I've been to weddings of near-strangers, and that's weird and uncomfortable enough, but this went way beyond that. You could feel the circling of wagons—the coming together of family and community. You could feel people reaching out to each other for support and comfort, and overhear them sharing stories of the person they had lost. You could sense all of that…but you weren't really a part of it. You didn't know the friends; you didn't know the family; you didn't know the stories. You were just…there. To witness.

The upside—for me, anyway—was that I could see things the insiders probably didn't, because I wasn't in the moment like everyone else. Which isn't to say I didn't feel bad. I felt awful. But that was just me—my own feelings. They didn't connect me to anyone else. So I sat, unconnected, and I watched.

The information I wanted was all right in front of me, across that expanse of chapel—it was all there with Chris's classmates. All the secrets. Whatever happened to him, it happened among them. I searched faces, looking for something telltale, some sort of giveaway, but everyone seemed locked up tight. Which of them was the key here? Which of them had been so strung out that they had pushed Chris to come to me for help? Was it just the girlfriend, or was it all of them? And which of them *was* the girlfriend? Was it the little, doll-faced blonde? The girl with the dark, frizzy hair? The tall redhead? Who was Chris trying to take care of and protect? Whose mess had he been trying to clean up?

It was right then that the tickling feeling I'd had with Carter came back—the feeling that something was wrong with the whole story. And now I knew what it was.

4

"I don't buy it," said Carter, watching me from his desk. I was pacing back and forth, spooling out my story, and he was tilting back in his chair, chewing gum, and saying little.

"He didn't do drugs," I insisted. "Ever."

"Says him."

"I think he was telling the truth."

"Says you."

"Come on, Carter…"

"Maybe he didn't never do it but that one time. You don't know."

I paced some more, shaking my head. "You should have heard the way he talked," I said. "How his dad was an alcoholic, how he always had to be the one who cleaned up after him— picking him up off the floor. Now here he is at college, doing the same thing for his friends. This is the poster child for Just Say No. This is not a kid who suddenly starts using."

"Except he did," Carter said, trying to be patient. "They tested his blood. It's drugs killed him, sure as shit."

"What kind of drugs?"

"They won't tell me that."

"Well, somebody gave it to him, then."

"Course somebody *gave* it to him. Nobody thinks he was brewing shit in his room."

"It doesn't make any sense. There's something else going on here."

Carter puffed out his cheeks, thinking, and slowly let the air out, like a dying balloon. "I see two ways it goes down. One: accidental OD, like the Baby Cops say. He's a user and he fucked up. Maybe he's habitual, maybe he's a first-timer. Either way, he fucked up and it's an accident. Two: he got depressed and he offed himself. Did it on purpose, we'll never know why. Either one's possible, both of them fit the evidence, and neither one of them's a mystery to solve."

"I know, I know."

"You want a case, you got to be able to call it equivocal death, and this shit ain't equivocal."

"Okay."

"But you don't like either of them stories I told. So what are you looking for?"

"I don't know. Whatever *he* was looking for. Whatever he came to me to talk about."

"Well, if there's anything there, you ain't gonna get your hands on it," Carter said. "'Cause unless you get the parents to give you permission, this thing's shut tight. They don't even want to know suicide or accident—they just want to go home."

I gave up my pacing and sat down across the desk from him. "Look, he comes to me and he says they're all on some drug, he says they're all paranoid and defensive and sick, he says he's going to bring me evidence. Okay, I never hear from him, I don't care, I don't think he's going to do it. But what if he *did* start poking around, making trouble? What if he *was* going to come back to me, and he just got in someone's way? Some dealer?"

"What if, what if," said Carter with a shrug. "You ain't got a shred of evidence."

"Yeah, well…that's never stopped me before."

"Jordy…" he said, in a warning voice.

"If I could talk to the parents—"

Carter laughed. "Yeah, Baby Cops'll *definitely* let you do that."

"Are the parents still here?"

"I reckon. They were gonna head home, but they got all tangled up about personal effects or something."

"Tangled up how?"

"I don't know. They couldn't find something. A cell phone, I think. Minor shit, but I guess they're obsessing. You know how it is—latching on to something physical, since the thing they actually care about is…you know."

"Yeah," I said. "So his cell phone's missing?"

"Shit!" he said, crashing down on all four legs of his chair. "Goddamn! Of course. The cell phone's got the microfilm."

I stared at him for a moment, then said, "You're an asshole."

He laughed.

"All right," I said, surrendering. He was right.

"Sorry I can't do nothing for you. I just don't think there's shit to do."

"Yeah, I get you."

I left Carter's office with the nagging feeling that I was missing something, but I gave up. Usually, I'm pretty good at knowing where the music is going—hearing the patterns and figuring out where the shift is coming. You can't improvise if you can't intuit things like that, and a lot of my job is improvisation—jamming, riffing, making things up as I go. On the one hand, that's hard to do, because life is mysterious, and the human heart is dark, and how can you really know the truth, and all that crap. But on the other hand, life is also a series of patterns, and there's not that many of them you can play. My bull fiddle's got four strings, and the human heart probably doesn't have a whole lot more.

But maybe this time I was just out of tune. Maybe this was all just my guilty conscience talking to me, wanting there to be something more—something I should have done…something I could still do now. I had emailed the dean before going to see Carter, telling her I had suspicions, but now I just felt bad about planting ideas in her head, stringing her along. This was a dead end, and I was butting my head against the wall.

I left Carter's office and drove over to the Candler campus to walk around a little. I don't know why. To close the door on the story? To figure out a way past the brick wall? I guess I would have been happy with either. I hate an unresolved chord.

I stopped in front of the Heywood dorm, where Chris had lived and died. I looked up at the old marble building and wondered what had gone on inside. It was like looking across that cold, wide chapel at Chris's friends. There was an answer in there, but it was far away from me, and it bugged me.

I pulled out my cell phone and took a few pictures of the building—out of habit more than anything else. But it was totally the wrong thing to do at that moment, because a Baby Cop had been watching me from across the street, and now he came over to hassle me.

"You got some business here?" he asked.

"Just taking a few pictures," I said.

"You got a kid here?"

"No!" I said with a laugh. "Do I look old enough for that?"

He didn't find it amusing. "Lemme see some ID," he said, holding his hand out impatiently.

This was ridiculous. How many times had I been on the Candler campus over the years? Hundreds? And suddenly, today, I looked suspicious? I took out my wallet and handed him the whole thing, refusing to pull out my driver's license for him. Which was the second wrong thing to do, because my PI license was in there, and he yanked it right out.

"All right, Mr. Greenblatt, private investigator," he said, putting on cop attitude like it was a Kevlar vest. "What the fuck are you doing here, taking pictures of this dorm? This particular dorm?"

This particular dorm. Ah.

"I'm just a friend of the kid who died here, that's all. I was…curious."

"Curious, huh? You working for the family?"

A lie might have been a good idea at this point, but I didn't think about it in time. I told him No. He looked me over, considering how much of an asshole he felt like being, and then seemed to back down a little.

"Well, look here," he said. "You got questions, I reckon you can go ask my sergeant. He might help you out—I don't know. But we can't have folks prowling around here, taking pictures and gawking and shit."

I looked around to see what kind of trouble I might have been causing. "Kids are all home for the holidays, aren't they?" I asked.

He took my arm firmly and turned me to face him. "I said we can't have folks prowling around here, and that ought to be enough for you. First of all, you're loitering, and that's enough for me to cite you, and second of all, we don't want this turning into some goddamned circus. Now, if you got business, like I said, you go take it to my sergeant. Otherwise, I need you off this campus. You hear me?"

"Yeah, yeah, I hear you," I said, annoyed. He let my arm go, and we stood there for a moment, face to face.

"You mean *right now*?" I asked.

"I mean right the fuck now, yes sir," he said grimly. "And if I see you hanging around here again, it's gonna be trouble for you. You got me, Mr. Greenblatt?"

"Loud and clear," I said. I wasn't sure he really had the authority to ban me from campus, but I didn't press it. It was bad enough he was going to remember my name.

He handed my wallet back to me and then watched me walk away from the dorm and down the street. For all I know, he followed me all the way to the edge of campus, where I had parked. I don't know. I refused to look over my shoulder.

5.

So Chris Tremaine's story was over, full stop, and for everyone else, life moved on. His friends were all home for the holidays, probably telling their high-school buddies about the crazy shit that had gone down on their campus, perversely proud to have the best anecdote.

For those of us left in Atlanta, the weather finally turned cold, and families did that winter thing of hunkering down together, becoming a little more private, a little more closed. Since I didn't have much of a family, I hunkered down with my bandmates. On the weekends, we practiced at Oticha's house, which had more open space, but if we had to meet at night, we set up down the street at my house, so Oticha's kids could get to sleep.

Usually we didn't practice much during the week unless we had a gig. But amazingly, we had managed to land a job for the week right before Christmas, at a bar in Little Five Points that had changed hands six or seven times in as many years. It had been hippie, punk, goth, even country. Now it seemed kind of nondescript. It was cleaner and brighter than in previous incarnations—I noticed the walls were no longer painted black—but it didn't seem to have a theme. Theme or no, though, they had hired us to play, so we needed to gear up and get ready. It was going to be our first public gig with Lydia on board, so we wanted to make sure we featured her and gave her some spotlight.

She didn't make it easy. "Lydia, what do you think of this song?" Shrug. "Lydia, do you think sax or clarinet for this piece?" Shrug. Either she was happy to go with the flow, or she just felt like the new kid and wanted to defer to the rest of the group for a while. Or maybe she was just an uncommunicative person in general. I couldn't tell.

But if she didn't reveal much in conversation, she spoke volumes when she played. For Lydia Sinclair, jazz was a total-body experience. I sometimes grooved to the music behind my bass, but that was just your basic toe-tapping and swaying from side to side. Oticha and Pete were rock steady and still—at most, Oticha closed his eyes. But Lydia danced. It was like her whole body was playing the music, and her clarinet was just the opening where the sound came out. The way she moved had something to do with how she felt about the music, and something to do with how the music made her feel. Or maybe it just *was* the music, playing her. You could get seriously mystical, watching Lydia play.

"It's not just that," Pete said one night, after practice had broken up and Lydia, Oticha, and Drummer du Jour had gone home. Pete was splayed across our couch, beer in hand. "She's not even the same person when she's playing."

Susannah and I were moving back and forth between the living room and the kitchen, clearing away shot glasses and beer bottles. She snorted in derision as she passed me. I thwacked a warning shot across her stern as she passed me, and then asked Pete what he meant.

"Her whole affect," he said. "Her waddyacallit? Her kinesthetic…thing."

"What the hell are you talking about?"

"I don't know. I did some work for a dance company once. I was trying to remember some of the words they used."

"Yeah," I said. "Don't do that."

"It's like, the whole way she carries herself, the way she moves, the way she just *is* in her body. It's *different* when she's playing. Like she's not the same person at all. There's jazz Lydia and life Lydia, and they're…different."

"So she's bipolar," said Susannah, coming back into the room. "So what?" She grabbed Pete's beer bottle out of his hands and went back to the kitchen.

"Hey, I wasn't finished with that!" he yelled. Then, "What's with her?"

"I don't know," I said.

"I don't like her," she said, returning with two fresh beers. "I told you that." She plopped down on the couch and handed a bottle to Pete.

"You didn't tell *me*," he said. "Why don't you like her?"

"Dunno," she said with a Lydia-esque shrug.

"Well, that's helpful."

"I don't have to explain myself," she said haughtily.

Pete looked up at me. "Seriously?" he asked.

"Yeah, that's true," I said. "It's a girl thing."

"Totally unfair."

I shrugged now. "Fair's got nothing to do with it."

He nodded and said, "See, this is why I haven't had a date in three years."

"Ho ho," my wife chuckled into her beer bottle.

I sat down in a ratty old rocking chair facing the couch, put my feet up on the coffee table, and pushed myself back into a recline. "Well, *I* like her. I like her sound."

Pete nodded. "Her sound is solid."

"So fine," said Susannah. "She's solid."

"Don't sulk."

"I'm not sulking. It's your band. I just don't like her. She bugs me."

"Okay," I said. "Something to talk about on the way to Macon."

"I don't think so," she said coldly.

"Okay," I said. "Something to totally avoid talking about on the way to Macon."

Pete staggered to his feet. "Gosh, you kids are fun," he said, "but I better be getting home." He looked over at his keyboard and amp, which we had pushed against a wall. "Okay if I leave my stuff till tomorrow?"

Susannah nodded lazily. I walked him out and said goodbye. When I came back, Susannah was already in the bathroom, getting ready for bed. She came out, book in her hand, and stayed like that until she turned the light out.

I wanted to say something, but I didn't. And the longer I didn't, the stupider it felt to bring it up. This is how I operate. I have this feeling in the moment—this thing I think I should say, this feeling I want to vent—but then I don't say it, I hold it back, and the longer I hold it back, the stupider and pettier the thing sounds in my head, so I keep it inside and never say it.

I *think* it, for sure. I say it to myself. I have lots of good arguments with my wife in my head. Just not out loud. Because they never seem to be worth it, in the end. Not compared to all the good stuff.

Susannah does not have this problem. Anything I'm doing that bothers her, she says it right away. Loud and clear. Which is why this thing with Lydia was weird. Whatever was bugging her about our new band member, it was something she wasn't comfortable sharing. And that was strange. But God knows I wasn't going to push it tonight. Maybe tomorrow. Or later. Definitely sometime before our road trip for the holidays.

But I never got the chance. Because the day after our gig, just as we were packing up the car to head south to see

Susannah's family, I got a phone call from Dean Whitman. She wanted to see me at her house. Right away. I told her we were heading out of town, and asked if it could wait till after the holidays.

She said no. She was angry.

Shit.

I had told her a few days earlier that I thought Chris had stuck his nose into something ugly and gotten killed for it. That's what this was all about. It had been a stupid thing to say, and she was angry about it. When would I ever learn to stop sharing my idiot theories before I had any evidence?

"Dean," I said, "I'm sorry I overreacted. I shouldn't have dumped all that stuff on you. And I promise I'll apologize in person. But it's Christmas eve tomorrow, and we've got to get down to—"

She cut me off before I could finish. "Jordan," she said—several times, until I stopped whining—"Listen to me. I need to talk to you. I need to talk to you now. In person. And I need it to stay between the two of us. Do you understand?"

I said I did, even though I didn't.

"You can head to Macon as soon we're done," she said. "Or you can take a bus, if your wife needs to leave right away. But I need to see you *now*."

"Why?" I asked. "What's this all about?"

But she had already hung up.

6

I stood at the dean's front door, waiting for her while giant animals threw themselves against the thick front door and scratched at it with razor-like claws. It was not a very inviting sound. When the door opened, I was pounced on by dogs large and small, and hooted at by various other animals. I was grateful it was December and I was wearing heavy clothes.

The dean led me through the wildlife to her home office, where we were safe from attack. She sat me down in a large, leather chair that swallowed me up and made me feel about ten years old. I pulled myself out and perched on the edge of the seat. The dean was looking at me from behind her desk.

"Why are you stirring things up, Jordan?" she asked.

I was immediately on the defensive, as I usually was with her. "What stirring? I'm not stirring anything."

"Yes, you are. You've been talking to people. Who?"

"Nobody. You."

She waited.

"And maybe a friend at the midtown precinct."

She sighed and closed her eyes. I could feel her headache from across the room.

"Just for advice," I said. "He's a friend. Anyway, if it makes you feel any better, he thinks I'm nuts, too."

She opened her eyes and looked evenly at me. "I didn't say you were nuts."

She picked up a little stuffed bird toy, of which she had many on her desk, and gave it a squeeze. It made some kind of birdcall noise. She turned the thing around in her hand and kept looking at it as she spoke.

"I don't know what's going on, Jordan, but I don't think it's as simple as the police are saying. I've looked at Chris's file, and I've talked to some of his friends. Chris using drugs? Hard drugs? That doesn't wash."

"I agree."

"All right, then. So something happened to him. What?"

"I don't know. Something."

"You said he might have been snooping around, trying to learn something about who was moving drugs on campus."

"Yeah, that's what I was afraid of."

"Well, your theory makes as much sense as anything else right now. And if it's true, then we have a very...volatile situation out there, and it's only a matter of time before somebody else gets hurt."

"Okay."

"I'm in a tough position, Jordan. Obviously, I can't condone or allow illegal drugs to be sold and consumed on campus. But I'm also not an idiot. I do live in the real world. I know what goes on, and what's always gone on, since *I* was in school. I know there are limits to what anyone can do."

"Sure."

"If kids want drugs, kids are going to get their hands on drugs. But if Chris got killed for asking the wrong questions, well…I can't wait around to find out who's next."

I nodded, but said nothing. I knew what was coming. I could feel it in the music.

"So where does that leave me? The family doesn't want an investigation. The campus police don't see a need for an investigation. If I pushed them to open one—and I'm not even sure I could—but if I did, you know they'd come at it like a blunt instrument, and the whole thing would go underground. Our Baby Cops don't exactly tread lightly."

I smiled, amused to find out that the administration had the same nasty nickname for them that we all did.

"So that leaves you."

Bingo.

"Police are going to focus on supply. Our office tries to lessen demand. We do a lot of good, believe it or not. We're ready to do even more, after what happened to Chris. We've got new drug awareness seminars ready to go, as soon as the kids come back to school. A whole series of them, not a one-shot deal. For the whole campus."

Now *she* sounded defensive. "Okay," I said.

She looked up at me. "But that's not enough, is it?"

I shrugged. This was her party, not mine.

"Never mind," she said, with a tiny smile. "I can read you like a book."

She got up and began to pace.

"I've been a good friend to you, I think, over the years."

It didn't sound like a question, but I agreed with her.

"There are limits to what I can do in this office. Even within those limits, you already told me I'm not going to hear much truth, if I ask officially, and I agree with you. So. I need someone who can find out what's going on out there. Someone who can tell me what we're dealing with, in case we need to take…some kind of action." She stopped pacing and looked at me again. "I need a friend, Jordan."

I nodded. "I understand."

"Do you?"

"I think so."

"You need to understand, Jordan, this would just be a favor. A favor to me personally. The university isn't asking for an investigation, so it's not like I can hire you."

"So this is just between you and me."

"Completely between you and me," she said, nodding. "Now, I have a friend over at the registrar's office. I think I could talk her into helping me out on getting you a student ID and all that. Under the table. It would get you on campus, at least."

"That would be helpful."

"But after that, well…you're on your own."

"Got it."

"We can put you in the Ph.D program so you can get in close to see what's going on. I don't think you can pass for an undergraduate anymore."

I thought about that for a moment. "I don't know," I said. "I don't think I could get away with being a grad student. I don't know anything about theatre. I don't even like it all that much."

She nodded. "So how do we get you close to Chris's friends?"

"I could probably handle music," I said. "I mean, I'm no scholar or anything, but I can play an instrument and read music. I could probably handle being a grad student there, if I didn't have to do it for too long."

"That might work," she said. "The departments work closely with each other, and they share a lot of students. It ought to give you access to whatever is going on. Let me see what I can do."

I watched her scribble a note to herself, and said, "And maybe a Masters instead of a Ph.D? I don't know how much heavy scholarship I can handle."

She smiled and kept writing. I wondered whether I should say the rest of what I was thinking. But I *was* a grown-up, now, more or less. "Listen," I said. "I hate to bring this up, but, you know, this *is* my day job, and…"

"I understand," she said. "You have bills to pay." She scribbled some more notes to herself. "I can't use university funds, but…I'll take care of you. somehow. I'll figure something out."

"As long as it pays the rent, I'm happy to do it for you. It's just, you know…a job like this, you have to be kind of all-in. I mean, to do it right, you have to put everything else on hold."

"I understand completely," she said.

But she didn't understand—not completely. And neither did I.

7

My friends and family were dead set against the gig from the moment I told them about it. Unanimously.

Yeah, I know—I wasn't supposed to tell anyone. Oops.

My father: "I always hoped you'd pursue graduate work, but not like this."

Oticha: "Unwise, man. You can't step into the same river twice."

Carter: "I reckon it's either a goddamned waste of time or you're gonna get yourself killed."

And from Porkchop, predictably, something about undergraduate poontang that I'm not going to repeat.

Susannah just got quiet when I told her. She started doing unnecessary busy-work in the kitchen—recleaning dishes that were already clean, reorganizing the spice rack. I came up behind her and wrapped my arms around her.

"What's the matter?" I asked, pushing the issue for once. "This isn't like you."

She shrugged. I held her tighter.

"I don't like it," she said, quietly. "I don't like you going away."

"I'm not going away. I'll be on campus during the day, like I'm at my office. What's the difference?"

"I don't know," she said. "It just feels different." She sighed and leaned back into me. "New people, new friends. I don't know. It just feels like everything's changing, all of a sudden. Nothing feels normal anymore."

"Change is good," I said, hopefully.

She sighed again. "Change is bullshit. Everyone says it's good, but nobody believes it."

"All right then, change is bad. But nothing's changing. This is just another job. I'm in, I'm out."

"No, it's going to be weird and complicated, I can tell. You're going to get *immersed* in shit, and come home telling me stories about this kid or that professor, or whatever—all these people I don't know, doing all these interesting things."

"I don't care about any of that," I said.

"You will," she said. "You're not going to be watching them from a distance—you're going to be right in the middle of it. It's different. Don't act like it's not."

"You've seen too many movies."

"And then the band comes over to practice, and even that's not the same anymore."

"Lydia's all right…"

She turned around to face me, still in my arms.

"I know she's all right, Jordan. I'm not an idiot. She kicks ass. It's just different, that's all. I liked how things were, and you changed it. That's all. I know you needed to change it. I know it's better. But it's different. It changes the whole dynamic, and I had nothing to say about it. Your job. Your band. I'm just the wife."

"I'm sorry."

"Don't be sorry. You did what you had to do. And you have to do this thing, too. I get it. Doesn't mean I have to be happy about it."

"True."

She leaned her forehead against mine.

"Just don't go falling in love with any college girls, all right?"

"Are you kidding? All those serious chicks playing Beethoven? You know that's not my thing."

She reared back and butted my head. Hard. I yelped.

"I'm serious, fuckhead."

"All right, all right," I said, wincing.

"No college girls, no sudden appreciation of theatre. And home in bed with me every night. Deal?"

"Deal," I said. I pulled back a bit to get her face in focus. "Are we good?"

She sighed again, but smiled. "Of course we're good," she said.

"Then it's all good," I said. "That's all that matters."

8

"Well, well, if it ain't Bulldog Barnes," Carter said, with a shit-eating grin, when I stopped by the precinct to check in with him.

"Quit that," I said. I hated the nickname, and he was the one who had come up with it.

"If the shoe fits, chew on it."

"I am not a bulldog," I said, sitting down and handing him the overpriced coffee I had picked up for him.

"Naw, not hardly," he said. "You got *no* problem letting go."

"I know, I know. You think I'm all fucked up on this Tremaine thing."

He shrugged. He was just a bystander, this time around—he didn't have to have an opinion.

"Fifty bucks says I'm right," I offered.

He shrugged again. "If you're right, you're a dead man."

"So pay Susannah then."

"You're an asshole."

"Yeah, I'm an asshole. Meanwhile, what do I need to know, before I head over there?"

Carter leaned forward and searched for one legal pad among the many strewn across his desk. He grabbed it and flipped through a couple of pages.

"I don't think there's nothing new since I talked to you," he said. "Family took the body, Baby Cops closed the case, that's it."

"No loose ends?"

He scanned his notes. "They lost his cell phone. That's all I got."

"Okay. And what about the roommate who found him?"

"Randy Youdin. He's out of the picture. Parents took him home to sit out the semester and get his shit together."

"Okay. I had the roommate and I had a girlfriend named Maddy. You get any other names?"

"No, I didn't get that kind of detail from CPD, and I didn't want to ask. If it sounds like professional curiosity, they'll talk to me. If I push it, they're gonna clam up."

"Right."

Silence.

"Listen," he said, seriously. "You be careful over there, all right? Keep your eyes open, but don't go jumping in over your head. You don't know what the fuck's going on."

I shrugged it off. "You know me."

He nodded and smiled crookedly. "Yeah, I do know you. That's why I'm saying it. Just on the off chance you're not full of shit."

"I'll be fine."

"Yeah, yeah. You'll be fine. You ever done one of these deals before?"

"What?"

"Go undercover."

"Undercover? What is this, *21 Jump Street*?"

He looked evenly at me, no longer amused. "You got a fake ID and a fake name, and you're embedding down at a fucking college where you don't belong. That's legit undercover, far as I'm concerned. Hell, that's legit, far as *anyone's* concerned."

I waved it away. "It's just an excuse to be there. It's my usual snoop job, that's all. Eyes and ears."

He nodded, noncommittally. "Maybe yes, maybe no."

"Fifty bucks," I reminded him. "You're gonna owe me by midterms."

He laughed, finally. I thanked him for his help and left him to deal with his real work. And I drove to campus to buy books for my classes.

Books for my classes! Jesus Christ. What was I doing?

9

I came back to campus bright and early on a Monday morning, with a freshly minted student ID in the name of Joshua Green and a brand new backpack slung over my shoulder.

I had been on the Candler grounds hundreds of times over the years, but usually on weekends or in the evenings. Now, though, heading across the quad toward my first class, I got this weird wave of memories—this visceral, time-travel-y feeling like the last fifteen years had never happened, and I was right back where I had started. Like all the things I had done, and seen, and been through, were just a long dream, and now I was awake, with all those days and years still stretching out in front of me, waiting to be lived.

What a rotten feeling!

I looked around as I walked to class, feeling like I was eighteen again and wondering: Where the hell am I going? Biology? Or have I already failed that? Is there a party tonight in the dorm basement? Is our band going to play, or are we just going to get drunk and write graffiti all over the walls? Or did I do that already?

Then I shook it off and remembered: no, no—I'm not back there; I'm *here*. I'm not a kid again. I'm a...grad student? Which felt even weirder, because I had barely made it out of college the first time, and grad school had *never* been something I had thought about. Ever. In any field.

And yet, here I was, marching into the lion's den.

Once the weird time-travel feeling wore off, I started noticing how different the campus felt. It wasn't just the new buildings that had sprung up since I had been a student there. Even the people looked different. I remembered the guys I went to school with being a variety of shapes and sizes and types, but everywhere I looked now, all I could see were enormous, steroidal monsters with broad chests and arms like tree trunks. Like everyone was suddenly majoring in Gym.

Now, maybe you don't find this unusual. I guess it depends where you went to college. But Candler was *never* a sports school. We never had a football team or a top-ranked basketball team or anything like that. I mean, there were teams, but they kind of existed in the background, and they didn't take up much oxygen. Even the guys on the rugby team didn't look like the guys I was seeing crisscrossing the quad. Those guys had been tough, and as strong as crazed bulls, but they never looked...inflated. These guys looked like they had bicep balloons. All of them.

The good part about watching this parade of Aryan Pride was that it took my mind off the scam I was about to start running. But as soon as I entered the music building, I remembered what I was doing there.

Fortunately, the first class the dean and her registrar friend had signed me up for was a tiny seminar on pre-Columbian and Chicano musical performance, where none of us were expected to be experts on the topic. So it would be easier for me to pass...at least for now.

The course was listed jointly with the theatre department, which meant I'd have access to a few kids from Chris's department. What I did with that access was going to be up to me.

I found an open seat around a big conference table and plopped down my bag. The student next to me was scrawny and shapeless, a giant lasagna noodle of a guy leaning way back in his chair, his boneless body and long legs cascading down the chair and onto the floor. He had a wispy beard and a pseudo-Rasta cap on his mop of red hair. Basically, he looked like every kid I had gone to college with. Finally. It was good to know they were still out there, somewhere.

He looked me over, trying to figure out what I was. "Theatre or music?" he asked.

"Music," I said.

"Thank fuck," he said. "I'm going to be so lost it isn't funny."

Theatre student. First try. Not bad.

"You help me with the theatre parts," I offered, "and I'll help you with the music."

"Awesome sauce," he said, extending his fist for a bump. "I'm Blair."

"Josh," I said.

The professor walked in, a striking-looking Hispanic woman in her fifties wearing a long, blue scarf draped dramatically around her neck and across her shoulder, pinned in place with an ornate pin in the shape of a bird. She had an equally dramatic streak of grey in her otherwise dark hair, and she stood in a posture that made you sure she had once been a dancer.

"Good morning," she said, with just the slightest accent. "I am Doctor Villareal. Please call me Claudia."

She sat down and arranged some papers in front of her—and, with a toss of her hair, we were off. Over the next two hours, I learned more about the Popul Vuh and the ancient Mayans than I ever thought I wanted to. I learned that the professor's pin was supposed to represent a flying serpent god named Quetzalcoatl. And I learned that folk music can be a great resource for finding cool band names.

I spent most of my time ingratiating myself with Blair—whispering definitions of musical terms when he looked bewildered, rolling my eyes when Villareal went into some obscure digression about Olmec religion, and otherwise making myself of use to him so that, when class finally ended, he'd invite me to lunch. Which he did.

I figured Blair would be eating with a crowd, being a social butterfly theatre-type, and I was right. A flock of friends was waiting for him, perched around a café table outside the cafeteria. When they saw us coming, they pulled over a second table to make room for us. I went inside to get some food, but Blair stayed behind to talk. That didn't surprise me—from the look of him, he didn't eat more than one meal a day.

Now, I had been on this campus a hundred times over the years—to see my father, or to stop by the library, or to see shows, or whatnot. But I hadn't really spent any time in any of these new buildings. And one of those buildings was the new dining hall. So I was not prepared for what I walked into.

The old dining hall had been just that—a hall. It was a huge, beige building with massively ugly chandeliers hanging down from an airplane-hangar-like ceiling—cold and echoing and personality-free. It was your basic, old-fashioned cafeteria, with one line of students snaking past three or four terrible entrée choices and the usual limp salad and old Jello side-dishes. If they ever served anything unusual, like tacos, it was only because they had a lot of hamburger meat leftover from the day before, and needed a way to get rid of it. You could usually see the remains of hamburger patties sticking out of the pile of ground beef—like they were too lazy to crumple it up and didn't care who knew it. Campus dining was the main reason half the freshman guys pledged fraternities.

But all that was a thing of the past. Now there were four or five different food stations anchored to different sections of the room, each one with a differently colored faux-roof or awning, painted in a different cheery style. You could have Mexican food; you could have Italian food; you could have falafels or wontons; you could have gluten-free; you could have dairy-free; you could have vegan. There was even a frozen yogurt stand. It was incredible. The long, straight, prison-like tables had been replaced by round-tops, and the linoleum floor had been replaced or covered up with carpeting. It looked like the food court at a high-end shopping mall. And all the students sitting around those lovely tables looked like goddamned catalogue models—the best and the brightest, showing off their new clothes and looking unspeakably healthy. I wondered, for a second, whether we had all looked like this, back in our day, but it didn't seem possible.

When I got back outside with my modest chicken wrap, I pretended to be intensely interested in my food so that I could let my ears wander around the table and tune in to what everyone was talking about. I discovered that Blair was a directing student with a fondness for German theatre, which sounded very strident and angry. Which was funny, because there was nothing angry or strident about Blair. He seemed like a happy, harmless dude, the kind of guy who would be content to smoke pot and play Hacky Sack for the rest of his life. And yet there he was, talking about all of this angst-y stuff with an actress who was introduced to me simply as Gates, and who seemed to be his constant companion. She had long, severe, straight hair parted in the middle, a prominent jaw, and a loud, commanding voice. She, at least, looked like she should be into Valkyries or whatever. They leaned toward each other, talking intently about stuff that made no sense to me, so I kind of tuned them out and aimed my ears elsewhere.

The other conversation was between two floppy-haired, blandly good-looking actors who were talking about a movement class they had just come out of, that had apparently been more punishing than usual. I was able to follow most of what they were talking about, but there wasn't any way into the conversation for me. So I just sat between their conversation and Blair's. Being a snoop by nature, it wasn't an uncomfortable position for me.

There was one other person at the table, and he was watching and listening in silence, like me. He wore round glasses and was dressed in a black, mock turtleneck and grey cardigan.

With that outfit, and his antennae so obviously deployed to pick up something interesting, I figured he was probably a writer.

I ate quietly, listening vaguely to Blair and Gates talk about people named Muller and Handke, and the two floppy-hairs talk about something called Alexander technique, until Gates started talking about a play she was working on. The name of the writer jumped out at me—I had heard it before.

"Brecht?" I said, butting into their conversation. "Is that what you just said?"

"Yeah," said Gates. "I'm doing a scene from *Mother Courage* for Directing."

"You're a Brecht fan?" said Blair, not quite believing it.

"I don't even know who he is," I said. "I just remember hearing his name, a few months ago. Somebody was talking about him after a show I saw here. It was the one with that meat bikini thing."

Blair and Gates nodded sadly and both said, "Chris."

Gates said, "He was big into Brecht."

"Was?" I said innocently.

That stopped even the floppy-hairs' conversation. I looked from face to face, faking confusion as best I could.

"What?" I said again. "Did he flunk out or something?"

"Dude," Blair said. "Chris is the guy who died. You didn't hear about that?"

"Fuck, no," I said quietly. "I'm sorry, man. I just started, this semester. I was barely on campus before."

Yes, it was ham-handed and obvious, but these guys didn't seem the suspicious types, and they took the act at face value. Most people do.

"What happened to him?" I asked.

"Drugs," Blair said. "So fucking sad."

The others nodded. I waited for elaboration, but there was none.

"That's a shame," I said, fishing a little more. "His show was pretty cool. He seemed like a talented guy."

"He was," said Gates, a little more aggressively than the situation called for. She caught a warning glance from the two actors, and backed down.

"What?" I asked innocently.

"It's nothing," said Blair. "Gates thinks they work the undergrads too hard. It's a pretty competitive program. There's too many kids, and not enough parts to go around. Things get intense."

"Chris was an actor, too?" I asked.

"Everybody does everything," one of the floppy-hairs said. "That's the program. But he only ever got shit parts, you know? Like, Spear Carrier Number Four? So he started doing more writing and directing."

"Which is how Cyrus got his hooks in him," said the other.

"What the fuck is that supposed to mean?" said Gates.

"Jesus, Gates," Floppy 1 said. "Chill."

"Got his hooks in him—what the fuck?" she said again.

"Who's Cyrus?" I asked.

Blair sighed. "Cyrus Calendar," he said. "He runs the directing program. He runs my whole fucking life, actually. He kind of took Chris on as his project."

"His little pet," Floppy 2 said.

"Fuck you," growled Gates. "You should be so lucky."

Floppy 2 just laughed.

"Come on," the other one said. "You know Chris never said a single word that didn't come out of Cyrus's brain—not all year."

"Was that a bad thing?" I asked.

"He was turning into a little Cyrus," Floppy 1 said. "If you think that's a good thing, then…"

Blair stepped in to translate. "Cyrus doesn't do much with the undergrads, so it was…kind of strange. Made some people jealous, probably."

"As if," said Floppy 1.

"Directors, I mean," Blair said. "Guys in the MFA program."

"Like you?" Floppy 1 sneered.

"No, not like me. Guys who didn't have access—that's what I'm saying."

"Was he a friend of yours?" I asked Floppy 1.

"Yeah," he said. "We were in the same hall, freshman year. He was a good guy. Till he went off the deep end."

This was more than Gates could take. "Anything that isn't a sitcom is the deep end to you."

"Gates, you're a fucking freak," the actor said, not unkindly, "but you've always been a freak. Chris wasn't. He was a normal, ordinary kid from the suburbs till Cyrus got hold of him. That's all I'm saying."

"Was he unhappy?" I asked. "I mean, was he forced to do stuff he didn't like, or…I don't know…believe in?"

That stopped them all. They thought about it for a minute, then shrugged.

"No," Floppy 1 said. "He loved the shit he was doing. He was just intense about it. Like freaky intense. I don't know what was going on with him."

"Yeah," said Floppy 2. "We didn't even see him anymore. I don't know what he was doing, but he was never around. I don't think he slept, like, ever."

"He was working on something," Gates said. "Some project. But he wouldn't tell anyone what it was."

There was a pause. A lull, as my friend Kitty would shout—not that she would have dared to make a joke about this one.

"Could we talk about something else?" asked Floppy 1, a little deflated. "I'm so tired of digging this shit up."

There were nods all around, and I apologized for bringing it up. But no one seemed to have another topic, so everyone just focused on their food in silence. I looked across the table at the writer, who hadn't said a word the whole time. He met my eyes, raised his eyebrows, and shrugged a little, but said nothing.

I looked at the faces of the students around the table— grad students and undergrads, actors and directors. There was a whole world going on here—a whole, intense world with just these four kids (or five, if you counted Silent Sam). Drugs had killed their friend, but that barely got a mention compared to all the other things that were going on. Was that just cover in front of a stranger, or was it the way they felt? And then, beyond this little group...what? The department was huge, with probably dozens of cliques and sub-groups, each with its own reality.

All these lives—all these dramas. I wondered how long it would take me to figure out what the hell was going on.

10

The first week of classes went by painlessly. I had to play piano every day, and it had been a long time since I had oiled those gears, so…that was a little embarrassing. But other than that, it was quiet. Which was bad, because a quiet education wasn't what I had gone there for.

I came home dutifully every night and told Susannah all of the nothing that I had experienced. And I begged off rehearsals with Oticha and the gang until I could get control of my homework.

"Homework?" said Susannah, staring down at the pile of books I had dumped on our dining room table. "Seriously?"

"Yes, dear," I said. "I've got a twenty-page paper due next week, and a hundred pages of shit to read."

She looked over the mountain of books in front of me and said, "This is officially no fun."

I agreed. I really didn't want to have to keep this crap up for a whole semester.

Fortunately, opportunity dropped in my lap just a few days later. I was walking to lunch with Blair, trying to make small talk while he gazed zombie-like into his cell phone. I've never gotten the hang of walking while reading, but Blair was a pro. Suddenly, he stopped dead in his tracks and said, "Dude…"

"What?" I asked, not knowing how else to respond.

"Calendar's having one of his parties this weekend. You're coming."

"Why?"

"Because we're fucking grad students, dude. Nobody invites us to shit."

"But why do I want to go to *your* party?"

Blair put the phone down for a second and looked at me.

"First of all," he said, "it's the only thing we've got, unless you're holding out on me."

"Nope," I said. "No music parties. None *I* know about, anyway."

"Okay then. And second, Calendar's parties are sick. He gets people from every department, there's always somebody doing a slide show from some archaeological dig or whatever, and then he makes this huge vat of curry and everybody gets shitfaced. Professors, I mean. Shitfaced drunk professors. You got your education, you got your entertainment. It's the total package."

"Hmm," I said, pretending to think it over.

"Plus," he said, "there are some seriously hot girls in the theatre department, and Calendar always invites them."

"Well," I said, "you make a strong case."

"Dude, if you don't come with me, you're not going to understand any of the shit we talk about at lunch for, like, a month," he said.

Eventually, I told him I'd go—not that I had been wavering. It was the perfect chance to meet more of Chris's friends and professors, and observe them at close, drunken range.

I told Blair I would meet him at the party about an hour after it started. I didn't want to be too conspicuous in the early, de-populated stages, just in case any faculty recognized me from my previous life. I figured an hour in would be safe, and Blair would be a good tour guide.

Cyrus Calendar lived not too far from me, in Little Five Points, the most conspicuously artsy and edgy neighborhood in town. There are plenty of arts enclaves all over Atlanta, plenty of interesting, diverse, and funky neighborhoods with cool shops and galleries, but none of them flies the freak flag as aggressively as Little Five Points. And yet, once you get off the main strip of stores and restaurants that are adorned with skulls and crystals, the streets are quiet and tree-lined and peaceful, with handsome old houses in various states of dignified decrepitude.

Calendar lived on one of those side streets, and he had one of those houses that, when you drive by it, you think, "If I lived there, I'd have a party every night." He had a corner lot with a good lawn, and a big, old, two-story house with wide stairs leading up to a wraparound deck with plentiful rocking chairs. When I drove up, there were already people sitting on the steps and milling around the deck, even though it was a cold, January night. There was a keg of beer on the deck, and a cooler of something right next to it. When I walked inside, I was hit with a blast of warm air, the smell of beer, and a wall of sound. The place was already packed.

Blair was sitting halfway up an open staircase, talking animatedly with Gates, as usual. I caught his eye and he gave me a helpless look, holding up two fingers, as if he had any chance of breaking free from that conversation in less than half an hour. I nodded and walked on to scope out the place by myself.

It was early enough in the evening that the distinct groups Calendar had invited hadn't broken apart yet; the undergrads were still huddled together in pods, the grad students were arguing theory in their own little groups, and the professors were keeping to themselves, as well. All of a sudden, I spotted my father's girlfriend, a poli sci professor named Amina, walking toward me with a big smile on her face. I stared back at her like a deer in headlights and shook my head as subtly as possible. She looked confused, but seemed to get the hint, turning and going into a different room.

Well, all right, so maybe I *hadn't* thought through this whole undercover gig. I had worried about running into professors I had known fifteen years ago, but I hadn't thought about those other, more modern-day connections I had to the damned place. For all I knew, my father was in there, too.

I ducked into a corner and quickly texted my dad's cell to let him know where I was and what was going on, so he could fill in Amina, since I didn't have her cell number. Tomorrow, I'd have to figure out who else I might need to warn.

I felt a thump on my back, and turned to see Blair grinning at me.

"Dude!" he said. "You came. I didn't think you would."

"I told you I would," I said.

"Yeah, I know, but you always disappear the minute class is done or lunch is over or whatever. I never see you hanging out. You're like Rocky freaking Raccoon."

"Falling back to my room?" I said, giving him the song lyric he was clearly asking for.

He laughed and nodded. "Totally," he said.

"Well, I'm here," I said. "So tell me who's who."

"Well, that's our host, over there," he said, pointing to an enormous bear of a man with a wild mane of uncombed hair, a greying beard, and a hideous, multicolored sweater. He was leaning his head back and laughing loudly at something another professor had just told him. The laugh boomed across the room, cutting through all the other party noise.

"He looks like the Ghost of Christmas Present," I said.

"He could play it, too," said Blair. "He's a Brit. Voice like Michael Caine, or God. Take your pick."

The man Calendar was talking to was just as tall, but rail thin where Calendar was stout. He had long, wispy hair sweeping down to his shoulders, and a bandanna or an ascot or something around his neck. I didn't know who he was, but his picture could have been in the dictionary next to the word "artsy." His arm was draped over the shoulder of a girl way too young for him, and he was leaning into her in a way that let his hand drift obscenely close to her breast.

"And that's Arlo," said Blair.

"Of course it is." I started moving across the room to get a better angle on them. Blair followed.

"Arlo Alden," he said. "He's Classics, technically, but he does directing work sometimes. I'm working with him this semester. He and Cyrus are old pals."

I stopped a few yards away from them, with Calendar's back to me, so I could see the man's face. His expression was just what I figured it would be: smug. Self-assured. Exactly the kind of look a guy in his forties would have if he had been surreptitiously feeling up a pretty girl and getting away with it. The girl was looking at the floor, her long, dark hair covering her face. Whatever she was thinking, I couldn't tell.

"Who's the lucky girl?" I asked.

"That's Maddy Taylor. Undergrad."

Maddy Taylor.

Maybe she heard Blair say her name—or maybe something else caught her attention—but either way, she chose that moment to look up from the floor, and her eyes locked onto mine. Even from a distance, I could tell there was something interesting about her eyes. They were a bright blue—a light, electric blue that cut right through the distance and grabbed you. She cocked her head to the side a little, as though she had seen something amusing, and she smiled a small, closed-mouth smile. She turned to the skinny Classics professor and whispered something, then she slipped out of his grasp and walked over toward me.

"Blair," she said happily, giving him a sloppy, drunken hug. "Blair without Gates. How'd you manage that?"

"She's on the stairs," he said, "explaining alienation to some freshmen."

"Freshmen?" she said, rolling her eyes. "Who invited *freshmen?*"

"Hey," he said, pulling away from her a little. "This is Josh. New guy. Music."

She pulled herself together a little and said hello to me, and I got to see her eyes up close. They were like ice, or a glacier, or something, but they didn't read cold. Maybe it was her dark hair, or the softness of her face, but there was nothing sharp, angular, or cold about her. She was all curves and softness—her cheeks, her lips. Maybe that's what made her eyes stand out so dramatically.

"Music, huh?" she said. "You gonna be working on the Festival of Fucked-Over Women?"

"The what?" I asked.

"Oh, shit!" said Blair, smacking himself on the forehead like a cartoon character. "I didn't even think about that. You totally have to!"

"Have to *what?*" I said, hopelessly lost.

"Arlo's show." He searched my face for comprehension and found none. "It's a Greek play. Ancient Greek. That's his thing."

"And it's called the Festival of Fucked-Over Women?"

Blair and Maddy both laughed.

"No, it's *The Trojan Women.* Euripides."

"But you've got to admit it's like a theme, this year," said Maddy.

"That's right," I said, pretending to remember. "You were in that crazy play last semester—the beauty pageant…thing."

"Yeah," she said nonchalantly. "No steak bikinis this time, though, thank God."

"Don't be so sure," said Blair. "Arlo's directing."

They laughed again, and then Blair smacked himself in the head again like the cartoon character he was rapidly becoming. "Which is what I was trying to tell you. Arlo's directing this thing, and he said he needs musicians to help out, maybe even be on stage as part of the action. You should totally get involved. We could hang out and work together. It'd be fun."

"I don't know," I said.

"Come on," he said. "I can talk to Arlo about it tomorrow."

"But I don't...you know...I don't play a whole lot of different instruments or anything. I just do what I...do."

Blair laughed and started singing. "Rocky Raccoon fell back to his room..."

"Whatever," I said. But my mind was racing. On the one hand, it was a perfect way to get in close and snoop around. Maybe the best chance I'd ever get. But actually being *in* one of their plays? On stage, front and center? No thank you. I'm a sideman. That's the view I like. It's hard to snoop when people are watching *you*.

But there was Maddy Taylor, smiling at me and telling me I should talk to Arlo. Maddy with the electric eyes and the pretty smile, telling me how much fun it would be to work on the show together. Maddy, who had been Chris's girlfriend. Who Chris had been so worried about, but who seemed to have moved on without a care in the world. Maddy, who might hold the key to this whole stupid business.

"All right," I said. "I'll do it."

11

Arlo Alden had an office in the Humanities Building, but Blair said he spent most of his time hanging around the Theatre department. As I walked down the hallway of the overheated, old building, it made sense why he'd avoid this place. The air was stuffy and close, the hallways were sterile and bare, and the professors I saw looked to be about thirty years older than the man I had seen at Calendar's party. With all the things that had changed at Candler since my years, this building had remained frozen in time.

I knocked on Arlo's door and then pushed it open. His office was small and dark, lined with shelves full of books, old magazines, and loosely bound manuscripts. There was a single, small window which was covered from the outside by dense shrubs and half-covered from the inside by books piled up on the windowsill. Strange-looking masks hung on the walls in the few spaces not covered by bookshelves. Larger masks dangled over his desk, suspended from the ceiling. Some of them looked Asian; some looked African; some just looked kind of Space-Alien. None of them looked like anything I'd want hanging over my head.

Arlo was at his desk, hunched over a pile of papers and leaning into a pool of light given off by a desk lamp, his long hair tied back to keep it out of his face. He was wearing a bandana or an ascot again, and he had reading glasses perched on the tip of his nose. In the low light, I could see creases and age lines on his face that I hadn't noticed at the party. He was no kid.

"Professor Alden?" I said

"Arlo," he said. "I'm only Professor Alden when someone's begging for a better grade." He took off his glasses, smiled, and gestured for me to sit.

"I'm Josh Green," I said. "Blair said he talked to you about me working on the show?"

He nodded. "Tell me about yourself. Musically, I mean."

"Well," I said, trying to figure out how much to give him. "I play bass, mostly. Electric when I was younger, now mostly bull fiddle. I've played in rock bands, jazz, done some side-work, accompanied gospel choirs and stuff like that."

"And you're in the MFA program here?"

"Yes."

"Why?"

I stared at him for a moment, feeling caught. I hadn't rehearsed an answer to that. Why did anyone get an MFA in anything? Wasn't it just to get better? Or was it to get a teaching gig? I had no idea.

"Right, well…my theory's pretty weak, so I wanted to work on that a little…"

He nodded.

"And, you know…I figured I could maybe teach."

"University?"

"No, just high school or whatever. I'm not a Ph.D kind of guy."

He smiled at that, and seemed satisfied.

"Blair said you were into jazz primarily. Is that right?"

I nodded. "Yeah. Dixieland, mostly. Hard bop. Swing. I don't much like fusion or contemporary or whatever you want to call it."

"Okay," he said. "Let me tell you what I need."

I realized my shoulders and neck had been tensed up through the whole conversation. I forced myself to relax them.

"So. We're doing this production of *The Trojan Women*, and…I'm not saying it's going to be a modern production, *per se*, but it's definitely not going to be traditional. So: chorus, yes; masks, probably; togas, no fucking way." He smiled. He thought he was being hip. I smiled back.

"The subjugation of women is too fucking eternal to put it in togas and call it history, so we have to break out of that from the word Go. The music has got to match the style, and the style is something we're going to work out organically as we go, so I need someone who can improvise with us. That's why you sounded like a good fit. I'm not saying it's going to be jazz. It's definitely *not* going to be jazz. But that aesthetic—the deconstruction of a melody, the sharing of an impulse from one to the other, the idea of the solo, the riff—*that's* what I'm looking for. You with me?"

I nodded. It seemed like the right thing to do.

"The whole thing is an experiment, yeah? And I need people around me who can get with that and not be afraid of it. Some of the shit we come up with could be kind of weird, kind of extreme, kind of who-the-fuck-knows-what-it-is? I don't need people around me who are going to self-edit or self-censor out of some preconceived notion of what's right, or what works, or what's appropriate. You with me? Because…well, that's it, actually. That's the whole thing: are-you-with-me? Because if you're going to take this trip, I need you to take it all the way. You know what I'm saying? You're either on the bus or you're off the bus."

I was at about 25% comprehension, but I nodded anyway. It was too late to back out now.

He grinned. "I like you. Yeah. All right. I think we can work together."

I smiled back at him, matching him, grin for grin. And I knew I was in.

I had told him nothing, really—nothing of any use. I could have made up more bullshit if he had asked for it—I was working like crazy to think up some interesting lies for him. But he didn't care. He didn't want to hear about me; he just wanted to hear himself talk. And that was fine.

There's a certain type of guy who, if you listen with respect and nod in the right places, they think you're wise even if you don't say a word. In fact, the less you say, the smarter they think you are. They can talk at you for an hour, uninterrupted, and walk away thinking you're a genius. Because all they're looking for is a mirror.

I can work with that.

12

The dean was not impressed.

"You're in a *what?*" she said, loudly enough to make me pull the cell phone away from my ear.

"A play," I said.

"What happened to keeping a low profile?" she asked.

"I'm just going to help out with the music," I said. "It's the fastest way I can get close to the action."

"Well, yes, I understand that," she said. "But did you have to put yourself on stage?"

"The thing doesn't open for months," I said. "I'm not planning on hanging around long enough to get my name in the program. Don't worry."

She sighed. "I do worry, Jordan," she said. "Please don't forget we have no permission to be doing what we're doing."

"That's all right," I said. "I usually don't."

She groaned. "Your humor is not making me feel calmer."

"Listen. The faster we get some information and get me out of here, the better it is for both of us, right?"

She agreed.

"The problem is, doing it fast means I have to be a little more exposed. I've got to put myself out there, make them feel like I'm one of them. And just being here, taking classes, isn't going to cut it. I've got to get in closer and be where Chris was, see what he saw. Otherwise, I could be here all year and learn nothing."

"I understand, Jordan," she said. "Believe me. I understand. It's what all of us in my office deal with, every day."

I nodded, forgetting she couldn't see me.

"All right," she said with a sigh. "Do what you think is best. Just stay in touch, and let me know what you're learning."

"I'll fire up the Bat-Signal if I have anything for you," I said.

She sighed again. I almost felt sorry for her.

13

Arlo wanted me to stop by rehearsal the following night
to meet the cast and pick up a script. I emailed Oticha and Pete
to ask if we could push *our* rehearsal off to the next night, and I
texted Susannah to give her a head's up. Then, feeling extremely
efficient and organized, I promptly forgot where the rehearsal
was going to be.

I stayed on campus through the afternoon, plowing
through some dense music theory and drinking too much coffee.
Then I walked over to the student center, where the theatre was
located. The two big, main doors were unlocked, but when I
pushed one of them open, the room was pitch black. I stepped
inside, stupidly called out a few Hellos, then shrugged and
backed away, letting the door thud closed. I stood there in the
silence for a minute, trying to figure out my next move. Then a
voice behind me, out of nowhere, said "You looking for
someone?" The shock pumped about a quart of adrenaline into
my blood. I turned around and saw my silent writer friend from
the first day at the lunch table.

"Jesus," I said. "You scared the hell out of me."

He smiled a crooked, closed-mouth kind of smile, pushed his glasses up on his nose, and said, "Sorry." He didn't seem to mean it.

"I was looking for Arlo Alden," I said. "I'm supposed to be at his rehearsal."

My companion nodded and said, "He's in Curry tonight." When he realized I had no idea what he was talking about, he added, "It's a rehearsal room. Over in the theatre department. The theatre's here; the department's over there."

"Ah," I said. "Got it."

"Come on," he said. "I'll go with you. I'm supposed to be there, too."

"Oh yeah?" I asked. "Are you in the play?"

He smiled that crooked smile again and said, "I am *of* but not *in*. I'm the dramaturg."

I didn't know what that was, so I just nodded, and we started walking.

"I'm Scott, by the way," he said over his shoulder.

"Josh," I said.

"I know. You've been hanging out with Blair."

"That's right."

"You're a music student?" he asked.

"Well, I'm a musician," I said. "I'm still working on the student part."

This got a legitimate laugh out of him.

"I know, right?" he said. "So hard getting back into that mind-set. It took me a whole semester to get into the rhythm."

We left the student center and started walking across the dark campus lawns. "Are you in the same program as Blair?" I asked.

"No, I'm in the writing program. Blair's a director."

"So what are you doing on this show? That word you used...I have no idea what it means."

"Oh. Dramaturg? It's like having a researcher or scholar on staff. Which is ridiculous in this case, since Arlo's a classics professor and knows this stuff better than I ever will. But he's letting me help with the translation, making sure it's actable and all. So it's interesting."

"Blair's working on the show too, though, right?"

"He's the assistant director—which is also ridiculous, because Arlo's the only show in town when he's directing. Basically, we just sit behind the table and take notes."

"Huh," I said. "That doesn't sound like much fun."

"You haven't seen Arlo work," Scott said with a little laugh. "Fortunately, it's a big table, so there's plenty of room for you."

"Outstanding," I said.

We arrived at the theatre building and walked inside, squeaking along a quiet hallway in the direction of increasing noise. Scott opened a door and we stepped into a large room, painted all black, where about a dozen students in sweats were…well, I wasn't sure what they were doing. They weren't exactly dancing, but they were flailing their arms around and walking with very slow, exaggerated steps. There were backpacks and coats strewn all around the room, kicked under chairs or lumped up against the wall. Plastic water bottles dotted the floor. At the far end of the room was a long, rectangular, folding table, behind which sat Arlo Alden, who was staring very seriously at the weird gyrations in front of him. Blair sat next to him and was leaning in to whisper something in his ears. Arlo nodded, but didn't take his eyes off the students.

Scott and I stood in the doorway for a moment, not wanting to interrupt anything. I turned toward him and said, "This is what the ancient Greeks did?"

He smiled, but didn't say anything.

Suddenly, Arlo yelled, "Right. That's good. Take a seat." The students ran for their water bottles, took a few swigs, and then sat or splayed themselves on the floor, awaiting instructions. Scott motioned for me to follow him, and we trotted back behind the long table. Blair grinned at me and pulled out a chair. I gave him the "what the fuck?" look that both of us had been practicing in our pre-Columbian theatre class, and he laughed.

"Warm-ups," he said quietly.

I nodded and sat down, just as Arlo popped up and began to pace.

I looked around the room while Arlo talked to his troops. The students were a little more diverse in body-type than I had seen in my walks across campus—no pumped-up gym rats in this crowd. But they were all so damned *pretty*. Not a scar or a blemish on any of them. Long, strong arms, long, beautiful hair, and bright, shining eyes staring up at their director with excitement and wonder. It was a little nauseating.

More importantly, though, I didn't see a single desperate-looking, hollow-eyed, strung-out addict in the bunch. Whatever Chris had seen in this room, I wasn't seeing it.

Except for Maddy Taylor. He had seen her—a lot of her. And she was here, her long hair pulled and tied back, and her electric blue eyes staring worshipfully up at her director. I looked around the room, to see if that was a general reaction, but it didn't seem to be. They were all paying attention to him, but there was something else going on in Maddy's eyes. I thought back to the party where I had met her, and how she had been leaning drunkenly against Arlo, and how his arm had been wrapped around her, his hand oh-so-casually brushing up against her breast. Had that been going on for a while, or was it new?

"The Greeks would not have shown the bloody axe, of course," Arlo was saying, as he paced back and forth. "But we will sure as shit show it. Oh, I know, I know, it's not actually part of the play we're doing, but who cares? This is not a museum piece. This is living theatre. We have no obligation to the past.

We have an obligation to today! To speak the truth!" He was shouting, but I wasn't quite sure why. "The glories of so-called victory? The hubris of sending violence out into the world and thinking you can remain *untouched*? No. No. While our Trojan women weep on the shore, we will show the audience what the so-called conquerors have reaped." He reached down into a duffel bag, pulled out a large axe, and held it up over his head. "There will be blood!" he yelled, and he threw it as hard as he could straight over the heads of the students.

A few of them saw it coming and flattened themselves. The rest just screamed. The axe sailed over them, struck the wall with barely a sound, and bounced off, hitting the floor.

I looked at Blair, wide-eyed. He smiled and said, "Plastic."

"And now," Arlo said, "I want to introduce the newest member of our team." He reached back to point to me. "Josh Green's going to be helping us out with music. That doesn't mean he's going to be composing songs or anything—this isn't The Sound of Fucking Music. But he's going to be working with us on ambient music, environmental sound, that kind of thing. And figuring out what we do with the chorus, of course."

The chorus. Of course. Just like in Chris's show. What the hell had I gotten myself into?

Fortunately, Arlo didn't want me to do anything on this first night. Which was exactly what I had been hoping for. I sat there as he lectured and had them do strange movement exercises, and I watched. But all I saw, for two and a half hours, were young, strong, healthy-looking students doing ridiculous things on command—the same thing I had seen when I first walked into the room.

Maybe it was because it was a new semester, and there wasn't enough stress to drive these guys to use anything harder than weed or beer on the weekends. Maybe whatever Chris had seen had settled down and washed away over Christmas break, and things were back to normal.

Or maybe Chris had been imagining the whole thing.

No, that wasn't possible. Something nasty must have been floating around campus, back in November. Something dangerous had been sitting in that dorm room with Chris—and whether he had chosen to take it or had it forced on him, it had killed him. I still had no idea what *it* was, since Carter hadn't been able to get the Baby Cops to share the toxicology report. But it was real, and it had been here.

And now? Now it had all gone underground. But buried didn't necessarily mean dead. The whole thing could have been sitting, waiting, like a cancer in remission. I knew how that worked. I had seen cancer firsthand. You think the shit is gone, you think you can relax and celebrate. You think the nightmare is over, and you can be a happy family again. But it's just biding its time, sitting on the sidelines, waiting for a moment of weakness.

And there's always a moment of weakness. There's always a second of vulnerability. And right then, when your defenses are down, it lashes out again, stronger than it was before, and it wipes out everything it touches.

Yeah, I knew that scene way too well.

Somebody—maybe somebody right here in this room—was going to have a moment of weakness. Sooner or later, it was going to happen. Somebody was going to need some kind of escape. And somebody else, somewhere on this campus, was going to be right there, ready to provide it. And the cancer would be back.

Could I find where it was hiding before it woke up again? That was the question. And if I couldn't, would I be there, in the right place, when it did wake up?

I had no answers. I didn't even have a lead. All I had was Chris's girlfriend. He had been worried about her—worried enough to talk to a private investigator. But what was it he had been worried about? What had he seen, that I wasn't seeing?

It was time to start snooping for real.

14

Rehearsal let out at 10 p.m., and when we emerged from the theatre building, the campus was quiet. I watched the actors zip up their coats, shift their backpacks onto their shoulders, and trudge off, singly or in pairs, toward dorms or cars. Blair asked me if I wanted to go get a beer, but I begged off. I had work to do. Not grad school; old school.

Maddy was walking alone toward the quad. I started walking behind her, keeping a good distance between us and keeping an eye on her feet to match her stride. I was wearing sneakers, so my shoes were quiet, but the quad was deserted and I didn't want to give her any reason to turn around and look behind her.

She kept her head down, hands in her pockets, lost in her own thoughts as she crossed the quad. Then she turned right and walked toward Heywood Hall, the dorm where Chris had lived. I stopped across the street and hung back in the shadow of a tree that was blocking the light of a streetlight. I wasn't sure what I was waiting for. She was just going home, but something told me not to leave until she went inside. And my Spidey-sense was rewarded, because she *didn't* go inside. She walked up toward the door, then stopped, turned around, and faced the street. I was glad I had kept my distance and was standing in the shadows. She didn't seem to see me—but then, she didn't seem to see anything. If she was waiting for someone, she wasn't looking for him. She just looked straight ahead, in a vague and unfocused kind of way, as though her engine had shifted to neutral.

She waited there for about two minutes, and then a car pulled up and stopped in front of the dorm. It was an old Mazda Miata—one of those two-seater, sporty cars that people used to get when they wanted a Porsche but couldn't afford one. Driving the car was none other than Arlo Alden. Well, well.

Maddy didn't look particularly happy to see him, but she didn't look sad, either. She didn't have any expression at all. She just opened the door and climbed in, and the two of them drove off.

Where they were going, I had no idea, and there was no time to get my own car and find out. But it was obviously something they were trying to keep secret.

I wondered how long this little scene had been playing out, because it seemed obvious from her expression that this was not the first time. How had it started? How often did it happen? Were they meeting every night, or just once in a while?

And more importantly: why? He had to be forty, forty-five. Maybe older. And he wasn't *that* good-looking. And her? She was what, nineteen, maybe? Young, beautiful, electric eyes and a mysterious smile—fine, I knew what he saw in her, but what was she getting from him?

All these questions swirled around in my head, but it was a hopeless game, and I was getting cold. So I went home.

It was after 11:00, and Susannah was not happy. I could feel it, the second I walked through the door. "Where the fuck have you been?" she asked, pacing around the living room. "You said rehearsal was over at 10."

"I had to follow someone," I said, putting my feet up on the coffee table, leaning my head back on the top of the couch, and closing my eyes.

"Dangerous?" she asked.

"No, just tedious," I said.

"And you couldn't call me?"

"I…yeah, I could have. I'm sorry. It just…developed, and I forgot."

"Just text me. You know? Something. Let me know you're alive."

"I know. I'm sorry."

She kicked my feet off the table, making me sit up and open my eyes.

"You don't sound sorry," she said. "Look at you. You're all *beleaguered* and shit. Like I'm nagging at you. What's that about?"

"I don't know."

She sat down across from me and said, "I'm not trying to be a bitch. Don't make me out like I'm some shrewish housewife or something. I don't care where you go. You know that. All I want to know is you're okay. The shit you get yourself into, I have a right."

I nodded. She absolutely had a right. And I was being an asshole. I wasn't sure why.

"I can't help it if I love you and worry about you," she said. "That's just how I am."

"I know. I like how you are."

"So fine. Cut the shit and talk to me."

"Right."

I opened my arms, and she moved across from the chair to the sofa, and then we were okay again.

15

Rehearsals stayed in the theatre department for the rest of the week, and every night, I followed Maddy Taylor back to her dorm. Every night, she did the same head-down, lost-in-thought walk across the quad. But every night, she went straight into her building and didn't come out again. I had my car parked strategically close so I could follow her if she took off with Arlo again. But she never did.

I watched her closely during rehearsal, to see if anything had changed. But it hadn't. Her eyes were still glued to him whenever he spoke, shining with admiration. He was obviously some kind of guru to her. But she wasn't alone—most of the cast stared reverently at him from time to time, and he knew it and loved it. He strutted back and forth in front of them like a peacock, making inspirational speeches between weird voice and movement exercises that didn't seem to have anything to do with the play. As far as I could tell, we weren't getting any closer to making a play, but what did I know? To me, "rehearsal" meant "practice." Like, you figure out what you need to do, then you do it till you get it right. But this wasn't that. I didn't know *what* this was.

Finally, toward the end of the week, Arlo let the actors use scripts, and it was my turn to do some work. Scott, the dramaturg, had been explaining to me that the chorus people in these old plays had long passages in verse that were either spoken or sung, or something in between. No one was really sure, anymore. So every director had to figure out something to do with them. They could break up the passages and have individual people speak them, or treat them like music and have people sing them together. It was kind of a crapshoot.

Arlo said he wanted to treat these sections as something totally different from anything else in the play. Not dialogue; not song; but something different. Something musical, but not music—that's how he put it to me. He knew what he wanted, but he didn't know what it meant. I had to figure out what it meant.

When I got to rehearsal that night, I found a pile of garbage on the floor: sticks, bricks, pieces of metal, old glass bottles. Six girls, including Maddy, were sitting cross-legged behind the garbage, scripts in hand, waiting for me. The guys were sitting off to the side, drinking from their plastic water bottles and watching the action.

"Ah, Josh—excellent," said Arlo, jumping up as I walked in—late, as usual. "Let's get into it. I want to see what we can figure out for this section. I pulled some stuff for us to use.

I'm not sure if this is *exactly* what we're going to use, but I think it's going to be something like this. We'll have items like this strewn all over the place, so anyone can use anything when they need it. Post-apocalyptic rubble—that kind of thing. Found objects turned into instruments—the detritus of civilization playing the music to sing its elegy by."

"Right..."

"So use whatever works for you. We'll get what you need as you nail things down."

He sat back down again and all eyes were on me. Six girls in their late teens or early twenties, gazing up at me and expecting something amazing. Suddenly I understood Arlo a little better.

"All righty," I said. "I guess let's start by just hearing the thing, yeah? Can we just read it aloud once?"

Maddy raised her hand and said, "How?"

"What do you mean, how?"

"Like, all together, or one line each, or what?"

"Well, how about *you* read it, since you already started talking?"

I *so* could have been a teacher.

Maddy laughed, picked up her script and read:

My queen! I share your shame and tears
But who will hear mine now?

My days at the loom are gone
I will not see my sons again
Tomorrow I scrub the floors
Or warm the beds of Greeks
Darkness is my queen now, and I curse her

Maddy lowered her script and looked back up at me. I nodded for a minute, thinking. Then I said, "Who wrote this shit?"

The girls all laughed, which was every bit as intoxicating as being on stage in a rock band. "That would be Euripides," said Arlo, also laughing behind me. "With an assist from our friend, Scotty Flynn."

I glanced back at Scott, sitting at the director's table next to Arlo, and grinned at him. "Sorry, man."

"No problem," he said, bright red.

"All right," I said, turning back to the chorus of Trojan women in front of me. "It's a happy little verse. So…let's take it line by line and figure out how to make it sound like it feels. If we're going to make it musical, or…sort-of musical…let's use the sound to give it some emotion. Right?"

I glanced back at Arlo, and he seemed happy, so I kept going.

"Cool. How about, each of you grab one of those…things in the pile, there, and just make whatever kind of sound you think makes sense with the…you know, with the emotion you're feeling, while we read it. With the instrument and also with your voice. Just…follow the feeling in the line. Like the words are the singer, and you're playing accompaniment. We'll do it one line, over and over, till we feel like we've got something."

They were game, and since there didn't seem to be any rules, I didn't feel like a complete moron. We worked on it for close to an hour, and by the end, we were exhausted. But I had to admit, the result was weird and different and interesting. I was actually kind of proud of it.

When it was over, I was too wiped out to play spy with Maddy, so I didn't hide myself as I walked across the quad toward my car. She noticed me walking more or less alongside her, and after glancing over at me two or three times, she decided to speak.

"You live on campus?" she asked.

"No—I'm parked over there, behind that dorm."

"Heywood? That's where I live."

I nodded, but I didn't say anything.

"It's a shit heap," she added, matter-of-factly.

"It's a dorm," I said, in the same tone.

"Yeah, but, I mean, some of the dorms are like resorts."

"They must be the newer ones. We didn't have any resorts when I was here."

"Oh, so you're a two-timer."

It took me a minute to figure out what she was saying.

"Yeah. Exactly. Back for more punishment."

"Well, take my word for it, there's beautiful rooms you can live in, these days. Meanwhile, I get this dump." She pointed to it, as we were closing in on it.

"Well, it's a place to crash, right? And it's close."

"Where do *you* live?"

"Me? Oh, I'm..." Shit. I hadn't actually figured out how to respond to that. Was it dangerous to give my real address? Not right now, probably. But what if things got hotter, later? What if someone wanted to find out more about this Josh Green person? "I'm down around Little Five Points," I said. Vague and safe.

Yeah? That's cool. I like hanging out there."

I nodded, not sure where this was going. We crossed the street and stood in front of her door.

"By the way," she said, stopping. "That was great, tonight. Really freaky."

"Yeah?" I said. "Thanks. I'm just making it up as I go."

"That's what you do, though, right? Isn't that the whole thing with jazz? Arlo said you—"

"Right, right," I said quickly. "Yes."

Lull.

"Well, anyway...*you* did a great job tonight," I said. "You found some really interesting stuff in there."

"Thanks," she said. "I kind of wish I could do more of it."

I had no idea what she was talking about, and it clearly showed on my face.

"I'm only with the chorus for that first section," she said. "I'm not even supposed to be there, technically, but Arlo wanted me with them for the opening."

"Why? Where are you the rest of the time?"

"Getting raped and killed," she said matter-of-factly. "I'm Cassandra."

"Wow," I said. "I've definitely got to read the script one of these days."

She laughed and looked like she was going to say more, but we were at her door, so she said good night and trotted inside. I walked past the building to my car. I opened the door and, on a whim, turned back to look at the dorm—just in time to see Arlo's little Miata pull up to the building. It sat there, idling—waiting—but Maddy didn't come outside. I stood there, watching Arlo watch the building, for at least two minutes...which can feel like an eternity when you're doing nothing but watching and waiting.

She didn't come out. Had she planned to meet him, and forgotten? Had she changed her mind? I had no idea. But Arlo wasn't happy. He gunned the motor and peeled off in a puff of rubbery smoke, making sure everyone in the building could hear him go.

16

I called Patty the next morning before heading in to class.

"I've got a stupid and embarrassing question for you, Tits," I said by way of introduction.

"Yeah," she said. "Like you ever call me with anything else."

"Back in school, was there any sex going on between theatre students and teachers?"

"Teachers?"

"Yeah, you know, like directors or acting teachers or whoever. Professors."

"Are you kidding me?" she said with a laugh.

"No, I'm not kidding you. I need to know."

"Yeah, Jordan. There was 'sex going on.' All the time."

"Seriously?"

"Isn't that the whole reason guys go into theatre? To meet girls? Just like music?"

"I guess," I said. "But I wasn't a music *student.* I never set foot in that place. I was pre-med, and I can't imagine *those* professors hooking up with freshman girls."

"Well, theatre's weird," she said. "We never really thought of them as professors. I mean, we were just working on shows together, and there are actors, and there are directors, and…there's definitely a thing that happens. I mean, it can be a pretty intense relationship."

"Right."

"You know, you're working together every night, late into the night, and it gets super stressful as it gets closer to opening night. It's like combat. A real pressure cooker."

"Okay."

"Can I ask what the hell is going on?" she said.

"Not yet," I said, distractedly.

Intense relationship, okay. That made sense. I had gotten a taste of it, the night before, and you didn't have to be a rocket scientist to see where things could go in a group like that, after weeks and weeks of working together. If the cast wasn't in bed together yet, it was only a matter of time, and I could easily see how a Blair or a Scott or even an Arlo could take advantage.

But I didn't buy that's what was happening here with Maddy and Arlo. It was still so early in the process, so not-yet-intense. And I kept thinking about that blank, listless expression I had seen when she was waiting for him to pick her up. Like she was...numb. Shut down. Out of juice, somehow. Where was the buzz? The electricity of the secret, illicit hookup? It's a palpable thing—a visible thing. I had seen it over and over in my work, spying on idiots who sneaked around on their spouses. Even from a distance, through a camera lens, I could read it on their faces. It was more than lust—it was the excitement of doing something they knew they shouldn't be doing. *That* was the drug.

And speaking of drugs...if Maddy wasn't excited about hooking up with Arlo that night, then what was she there for? If not the drug of secret sex, then maybe some other kind of drug? Something to recharge her batteries? The kind of something that could help a classics professor pay for his sporty little Miata?

Maybe, maybe. I could already think of ten reasons why I was wrong, but ten wasn't enough to stop me from puzzling through it. Because here's the thing about puzzles: you can't put the pieces together until you have some pieces to work with. And in real life, the pieces don't come in a box. You have to start somewhere, and sometimes it doesn't matter where you start. You gather up a couple of facts, see if they fit together, and either way, you learn something.

All I had to start with was what Chris had given me. If it was true that a couple of months ago someone was moving shit around the theatre department, then anywhere in the theatre department was a reasonable place to start digging for treasure. And if he had been worried about Maddy Taylor, specifically, then maybe Maddy's hook-up was the X that marked the spot.

I wanted to call the dean for some information on Arlo, but I held back. I had screwed up cases before by jumping the gun and handing over names before I had evidence. And the dean was definitely waiting for a name. I wasn't going to let that happen this time.

But if I wanted to know more about Arlo, I was going to have to do more than just watch rehearsals. All I could see there was Public Arlo—the act he was putting on for the cast. And from the looks of Blair and Scotty sitting at the table and being ignored, night after night, my chances of worming my way into a friendship with the guy were pretty slim.

But Maddy might work. Maddy, I could get to know. And Maddy knew a different Arlo than the rest of us. So I did call the dean, but I didn't ask her about the professor. I asked her about the student.

"Taylor?" she said. "With a Y?"

"That's it."

I heard her typing in the name.

"What do you want to know?" she asked. "There are privacy issues here, you know. Student records are confidential."

"Tell me whatever you can," I said. "She was close to Chris Tremaine, and I think she might be close to whatever he stumbled on."

"All right," she said, with one of those familiar sighs of hers. "Let's see…"

"Anything unusual happen to her last semester? She need a doctor, or treatment for anything, maybe?"

"Jordan!"

"What?"

"I couldn't tell you that, even if I had access to it. Which I absolutely do not."

"All right, all right. Just asking. How about her classes? Anything out of the ordinary there?"

"Well…it looks like she was on academic probation after midterms."

"Okay. And was that unusual for her?"

"As far as I can tell. Her grades look fine, all through freshman year."

"Fine like what? What are we talking about?"

"Jordan…"

"All right, never mind. So it was unusual."

"Yes. First semester, sophomore year is not when we tend to see grades bottoming out, unless there's some other crisis going on, like a family illness or something."

"And was there?"

She sighed again. This was obviously no fun for her. "I have no idea, Jordan. This is just a student record, not an FBI dossier."

"Okay. So she screwed up her midterms. Did she come out okay, or is she still on probation?"

"Well…" she paused for a moment, thinking or reading. "It looks like she took a couple of incompletes, but the probation was waived because of extenuating circumstances."

"Meaning Chris's death?"

"It doesn't say. But that would be unusual, since she wasn't family or a roommate. Those are automatic exemptions. But it's possible."

"Possible if she had gone to talk to somebody to ask for it?"

"Jordan, I told you, I can't—"

"I'm saying theoretically. If it wasn't an automatic thing, then it only could have happened if someone had intervened for her, right? Which means she…it means one could reasonably infer that she went to talk to someone, right? A dean or a counselor—at least once." I waited for a response, but there wasn't one. "Can you at least tell me if that's a reasonable inference to make?"

"Well…" I could feel her discomfort over the phone. "You are often a reasonable and intelligent person. Can we leave it at that?"

"Sure."

"One other thing I think I can tell you, which might be useful. I don't know. But it's unusual, if that's what you're looking for."

"What is it?"

"It looks like, when she applied two years ago, she applied as an emancipated minor."

"What's that?"

"It means she declared herself independent from her parents before she turned eighteen."

"Isn't that just a financial-aid thing or something?"

"No, it's bigger than that, usually. It's a thing you have to go to court for. It's a...it's a process. It's a lot of work. If you want to declare yourself independent before you turn eighteen, there's usually something big driving it. Child actors do it sometimes, when they want to control their own money. But most of the times I've seen it, it's been a sign of trouble at home."

"Hmm. But you can't tell me what."

"All I know is what's in the record. I can tell you Taylor isn't her birth name, for whatever that's worth. She was born Madeleine Bates. I have a copy of her birth certificate."

"So she was adopted?"

"I have no idea. You'd have to figure that one out on your own."

"Well, that is my job."

"Jordan…" She hesitated for a second or two. "Tell me the truth. Are you getting anywhere with this?"

"Well…" I said, also hesitating, not wanting to push things too far, too fast. "I'm calling you with direct questions, so…what would a reasonable person infer?"

"All right," she said. "Just be safe. And keep me informed."

"You'll be the first person I call," I said, feeling pretty certain it was a lie.

17

With Maddy moving off to work alone with Arlo, away from the chorus, the week became increasingly frustrating for me. It was just what I had been afraid of—putting me front and center made it hard for me to watch and listen. What I wanted to do was learn more about Maddy Taylor and Arlo Alden; what I was being forced to do was create weird-ass musical soundscapes for the chorus.

But just because I wasn't watching Maddy closely didn't mean other people weren't. So I dragged Blair and Scott out for drinks after rehearsal one night, to trade gossip and talk about the show. I waited a decent interval before I asked the one question I cared about.

"What do you think about Maddy?"

"As what?" asked Blair. "An actress or a piece of ass?"

"Blair...Jesus Christ," said Scott, disgusted.

Blair shrugged his bony shoulders. "The man asked a question. I'm just establishing context."

"She's, like, nineteen years old," said Scott.

"I didn't say *I* wanted to fuck her," said Blair. "I'm just trying to find out if *he* wants to fuck her."

"I don't," I said, trying to make peace. "I'm just asking."

"Blair is obsessed with undergraduate girls," said Scott.

"Blair is not *obsessed*," said Blair. "Blair is *intrigued*."

"Listen, I'm the dramaturg here," said Scott. "I'll give the context."

"I'm the director, and I interpret intentions, so fuck you."

They stopped, and looked at me.

"Don't look at me," I said. "I'm the bass player. I'm just trying to follow along."

They both smiled at that.

"So what did you want to know about Maddy?" said Scott.

"Nothing," I lied. "I was just thinking, it's a tough part she's got. Intense. And she's awfully young."

Scott nodded. "Hecuba's the main role, but Cassandra's right up there. And yeah, I don't think she's ever done anything like this before."

"I saw her in that play last semester," I said. "I don't remember it much, but it was just chorus work, wasn't it?"

"Yeah, Chris and his fucking chorus," said Blair.

"Why? Was that a special thing of his?" I asked.

"Oh, yeah," said Blair. "He's the whole reason I'm working on this nightmare. He totally badgered me into it. He was supposed to be the dramaturg. He was working with Arlo all last semester to get it ready."

"Oh," I said. "I didn't realize that."

"Yeah," said Scott. "I was a late-in-the-game replacement."

"I thought you said you wrote the translation."

"God, no," he said. "That's way beyond me. I *re*-wrote it to make it actable. Actually, Chris re-wrote it, and then I came in and tinkered with it some more. This was Chris's dream project from the start—for him and Maddy."

"Ahh…" I said. "So *he's* the reason she got the part?"

"Totally," said Blair. "Chorus girl to leading lady. It's a Cinderella story."

"Yeah, all right," said Scott. "But Josh did remember her from last semester."

"I did," I said.

"And I bet you can't remember any of the others."

"Well, I don't *know* any of the others."

Blair laughed. "Half of them are in this show, dude. You see them every night."

"That's my point," said Scott. "Maddy's the one you remember. That's the thing about Maddy. *That's* why Arlo cast her."

"Okay. But can she handle it?"

Scott shrugged. "She'll have to."

Blair chimed in. "She will. They always pull through in the end." Then, with a little smile, he affected a British accent. "Strangely enough, it all comes together."

Scott smiled, and said, "How?" Obviously offering up the straight line.

Blair nodded, and they both said, "I don't know; it's a mystery."

They both grinned. It was obviously a line from something I didn't know.

"Yeah, if only it *was* a mystery," said Blair.

"Why? What is it?" I said.

"Oh, you know…" he said with a shrug. "A little passion, a little panic. And a little chemistry."

"Don't go there," Scott said. "Come on. Maddy's doing fine."

"So far. It's early."

"Plus, she's getting help on the side with Arlo," Scott said.

Which made Blair snort in the middle of sipping his beer.

"What?" said Scott.

"I'll *bet* she's getting help on the side."

Scott sighed. "Seriously?"

"You said it. I didn't."

"Unbelievable," Scott said. "I'm surrounded by children."

"Yeah," said Blair. "None of the rest of us had the maturity to get married at twenty-two."

Scott growled and then punched Blair hard on his bony arm, which made both of them wince and say, "Ow!"

"You guys are cute," I said.

I steered the conversation away from Maddy after that, to make sure neither of them walked away from the night thinking I had some unnatural interest in her. But that "it's early" comment stayed with me. Something *had* happened, last semester—something Blair was worried he was going to see again. Which fit with what Chris had told me. Chris had been worried about her back before Thanksgiving. That was right after he had directed his play. Things got bad enough that it screwed up her classwork to the point where she got put on probation. According to the dean, she had something in her background that brought her to school as an emancipated minor, so maybe her home life was a little shaky—maybe she didn't even go home during breaks. Which meant she was alone and vulnerable when things got bad. Whatever happened, she seemed to be in okay shape now, even with a dead boyfriend. She was back in school, she was in a starring role for the first time, and clearly I wasn't the only one suspecting that she was fucking her director.

So…a little needy, maybe a little fragile, with midterms coming up and a big show on the horizon. And all her friends standing by, wondering if she would pull through.

If Arlo was selling more than art, Maddy Taylor looked like the perfect customer.

18

"Ew," said Kitty over lunch, after I told them what had been happening on campus—carefully omitting names.

"Which one is *ew*—the drugs or the sex?" I asked.

"The sex, obviously," she said. "Who cares about drugs?"

"Well, I do," I said. "It's kind of what I'm there for."

"What are you, the avenging ghost of Nancy Reagan?" asked Porkchop. "I distinctly remember you sucking up the good smoke like a vacuum cleaner, back when the world was young."

"Yeah, so do I, thanks," I said. "But this isn't weed. This is…I don't know what it is. Meth, crack…I don't know. It's harsh, whatever it is. And a kid died because of it."

"So let the police handle it," said my attorney.

"They didn't bite. So now it's on me."

"But getting back to the point," said Kitty. "*Ew.*"

"Yeah, fine, I agree. But what do you think?" I asked. "Is it just a thing that goes on in theatre and music and stuff, or do you think it happens everywhere? I mean…were you aware of shit like that going on?"

There was a minute of quiet quesadilla-chewing as my friends pondered the question. Then Kate said, "I don't remember anyone fooling around with professors. But I was an Econ major, and the professors were all boring and ugly."

"Yeah, I don't remember ever hearing stuff like that, either," said Kitty. "High school, yes, but not at Candler."

"High school?" said Kate. "Ew."

"I know, right?"

Patty shrugged. "Just because you never heard about it doesn't mean it never happened," she said. "You guys probably didn't hang out with faculty the way kids in the arts do."

"Well, I had a history professor steal my research and publish it under his own name," said Porkchop. "That was kind of spiritual rape. Does that count?"

"It's creepy as hell," I said. "Not your thing; this. I mean, if it was going on when we were there, I never had a clue. But I barely came out of my room, right? So what do I know?"

"What are you talking about?" said Kate.

"You know," I said. "Me in my room, headphones plugged into my bass. I was oblivious to pretty much everything."

Kate and Kitty looked at each other and then shrugged.

"The way I remember it," said Patty, "you were down in the study room every night with your friends, banging out really loud metal and downing bottles of cheap vodka."

"Yeah, Jordan," said Kate. "I saw you all over the place, freshman year. I don't know what you're talking about."

"Weren't you the one who started the whole graffiti thing on the dorm walls?"

"Yeah, the stuff we all had to clean up when the deans found out?"

"That was definitely you."

I looked over at Porkchop, but he just laughed at me. "With witnesses like that, I wouldn't touch your case with a ten-foot pole," he said.

"Huh. Definitely not how I remember that year," I said.

"I paint what I see, child," said Patty. She chuckled to herself, then realized everyone was looking at her. "It's an old cartoon I saw somewhere," she said. "There's an artist sitting at an easel, painting. And he's looking at this beautiful landscape, but the canvas is filled with all these monsters and ghosts and stuff. And this little girl is standing next to him, looking at what he's doing, and he says, 'I paint what I see, child. I paint what I see.'"

Lull.

"Well," I said, before Kitty could yell, "it sure is fun hanging out with you guys, but I've got to get back to campus. I have to help proctor an exam."

"Don't slip any answers to the co-eds," said Porkchop. "Or anything else, for that matter."

"Thank you, counselor," I said. "What's that little gem going to cost me?"

"That one's *pro bono*," he said.

The music class was one of those introductory survey classes that freshmen and sophomores take to satisfy general requirements. There were a couple hundred kids in the lecture hall, all of them looking bored and annoyed. I wondered if they looked more engaged on a non-test day, but I doubted it. The teaching assistant for the class had called in sick, so they had asked me to fill in. It wasn't a strenuous job; all I had to do was hand out papers, patrol the aisles to stop any talking or cheating, and then pick up the papers at the end. If the TA stayed sick, though, I'd probably get stuck with the grading.

I recognized a couple of faces from rehearsals, and they nodded at me as I passed by. And then, about halfway up the risers in the room, I saw a brighter, prettier face flash a grin at me, with a little, surreptitious wave of a hand. It was Maddy. I mouthed "good luck" to her as I handed her the test paper, and she rolled her eyes and laughed.

When the test was over, I collected the papers and handed them off to the professor, hoping they wouldn't get handed right back to me later in the day. As I started walking back toward my car, I heard someone running behind me, and then someone grabbed my arm. It was Maddy.

"Whew," she said, laughing. "You walk fast."

"New Yorker," I said.

"I hate sitting in the middle of that row."

"Claustrophobic?"

"Kind of. Sometimes I pick up on other people's shit, you know? Their emotions? And if their energy is all spiky and freaky, it can freak me out too."

"But now you're free."

"Yeah. Free at last."

"So…you do okay?"

She threw up her arms dramatically and looked to the heavens. "Who knows?" she said. "I can't keep all that terminology in my head."

"But you can memorize lines for a play."

"Yeah, but, you know…one or the other, right? There's a limit."

"Listen, you can't be failing classes. Arlo's not going to be happy if you get booted off the show."

"I'm not gonna get *booted*," she said. "It's not like I'm on the football team or anything."

"If we had a football team."

"Exactly."

"Still," I said.

"Yeah, I know. I know."

I stopped, and turned to face her. "Listen, if you ever need help—you know, with the music stuff—I'm happy to. It's like my job, actually."

"Yeah?"

"For the good of the team? Of course."

"Because I need to write a paper to make up for my *last* grade, and I'm totally lost."

"What's it on?"

"Gregorian fucking chant."

"Yeah...not exactly my specialty, but I can read what you've got so far."

"You're an angel!" she said, and she leaned in and kissed me on the cheek. "Can I come by your office sometime?"

"My office?" I laughed.

"You don't have office hours?"

"I don't have an *office*. I could probably arrange some table-outside-the-cafeteria hours, when the weather's nice."

"Well, it's supposed to be sunny tomorrow."

That was fast. "Okay. Sure. Around two—after the lunch crowd clears out?"

"Great," she said. "Thanks *so* much."

"Anything for the show," I said. But she was already running off to her next class.

19

Following Maddy home after rehearsal was one thing. Walking side by side and chatting was easy. But sitting right across from her in broad daylight, pretending to be her friend—that was a whole different gig.

"So you're saying I should move this paragraph down to where?" she said, scrolling up and down, lost in her own text.

"The bottom of page two, I was thinking."

"Yeah, but…" she wrinkled up her face. It was adorable. "My pages don't match up with yours anymore."

"It's the paragraph that starts, 'The prevailing culture of the medieval world…'"

She sighed. "I can't find it."

"You wrote it!"

"Don't be mean."

I got up and circled around behind her, to help her find the text. I leaned forward, my head next to hers, and pointed. She turned toward me and thanked me, her face dangerously close to mine. I felt the blood rush to my cheeks and backed away, returning to my seat.

"You're sweet to help me like this," she said with a smile. "The other TAs are useless."

"Well…they've got a lot of students to deal with," I said.

She smiled again, then leaned forward and said, with a breathy, southern accent, "I guess I just need more…personal assistance."

"And I need a little distance," I said, putting my hand on her forehead and gently pushing it back.

She gave a theatrical sigh and pouted. I tried to ignore her. And we got back to work.

It was probably the one honest thing I had said to her all day. I *did* need a little distance. Watching guilty husbands from the safety of my car…doing research at the library…that's what I do best. That's my comfort zone. Even when I'm with the band, I have this gigantic bass fiddle between me and the audience. The whole idea of being out front, totally exposed, *interacting*—that's not for me.

And yet, here I was, playing this weird role with no script and no safety net, having no clue how to get from Point A to Point B. You'd think as a musician, that wouldn't freak me out, since most of what I do is improvisation. But jazz is different. There's always a net. I've got key signature, I've got timing, I've got a chord progression. All that stuff gives you boundaries. It's like sports—you know where the lines are, and as long as you keep the ball inbounds, you're good. But there was no groundskeeper laying out lime here, and there was no sheet music to follow, so I figured the only way to see where the line was, was to cross it.

"So, what is it with you and us older guys?" I said, smiling to make it sound like a good-natured tease. "First Arlo, now me?"

She looked around in a panic, then said, "What are you talking about?"

"I saw you hanging all over him at Cyrus's party," I said, filing that look of panic away in my mental notebook.

She sat back up again. "Oh, that," she said. "That was just…drunk. I could barely stand up straight, that night."

"Uh-huh," I said. "Okay."

"And as for you," she said haughtily, "I'm just being nice so you'll help me with this paper."

I laughed, and she grinned, happy that I wasn't taking offense.

"So you're not sleeping with your professors?" I said, pushing on but keeping a teasing tone.

"No!" she said, horrified. "Shut up!" She picked some cold fries off her plate and threw them at me.

"Well, I'm glad to hear it."

"He's a decent guy," she said. "I know everyone thinks he's crazy, or weird, or whatever."

"I'm firmly in the Whatever camp," I said.

"But he's different outside rehearsal. You should see him. He puts on this act and all, but outside, he's quieter. Still intense, but quiet. He's like, artist *qua* artist."

"Qua artist?"

"Qua qua qua," she said, and laughed. "I took a Beckett class last semester. Now I can't stop saying it." She paused to eat some of her lunch, then added, "Plus, he's crazy smart."

"Beckett?"

"Arlo!"

"Right. So...you spend a lot of time with him, outside rehearsals?"

She shrugged. "Not a lot."

She bent back down to her laptop and made a show of working on her paper again.

"Blair says Arlo's been helping you with Cassandra."

She nodded. "He'd better. I need all the help I can get."

"Help *qua* help?" I asked, fishing.

She stuck her tongue out at me, but it was a half-hearted gesture.

"Guess that doesn't leave you much time for hanging out with friends."

She shrugged again.

"Hey," I said, trying to get her to look up. She did, but only briefly. There was something unhappy in her eyes.

"You do have friends, don't you?"

She rolled her eyes. "Yes, Father, I have friends."

"Is that like Dad Father or Priest Father?" I said, smiling.

"Take your pick."

"All right, all right," I said. "I just want to make sure you're okay."

"I'm fine. I have friends." She paused, thinking, then pushed the thought away with a "Whatever."

"I guess it's still kind of difficult, huh?"

"What?"

"You know—being out with people, doing things, after that friend of yours who killed himself."

She stared at me for a minute.

"Chris?" she said.

"Yeah, that's the one."

She narrowed her eyes at me, suspiciously. "What does that have to do with anything?" she asked.

"Well...weren't you two, like...a couple?"

"No," she said evenly. "Who told you that?"

"Well," I said, trying to remember. "Everyone, I guess."

She sighed—non-theatrically, this time. "Fuck everyone," she said. "Everyone thinks they know everything."

"And they don't?"

"No," she said. "Chris was hung up on me, but there was never anything between us. He was..."

"What?"

"He was like a twelve-year-old. I don't know. He was nice. He was, like, the nicest guy I knew, all freshman year. We were good friends for a while—I could talk to him about anything. But then he started writing all this poetry and shit, and putting stuff in my mailbox at the theatre department—"

"Like what kind of stuff?" I asked.

"Flowers. One rose, sticking out of the mailbox, where everybody could see it. Like that."

"Sounds romantic," I said. I was watching her face closely, trying to get a read on what was going on.

"It was totally embarrassing," she said, whining a little bit and looking away. "I caught so much shit from people, and I told him…I told him he had to stop it, but he was like this little puppy or something, following along after me and…" She shrugged again, dismissing the memory, and looked down at the table. "I don't know. I felt bad when he died, of course. We all felt lousy. How could you not? But he wasn't anything…you know…special to me."

She looked up quickly—just for a second—to see how I was reacting or to see if I was buying it. And in that single second, I could tell she was lying.

"He was just an NGB, you know?" she said a moment later, keeping her head down.

"NGB?"

"Nice-Guy-But. You know… a really nice guy, but…"

"But you wouldn't want to date him."

"*Date* him?" she laughed. "What is this, *The Suite Life?*"

"Again, I have no idea what you're talking about." I was starting to feel ancient.

"It's…never mind. It's an old Disney show. You know…clean-cut, fresh-faced, shiny people…"

"So nobody dates in college anymore? Is that what you're saying?"

"I don't know," she shrugged. "Not like *that*."

"Like how, then?"

"I don't *know*." She was starting to whine again.

"All right, never mind," I said.

She typed for a minute, then stopped and looked up at me for a moment. "What were *you* like, back in college?"

"Way back when?" I laughed. "What am I, a hundred years old?"

She giggled.

"I was exactly like this. It wasn't so long ago."

"I don't believe it," she said.

"I'm telling you."

She shrugged, and went back to typing. "Suit yourself."

I watched her for a minute, then said, "You're a very aggravating young woman."

She looked up, waggled her eyebrows dramatically, and said, "My evil plan is working."

Then, looking down at her laptop, she scrunched up her face and bent down to fix something.

"Are you finished with that, or what?"

"One second," she said, holding up one hand and typing with the other. "Done."

"All right. You want to read it to me?"

She looked quickly at her watch and grimaced. "Crap. I can't—I'm late. Can I email it to you tonight? I really want you to read it one more time, if you could."

Email. Another thing I hadn't figured out. I didn't have an email address for this Josh Green character I was pretending to be.

"Let me send *you* an email," I said. "I've already got your address on the rehearsal sheet. Then you can just hit reply and attach it." That should buy me enough time to set up a new account.

"Coolio," she said, gathering up her stuff. "Sorry I've got to run. Thank you so, so, so much. I really appreciate it."

"My pleasure," I said. "See you later."

She ran over, kissed me on the cheek, and then dashed off.

I stayed for a few minutes to process.

First of all, this was not a strung-out, drug-addled girl, whatever Blair had been implying. She was functional; she was fine. But there was definitely something going on under the surface. I didn't know if it was home life, or Chris, or Arlo, or something else. I was going to have to dig a little harder for that.

Also: Chris was something to her, but he wasn't her boyfriend. That was news, since everyone thought they had been together. Well…everyone my age. It was just like Chris had said—we were a million miles away.

But *he* hadn't been a million miles away, had he? He had been in way too close. Watching her every day at rehearsal. Being a Good Friend and wishing he could be more. Watching her and wanting her. And then getting up the nerve to send her poetry and give her flowers. You had to give him credit for that—he put himself out there.

But she had been embarrassed. She had said No. Stop it.

I was trying to imagine what that felt like—getting up the courage to lay everything on the line for a girl, only to get shot down—not just shot down, but told you had *embarrassed* her. That your gesture had been *humiliating*. What do you do with that? Where do you go with that, especially in a tight little group like this, where you see the same people every day? Was that enough to make you start doing the very thing you had hated in your father?

That was one song I never had to play. I may be the quintessential bass player—hanging back and letting others have the spotlight—but that doesn't mean I was ever one of those "NGBs." I mean, I didn't go out of my way to be an *asshole* or anything, though I definitely had my moments. One really bad moment, for sure. But most of the time, I didn't have to go begging for attention. There were always plenty of girls hanging around when I was in my headbanger phase—girls who thought I was mysterious and interesting, just because I was in a band. And the less I paid attention to them, the closer they came. They came to me—I never had to go looking for them. And I never had to watch a girl walk away from me, either. It was always *me* doing the walking—me saying, "too much, too close, got to go." Over and over, for years. Until I met Susannah.

Susannah.

Shit.

The show had the night off. I was supposed to be meeting Susannah for drinks.

I was going to be late again.

20

By the time we got home, Oticha was already in our living room, working on a solo. When your house doubles as a rehearsal hall, a lot of people have keys.

Pete and Lydia were sitting with some beers they had helped themselves to, while Oticha stood in the center of the room, doing some mournful variations on Ray Charles's "You Don't Know Me." He finished a phrase and then pulled the horn away from his mouth and looked at me.

"Well, look who-all decided to come by for a visit."

"Sorry, guys," I said. "I've been behind, all day."

Susannah trailed in behind me, gave everyone a half-hearted wave, and went into the kitchen. There was an awkward silence.

"Where's Ray?" I asked.

"Couldn't make it," said Pete. "Again."

"Between him and you, it's not much of a combo, these days," said Oticha.

"I'm doing the best I can," I said, reaching for the bass fiddle and getting set up. "So, no drums tonight? Nothing?"

"I brought this," said Pete, holding up an old washboard, circa 1850. "I thought I'd play around with it a little and see what I could do."

I just stared at him for a moment. "It was Lydia's idea," he said. "She said she liked washboards."

"I said I liked washboard *abs*," Lydia said, not even bothering to take the beer bottle from her lips.

Pete looked embarrassed, but he soldiered on. "I saw some guys in the park last weekend, and they were getting a lot of good sound out of one of these, so I picked one up. I soldered some tin cans to the bottom, see? Different sizes? And I bought some thimbles. It's something, at least."

I shrugged, happy to have the spotlight on someone else. Besides, I had been a fan of the old washboard thing since New Orleans.

"Does this mean Jordy's gonna have to get an old metal tub and string, and shit?" said Oticha. "Because I'm gonna draw the line right there."

"Just finish your haunting refrain, will you?" Pete said. "We're all waiting."

Oticha smiled—he always liked it when Pete got annoyed enough to fight back—and put the horn back up to his lips.

All snark aside, it *was* a haunting refrain. I followed along, giving him some support, but he didn't need much from me. It was spare, and slow, and plenty sad, even without the words. Of course, when Lydia decided to leave her beer and join in, it went from haunting to heartbreaking. She stood next to Oticha, closed her eyes, and swayed gently back and forth while she sang:

> *You give your hand to me*
> *Then you say hello*
> *I can hardly speak*
> *My heart is beating so*
> *And anyone can tell*
> *You think you know me well*
> *But you don't know me*

I listened to her rich, smoky voice singing alongside Oticha's warm trumpet, and all I could see was Chris Tremaine pining after Maddy. Watching her in rehearsal; watching her walking away from him.

> *No, you don't know the one*
> *Who dreams of you at night*
> *And longs to kiss your lips*
> *And longs to hold you tight*
> *Oh I'm just a friend*
> *That's all I've ever been*
> *'Cause you don't know me*

I could picture her walking across the quad at night, just like when I had been following her. But now it was Chris following—Chris hiding in the shadows, waiting to see who she would meet. Chris hiding under windows, listening, while she sat in a room somewhere, shooting up something, going down on someone, doing a hundred other things that broke his heart.

I looked up at my friends and realized that Oticha and Lydia had stopped. I was still playing.

"If you're gonna be sideman to the music in your own head, the rest of us might as well go home," Oticha said.

"It's not *my* fault I got carried away," I said. "It's y'alls fault."

"*Y'alls*—listen to him," said my friend. "You hear that?"

"You're not fooling anyone, you know," said Pete.

"All right, all right," I said. "I'm sorry."

We worked on the song for a few more minutes, and then Pete asked for something faster so he could try out his washboard. He had a strap attached so he could wear it around his neck. Once it was on him like a breastplate, he put some thimbles on his fingers so that he could strum the metal washboard to make a rattling sound, and whack the various tin cans he had attached at the bottom. He ran through some of what he could do and grinned at us. He was right—it was a great sound.

Lydia grabbed her clarinet and started in on "Won't You Come Home, Bill Bailey?" Pete stood by and supplied a wonderfully zippy, rattly percussion. I listened for a while, then came in on bass to give them some support. Oticha just stood by and watched, nodding appreciatively.

"Looks like somebody's been practicing behind our backs," he said, when they were done.

"We just played around with a few ideas," said Pete, his face bright red.

"Mm-hmm," said Oticha. "Only problem is, if Lydia's gonna sing a verse, and you're not gonna be on keys, we've got nobody to pick up the melody but me. And we've been doing that to death."

"Yeah," said Pete. "That's true. I guess I could run back to the keyboard."

"That's goofy," Lydia said. "Just keep it like it is. I don't need anyone else on melody."

So we tried it. And it worked. Pete and Lydia worked through the song like they had been playing together for years. And we all congratulated one another for being so clever.

Yeah, we were geniuses. Except none of us could see what was right in front of us. None of us except Susannah, who was watching from the kitchen doorway.

"He's in love with her," she said later, after everyone had gone home. "It's so obvious."

"He's not in *love*," I snorted.

"I warned you this would happen," she said. "Nobody listens to me."

"He'll get over it," I said. "Pete is *not* her type. He'll figure it out, sooner or later."

"You know everything," she said. She got up and started cleaning up—clearing away beer bottles and straightening out the furniture.

"What's the matter?" I said.

"Nothing," she said.

"Don't get all passive-aggressive on me," I said. "That's *my* thing."

She stopped what she was doing and said, "Fine." She marched over to me and stood facing me, inches from my face, which, even though I had just kind of invited it, made me uncomfortable. "You're dismissing me and I fucking hate it. Okay? How's that?"

"I'm not dis—"

"Fine. Fine," she said, getting angrier. "You're right. I shouldn't talk about what you're doing; I should talk about what I'm feeling. So here: *I feel* dismissed. *I feel* ignored. *I feel* like you're not paying any goddamned attention to me. And I hate it."

I didn't know what to say. I'm not good at these lay-your-cards-on-the-table confrontations. But Susannah's a pro. Susannah can stare you down till you break.

"Why?" I said, quietly. "What am I doing?"

"I don't *know* what you're doing," she said, exasperated. "I don't know what you're *ever* doing. You're fucking absent—all the time."

"I've been late a couple of times—"

"I don't mean *physically*," she said, like she was talking to a child. "I mean up here, in your head. I don't care if you're twenty minutes late to meet me for a drink. But I sure as shit care if your mind's a million miles away once you get there. Even when you're with me, you're not with me."

"I'm sorry."

"I told you this was going to happen, didn't I?" she said. "Nobody listens to me. I told you you'd get all...*engrossed* over there. I told you it's a whole other world, being on campus. *I* knew you'd get sucked in. How come *you* didn't? Don't you remember what it was like?"

I thought about it for a minute, and about what Kitty and Kate had said at lunch. "I guess not," I said. "I didn't realize how much of it I had...blocked."

"Yeah, well..." she said, foundering a little bit. "I'm not saying you can't do your job. You know? I just want you to come *home* from it."

"I know," I said. "It's hard. It's not like a regular job. I can't just leave papers on a desk and walk away. It stays in my head, all the time, trying to work itself out. I can't help that."

She walked away and sat down on the couch. "And there's no room for me?" she said. "That's what you're saying? You work a case like this, there's no room for me? Anywhere?"

"No," I said, sitting next to her. "That's not what I'm saying. You're...you know how important you are to me. Jesus..."

"Yeah, I know it," she said. "But it's nice to *hear* it every once in a while."

I nodded.

"That's why I thought...I figured if you had the night off, we could have a drink, go out to dinner, like a...you know, like a date, or something. Not like some old married couple, but like when we first met. And you weren't even in the room with me."

Suddenly, everything came into focus. The way she had been acting all afternoon—how angry she had been when I said I needed to get back to meet the band—all of it. "I'm sorry," I groaned. "I missed the whole...what you were trying to do. I totally fucked it up."

"It's all right," she said. "It's just a...date."

"No, it's not all right. And I *am* sorry."

"It *is* just the case, though, right?" she said. "I mean, you'd tell me if it was something else?"

"No," I said. "I'd be completely chicken-shit and avoid talking about it till it was way too late."

"Yeah," she said. "I figured."

"But really, it's just the case. If it even *is* a case. I don't know what it is, to tell you the truth."

"If it's not a case, then get out of there and call it a day."

"No, it's…something. There's something going on over there, and I can't figure it out. Whatever got Chris killed, it's still out there. It's all buried twenty feet underground, but it's out there."

"So dig deeper."

"Yes. And faster."

She leaned her head on my shoulder. "Faster would be nice."

21

Fine. So: how to make it faster? Obviously, it meant I couldn't rely on secondhand info from Maddy and learn about Arlo from a casual distance. I had to go after him directly.

The problem was, Arlo Alden was still basically a cartoon character to me, even after a couple of weeks of rehearsals. Maddy said he was a different guy outside of rehearsal. I needed to see what that looked like. It was probably crazy to think a professor would be selling drugs to his students, but, on the other hand, this was a guy who had hurled an axe at his cast members' heads. So, fine, it was a prop axe. It didn't have a blade. But still.

I decided to skip a few classes on Monday afternoon and keep an eye on the professor, but there wasn't much to see. He went from his office to a lecture hall. I sat in the back and watched him drone on about Homer. Then he went back to his office. I lurked in the hallway, hoping to catch some shreds of phone conversations, but I couldn't hear a word. He had an endless stream of Bob Dylan tunes playing on an iPod in an expensive-looking docking station, which made it impossible for me to hear whatever was going on inside. But whenever I could peek into his office, he had his head buried in a pile of old books. I had to give him credit for that. He may have been out on a crazy limb as a director, but the man did his homework.

And Maddy had been right; the guy I was spying on was definitely a different person from the guy I saw in rehearsal. He was just as pretentious and self-involved, but when he stood in front of a classroom, he took on a whole different persona—the Classics professor: urbane, witty. He spoke calmly and evenly, even when he was telling a joke. He was the voice of authority. And when he sat in his office, he stayed silent and focused on his reading or his writing.

So was this guy a scholar playing the part of Crazy Artist at night, or was he a crazy artist at heart, reining in the crazy to teach his classes every day? Who was this guy, deep down? What was driving him? What was he looking for? Was he the kind of guy who could find a way to justify selling crack or crystal meth to a bunch of vulnerable teenagers, just so he could buy a nice car for himself?

Watching him at work wasn't going to tell me much— that was clear. But at about 4 p.m., he left his office, coat in hand, and I perked up. His day was over, but he had a good three hours to kill until rehearsal started. What would Professor Alden do with himself during that time? Something weird, I hoped.

I followed him across the quad, much as I had followed Maddy at night—keeping a safe distance and matching my pace to his. He seemed to be heading toward his car, which was great—my car was parked nearby, and I wouldn't have any trouble finding his little Miata in traffic, once I caught up with him.

Unfortunately, long before we reached the parking lot, Arlo slowed down, as if sensing something in the air. Then, before I could do anything, he whipped around and looked straight at me. It was the only time I had ever been caught like that, and I was not happy about it.

If Arlo thought there was anything strange about seeing me behind him, he hid it well. He grinned, then reached one arm out to me across the expanse of lawn and yelled, "*Khai-re*, Orpheus!"

"Hey," I said, not sure what he had said, but taking it for something friendly.

"Where are you off to?" he asked.

"Nowhere," I fumbled. "I mean…home, I guess, for a while."

"Waste of petrol. Come join me for a drink." He waved me over to him, and we walked down a hill to one of the many bars sitting at the edge of campus. I reached into my pocket and switched on my digital recorder. Maybe I'd catch something more useful than his lectures on Homeric epithets.

When we got settled in one of the high-backed booths and had our beers, he said, "I like what you're doing. Have I told you that?"

"Uh…no," I said.

"I forget, sometimes. I don't get to direct as often as I like, and, you know…the people skills, they get rusty. I talk to Phidippides more often than I talk to Phi Delts, if you know what I mean. I spell *fuck* with a phi."

It was a well-rehearsed line, but he was proud of it, so I gave him a respectful laugh.

"Anyway, I like what you're doing with the chorus," he said. "It's striking and it's different."

"Well, thanks," I said. "You realize I have no idea what I'm doing, though, right?"

"Absolutely," he said with a grin. "That's why it works." He leaned forward, intently. "The hard thing—the hardest thing, really—is breaking free of tradition. Getting out of the rut. Because what makes a rut? It's just people taking the same route, day after day. The more they take that route, the more they guarantee the next people will take that route. They dig a track for the people who follow, and the track becomes a grave. It's only the pioneers, the trailblazers, the ones who come first, who get to make an authentic choice."

"I get that," I said.

"And that is the great thing about university theatre. You meet these kids before they get trained. Training is the great curse, Josh. All it teaches you is how to fit into the grave-rut. God save us all from training." He shook his head sadly. "You work with professionals, all they can give you is what they think they're *supposed* to give you. But with kids this age, you get authentic, genuine *response.*"

"Yeah, but you can also get crap, can't you?" I said. "I mean, if you asked me to play a new instrument before I learned how it works, it would sound like shit."

"Yes!" he said, clearly relishing the conversation. "But at least half of the instrument for an actor is emotion—feeling—genuine connection to the human heart, and the ability to express those feelings in a true way, not a prepackaged, sitcom way."

"I get that," I said. "But still, if they don't know what they're doing, how do you know you won't just end up with…noise?"

"You don't," he said. "That's why we do experiments here, at university. We play our little games here, where nobody cares if we make any money, or get people to renew season ticket subscriptions, or even make anyone happy. Subsidized experimentation—that's what this is all about."

"Huh," I said.

"Of course, if it works…" he trailed off, looking off in the middle distance somewhere. "If it works, then you've got your ticket. You can go the academic route and publish in a journal, *and* you can go the commercial route with a production. Two-pronged attack. And I'm talking about a *real* production, with grown-ups."

He seemed to have forgotten about how wonderful it was to work with students. But he kept going. "Regional, to start with, then you hope it catches on and spreads. That's the brass ring, Josh. You find something truly, legitimately *new*, that *works*, and you tie yourself to it and ride it. That's how you make your name." He thought for a minute, and nodded to himself. Then he focused his eyes on me again, and smiled.

"Do the students get any credit when something like that happens?"

He shrugged and said, "They get the experience." He reached for his beer. "That's what college is for."

"I guess."

"Insight. Wisdom. Opening the doors of perception…" He had slipped into his impress-the-undergrads routine, but I decided to play along.

"I've heard that line somewhere."

"I would hope so! It's Blake. Wild Bill. It's where Morrison got his name for The Doors: 'If the doors of perception were cleansed, everything would appear to man as it is, infinite.'"

"That's pretty intense."

"Only if you think about it," he said with a grin. "And then, man, it's so much more than intense. You want to know what it is? Really? It's the true and real purpose of what we're doing here. Not grade-grubbing. Not getting into some fucking graduate program, but *vision*. Satori. Seeing the world with new eyes. That's what this is all about. And you're either on that bus or you are *off* it."

"Well, you can sign me up," I said, raising my glass. "To art, and to vision."

He joined me, and added, "And to whatever chemical shortcuts we need to get us there."

And we drank again.

I tried to stay nonchalant, but my heart was racing. I had him on tape—but what did I actually have?

"Speaking of which..." I said, tossing out the bait to see if he'd bite. "If I was looking for something stronger than beer..."

"Oh, no," he said, laughing, holding up his hands as if to say Stop. "Talk to your comrades if you want to pursue *that* conversation."

"What comrades?" I asked, innocently.

"Your little MFA buddies. Blair, or Scotty, or whoever you hang out with in the Music department."

"Not willing to share your source?" I said, smiling innocently.

"My source," he said, rolling his eyes. "You overestimate me, Orpheus. My source is whoever passes something around at a party. I don't keep for myself anymore. Not in years."

And that was all I got out of him. The conversation drifted to more arty stuff, and then he left before I even finished my beer, to run home and get some things for rehearsal. I stepped outside to call Carter and give him an update.

"Outstanding," he said, unimpressed. "So you found a college prof who smokes a little weed, maybe drops a tab of acid now and again. Damn, son, that's front-page news."

"You're an asshole," I said.

"And you're jumping at shadows," he said.

"I know," I groaned, rubbing my eyes. The sun was setting, and it was getting cold. "But shadows is all I've got."

"So get the fuck out of there and go home," he said.

"You think I don't want to?" I said. "Trust me, I'd be more than happy to call this thing done."

"Thing was done before it started," he said.

"Easy to say from a million miles away. You're not involved."

"I'm involved," he said. "I got money riding on it, don't I?"

"What am I supposed to do?" I asked. "I feel like there's something here, but I can't get close to it."

"Maybe whatever *was* there is long gone," he said.

"No, it's still here. Players are the same, scene's the same. Nothing went away. Nothing changed, except a kid died."

"That doesn't mean it's murder," he said.

"What if this guy Alden *was* dealing, though? And what if something went wrong, or he panicked?"

"If, if, if…"

"I know." I paused for a minute, feeling the cold air start to creep in. "So you don't think there's a chance?"

"More than a chance he's using; less than a chance he's dealing."

"So who is?"

"Who isn't?" he snorted. "It's a fucking college campus."

I'd been over this so many times. "I'm not talking about weed, Carter. I'm talking about something hard core, something kids wouldn't usually use."

"You got no idea what kids use," he said. "You'd be amazed, son. Even down to middle school."

"Middle school?"

"We got a report last year about some shit moving through the middle schools called Strawberry Quick. Crystal meth flavored with fucking strawberry milk-shake powder to make it go down easy. Turned out to be bullshit, but we turned up all kinds of ungodly shit while we were looking for it. Ecstasy at the eighth-grade prom, roofies, you name it."

"Roofies? Are you serious?"

"All I'm saying is, don't go looking for some big-ass snake trying to sneak into your little garden. Snake's been there for years."

"Look," I said, getting exasperated and cold. "All I know is what the kid told me, and what he told me was that things were weird, people were acting different—it wasn't like what he had seen before. And his dad was some kind of falling-down alcoholic or something, so it's not like he was dewy-eyed and innocent about what people look like when they're fucked up. That's what he told me, and then he went back to gather more information and ended up dead."

"All right, all right," he said, picking up on my tone. "So there's a bad guy pushing bad shit on campus. Why do you want it to be *this* guy?"

"I don't know," I said. "I just don't like him."

He tsk'd at me. "Doesn't mean you got to like him for *this*," he said. "Classic rookie mistake."

"True."

"I mean, a guy like that? A professor? Why would he risk it?"

"Money, maybe. Some other reason. There could be reasons."

"So fine. If there's reasons, go find them, Bulldog."

"Yeah," I said, feeling a headache coming on. "I'm working on it."

"Lemme know if I can help."

"Seriously?" I said, pouncing on the offer. "You want to run a NCIC report for me?"

"You know I can't do that unless we've got an investigation open."

"Yeah, all right."

"Anyhow…you really think your boy's got priors?"

"No," I said. "I don't know. It's a long shot."

"Go search online. You got your own databases. You don't need mine."

"Then how about this?" I said. "How about you go back to your friends at the Baby Cops, find out how the kid OD'd? Without that, I'm just swimming in jello. At least I'd know what I was supposed to be looking for."

He tsk'd at me again, thinking, and then said, "It's a tough one."

"Well, you're a tough guy."

"You know they don't want to give up nothing, but…lemme see if I can pry it out of them."

"Thanks, man." I said. "I owe you."

"Naw, I already owed *you*," he said. "But either way, I'm still gonna collect my fifty."

I hung up and stood there in the parking lot. It was too late to go home, and too early to go to rehearsal, and I had nowhere else to go. So I just stood there, trying to figure out what to do next. I stood there for a long time.

It didn't help.

22

Carter was right about one thing—if I wanted Arlo, I was going to have to do my own research. So for the rest of the week, I decided to exercise my God-given right as a student to skip class, and I sat in my little office downtown, poring over the records available to me as a licensed investigator. I didn't think I'd find any kind of criminal record, but I thought maybe I could find a motive, or a hint of a motive. Maybe he was divorced and paying a hefty alimony. Maybe he was up to his eyeballs in debt. Maybe there was *something* I could hang my suspicions on.

But no. I spent two days digging through every database I could access and I found nothing even remotely incriminating. The man owned a fancy car and lived in a nice neighborhood because he could. He wasn't up to his eyeballs in debt. In fact, he had no debt. Zero. He must have been teaching classics and directing plays because he liked it, because he sure didn't need the money. Most of his income came from investments, and those investments were major, and old. Arlo Alden was some kind of Old New England Trust Fund Baby gone to seed. This was a guy who never *had* to do anything. His whole life was just hobbies and diversions.

Okay. Fine. So that was Arlo Alden. But if he didn't *have* to do anything, didn't that mean he thought he *could* do…everything? Massively Entitled definitely described the Arlo I saw every day. So if he didn't have to sell drugs for money, fine—maybe he just made drugs available because he thought it was fun—The Great Giver.

But, as Carter would say, "If, if, if…" I had nothing tangible. Nothing real. I was still at square one.

I needed a break in this case, and I needed it bad.

Now, in movies, you see Great Detectives finding tiny, obscure clues that no one else has noticed because they're amazingly perceptive, superhuman sleuths. And then they use their secret key to systematically unlock the truth—like how a piece of lint on some guy's sleeve reveals exactly where the guy had been nineteen hours earlier. They thwart the bad guys because they're geniuses. And, by the way, the bad guys are always top-notch, super-obsessive bad guys, planning every aspect of their crime to the last detail. Coincidence is never a part of these stories. Nobody just stumbles on a lucky break.

But in real life, it's lucky breaks and coincidences that make up about ninety percent of everything that happens. Just look at me: I go on a stakeout and just happen to look in the right direction at just the right time. Boom—I'm a minor league hero for catching a burglar. I follow some poor schlub to find out if he's gay, and the one day I happen to linger around a few extra minutes, boom—I catch him meeting someone in the park. Brilliant detective work? No: dumb luck. Sometimes you just catch a break.

My whole life is exactly the same. I go to a concert and set up my blanket in one particular spot instead of another particular spot, and I end up with a new best friend and music partner who changes my life. I go to a bar and smile at one particular girl instead of some other particular girl, and I end up marrying Susannah. It's all just random numbers. Dumb luck. Chance.

I'd been hanging around this campus for over two weeks (though it felt like two months), keeping my eyes and ears as open as possible, and I still didn't know anything about what had happened to Chris Tremaine. Why? No lucky breaks. I could have hung around for another two weeks, with nothing more to show for it. I could have hung around for another two years.

And then I caught a break.

"Hey...Josh...?" The voice was weak and whispery. Sloppy, somehow. She was drunk, or strung out, or something.

It was about ten o'clock on Saturday night. I had met up with Susannah at a nice Italian place in Virginia Highlands for a lot of wine, a little pasta, and some "marriage reconnaissance," as she called it. We were heading home, warm and cozy, when I got the phone call.

"What's the matter?" I asked. Because something was obviously the matter.

"I don't know," she said lazily. "I just...needed a friend."

"Are you okay?"

She laughed a weary, little laugh. "Oh, sure..." she said.

Susannah looked at me and mouthed, "Who is it?" I held the phone away from my head and whispered, "Witness." She nodded.

I put the phone back to my ear. Maddy was in the middle of talking. Rambling. She was upset. She had been out with some girls and they had said something. She needed someone to talk to.

"What about your other friends?" I asked, trying to get off the phone.

She laughed that sad laugh again. "Yeah, them." There was a pause. I waited. "You don't understand," she said. "Chris was the only one who...I mean...you *do* understand. You said it, but I was...too embarrassed. But then I thought, after the other day, after we were talking, maybe...I'm sorry. I'm being stupid."

I glanced over at Susannah. I was going to catch serious hell for this, but suddenly, I was seeing an opening—a crack in the door. Maddy was talking. She was looking for a sympathetic ear. And she was talking about Chris. This was exactly what I had been waiting for. The timing was just shitty.

I tried to imagine telling my wife I was about to go visit a drunk college girl in her dorm room. Unsurprisingly, the scene played badly in my head. I needed to see her on safer, more neutral territory. But where? I couldn't bring her home. Forget that. I mean, put aside how Susannah would react to it, which was bad enough. The whole idea was bad. I had to keep my worlds separate. My house was Jordan's, full of Jordan's life. I couldn't let the mess of this case get entangled with my actual life. Josh Green had to live somewhere else.

My mind was racing. I needed a place that looked like a grad student lived there. A non-married grad student. And I needed to invent it instantly.

"Can you get down to Edgewood? It's like, just below Little Five Points, off Moreland" I asked.

"Yeah, I guess so. I don't think I should drive, though."

"No," I said. "Call a cab." And I gave her an address.

"Thank you," she said, starting to cry.

"It's okay," I said, trying to avoid the angry glare coming at me from across the car seat.

I hit the End button and then typed in another number, as fast I as I could.

"What are you doing?" said Susannah. "We needed tonight…"

"I know. I know," I said, typing. "I can't help it. This is the only goddamned break I've had. If I let it go, I might not get another one."

"But—"

"Faster, remember? This is how I get there faster."

The phone rang on the other end and picked up. "Pete?" I said, before he could even say anything. "I need a huge favor."

23

Pete had been living like a grad student for as long as I had known him, so his place was perfect. He lived alone in a dark, little bat-cave of an apartment, in a fringe-y part of town, and he never invited people over. Half of his living room was filled up with keyboards, computers, and recording equipment, and the other half was taken up by an enormous TV screen, a ratty old love seat, and a chair that looked like he had stolen it off the bridge of the Starship Enterprise. It was a big, overstuffed recliner with built-in cup holders and TV-remote caddies—the kind of chair a guy could live in for days, if he had enough food within reach. And you could tell from the ground-up potato chips and Cheetos dust that Pete always had enough food within reach.

I'm not saying I *would* have lived in a place like this if I had never gotten married, but I definitely *could* have.

I dropped Susannah at home and raced down to Edgewood while Pete cleaned out his spare bedroom, trying to make it look like somebody lived there. He was still in there when I arrived.

"So who are you supposed to be?" he asked, watching me throw some clothes I had brought with me around the floor.

"Josh Green," I said. "Music student."

"Josh. Okay. And how long have we known each other?" he asked.

"What?" I said, distracted. "It doesn't matter. I don't think it'll come up." I stood up to survey my work. "Look okay?"

He looked around. "Well. If you're supposed to be a musician…"

"Fuck," I said. "No instruments."

"Does she know what you play?"

"I think so." I tried to think, but nothing was coming. "Don't worry about it. I'll figure something out. Maybe she won't notice. She's drunk, I think."

"You didn't mention that part," he said, looking unhappy.

"Pete," I said, putting my hands on his shoulders in a fatherly way, "if this is the first time you've ever had a drunk girl in your apartment, then I'm doing you a favor."

"Yeah," he said, not looking convinced. "When she throws up on me, remind me to thank you."

But we didn't have time to strategize any more than that, because Maddy was already knocking at the door. I opened it and saw her standing there, head down, looking beaten and bedraggled. Behind her, I could see a cab pulling away from the parking lot.

"Hey," I said. She looked up at me for a split second, then looked down again.

"Come in," I said. "It's cold out there."

She walked in, still looking at the floor.

"Come in. Sit down." I led her over to the love seat, sat her down, and took her coat.

"I'm sorry," she said quietly. "This is stupid."

I sat down next to her and tilted her face up to mine. "It's not stupid. Whatever it is."

I noticed her glancing over my shoulder and turned to see Pete standing sheepishly, not knowing what to do.

"That's Pete," I said.

"Hey," she said. "Sorry about this."

"No worries," said Pete. "I'll just go...do something."

Maddy looked around the room. "Are you a musician, too?"

"Yeah...sort of," said Pete carefully. "I do a lot of stuff."

"Computer stuff?"

Pete perked up, encouraged by the interest. "Yeah, actually, right now I'm doing some work with computer-augmented responsive performance environments."

We both stared at him. He fidgeted a little.

"It's stuff that, you know…fuses space, sound, image, and…sensor-based technologies," he added, hopelessly. He nodded for a second, as if confirming something to himself, and then pointed to his bedroom and said, "I'll be in there."

We heard his door close, and then there was silence. I watched Maddy, waiting for her to make the first move. She didn't.

"Can I get you anything?" I asked. "Water?"

She shook her head, then lifted her hands and covered her face. She was crying.

"Hey, come on," I said. "Whatever it is, it can't be that bad."

"It's all your fault, anyway," she said.

"Me?" I said. "What did I do?"

"Made me feel like shit."

"How'd I do that?"

"You kept *talking* about it, teasing me, and now I can't…"

"What?"

She sighed, dropped her hands, and leaned back into the sofa.

"It doesn't matter," she groaned. "It's not your fault. It's me. I deserve it when they talk about me."

"What? What are they saying?"

"Arlo. Arlo and me. The fact that we...we're...*you* know."

I didn't say anything, so she sat up straight, and looked me in the eyes. "We're fucking, okay? Just like you thought. Just like *everyone* thinks, apparently."

I took a moment to pretend to be shocked, and then said, "Okay. So...fine. If that's what you want to do, who cares? What do you care what the sorority girls say?"

She shrugged.

"Unless it's not what you want..."

She shrugged.

"Okay. How long has it been going on? Let's start with that."

"Just the last couple of weeks. Coming back after all the...stuff, last term, and then jumping into this show...it was hard. And I didn't have anyone to talk to."

"And he was there for you."

She snorted. "Yeah, he was there. He's always there."

"That sounds ominous."

"Not ominous. He's just always *been* there, ever since..."

"What?"

"I don't know," she sighed. "He was really nice to me, freshman year, the first class I took with him, and after that he always, kind of…made an effort, you know? Any time I saw him. To say hello, or help me run lines, or whatever."

"Run lines?"

"Rehearse. He was always just super nice and helpful and…stuff."

Stuff. I'll bet. I could just picture it.

"You think I shouldn't be fucking him," she said—more a statement than a question.

I put up my hands, defensively, and said, "I have no opinion on the subject."

She snorted again. "Yeah. Right."

"All I know is, you're drunk and upset, and you took a cab all the way down here to talk to me about something, so…"

She nodded. "Yeah, all right."

"So I'm listening. And I'm thinking maybe *you* don't think you should be fucking him. Maybe you think it's a little creepy for a professor to be sleeping with one of his students."

"He's not creepy!" Then she was quiet for a moment. "I don't know. Maybe he is. He likes giving backrubs. He's very…touch-y. But, I mean, he does that with everyone, right? And it's theatre, so… gah! I don't *know*!" She stood up, but didn't seem to know where to go or what to do, so she sat back down again. "We were at this party at Cyrus's house. He was going to give me a ride home, because everyone else was gone, but then we never…got there. Whatever. This is weird, talking about it." She got fidgety again, but stayed put.

"Okay, so what happened tonight?" I asked, trying to keep her on track. "Something got you upset. It's got to be more than some idiot girls teasing you."

"It's *you*. You happened," she said. "My guilty-conscience fairy godmother…father."

She looked at me with a sad, little smile, then closed her eyes and shook her head.

"It's not your fault," she said. "I knew the whole thing was…fucked. I mean, it's wrong. Obviously. I know that. It was just the only nice thing I had."

"But now you're thinking it's not so nice?"

"I mean, it's still nice when I'm with him, mostly. He's super attentive and stuff. But now, after we talked that day, I can't help seeing the whole thing the way *you'd* see it. You know—through someone else's eyes. And it's…yeah. It's creepy, I guess. I mean, it's not like he likes me *qua* me, right? I mean, it can't be. I was just this dumb seventeen-year-old."

That caught me off-guard.

"Wait a second, wait a second, hold on."

"Not *now*, I mean. Then. When I first got here. He's always looked at me that way. I could feel him looking at me, right from the start."

I didn't say anything. I wasn't sure what she was hoping for. She stared at me, waiting for me to speak, until finally, she said, "So it's *wrong*, right? I mean, obviously. I shouldn't be going over there."

"So why do you?"

"I don't know!" she yelled.

I watched her closely. "I think you do," I said quietly.

She shrugged, then nodded.

"Ever since he died, I just kind of drift around," she said. "No anchor, you know? Or no rudder. I don't know what I'm doing. I just...do things. Like...untied. It was too hard, and he was there, and I guess I kind of...drifted into him."

I tried to picture Arlo, watching and waiting to get at Maddy, and I wondered just how "drifty" the situation had been, but I didn't say anything.

"And then you and I were hanging out," she said. "And it felt so...normal. It felt like normal friends again, without the...you know. Like, maybe somebody might actually give a shit about me again, without...wanting something."

"You *qua* you?" I said.

"Yeah," she said quietly, looking down at her hands. "It's stupid."

"It's not stupid," I said. "Everyone deserves that."

She shrugged.

"Hey," I said, lifting her chin gently so she was looking at me. "What happened to him, Maddy? What happened to Chris? No one around here will talk about it."

"He killed himself," she said.

"I know, but why? Doesn't anybody know why?"

She turned away from me a little. "I think he just got…sad."

"About what?"

"He didn't tell me."

"He didn't tell you? I thought you were his best friend."

"No, that's the whole point. Don't you get it? *He* was the friend. He was the one who listened. He asked questions. He gave a shit. He was the one who fell in love and gave me flowers and…and wrote poems. I didn't give him *anything*." She stood up, paced a few steps, and looked around like she wanted to pick something up and throw it against the wall, Instead, she just beat her fists on her own forehead, yelling, "FUCK!" at the top of her lungs.

I jumped up and grabbed her hands, trying to keep her from hurting herself, but she yanked herself away from me and collapsed into Pete's big chair.

"Why do you do this to me?" she said, crying again. "Why do you make me think about all this shit and feel worse and worse about everything? Every time I talk to you?"

I walked over to the chair and kneeled next to it. "Maybe because I'm your friend," I said, "and I care about what happens to you."

"Yeah?" she asked drowsily, with a sad little laugh. "Why should *you* care?"

"I don't know. I just do," I said.

"Maybe you just want to fuck me," she said. "Like everyone else."

"No," I said. "Not everyone."

"Maybe that's all I'm good for."

"Maddy…"

"The fuck do you know? You barely know me."

"So tell me."

She shook her head, hard, and her long hair fell across her face.

This was getting weird and toxic. I didn't know what she wanted, or how to help her.

Finally, she seemed to pull out of it. She sighed, pushed her hair back, and leaned back. She wiped her face and said, "You guys have any pot?"

"Sorry. No."

"Seriously? Two musicians and no weed?"

I laughed. "Well, Pete has asthma, and I get paranoid. So we're strictly an alcoholic household."

"Fine. How about a beer?"

I had no idea whether Pete had anything on hand, but I went off to the kitchen to find out.

"Seriously, you get paranoid?" she called out to me.

I came back with two bottles and handed one to her. "Totally," I said. "I get all weird and introspective and self-loathing, judging every word that comes out of my mouth and every gesture I make—like I'm sitting there, behind my eyeballs, saying, 'Why'd you say that? Why'd you lift up your hand like that? You look like an idiot.' It's not a ride worth taking."

"Huh," she said, taking the beer from me. "At least I'm not the only one with issues."

"Not hardly," I said, clinking my bottle against hers and drinking.

"I was using this stuff last semester that did some seriously weird shit to me," she said. Then she stopped, lost in thought, shaking her head.

"What was it?"

"I don't know, for sure. Some weird combo platter of heinousness. It was supposed to be like ecstasy, or crystal meth, or something like that, but without being addictive or harmful. Make you think about all the happy stuff in life, like all the stuff when you were a kid, and push away all the now stuff that sucks."

Finally—the whole reason for being here.

"But it wasn't all it was cracked up to be?" I prompted.

She snorted a little laugh. "Not exactly." She drank her beer for a minute. "I mean, it got me through the show, I guess, but then I couldn't stop it. Or I didn't want to, I guess. The whole Chris thing happened, and my grades were getting fucked, and...you know."

"Same old story."

"Yeah. It took me the whole break to get my head straight."

I watched her, trying to figure out how much to push. But I didn't have to do anything—it was all coming out on its own.

"It felt so *good*, though," she said, leaning forward and putting her head in her hands. "I swear to God, if you had any, right now, I would totally take it. Even though I don't want to. I would. And I'd go fuck Arlo's brains out for, like, a day and a half, just like the first time, and I wouldn't even care."

"Like the first time? I thought you said the thing with Arlo just started."

"Yeah, I mean, officially. But there was that one night, last semester. After closing night. I was kind of..."

I tried to read what was going on in her eyes—what she was reluctant to say—but I couldn't figure it out.

"It was just that one time, and it was a mistake, and I tried to stay away from him, but then we all came back after break, and it's...it's just so fucking hard. I don't want to pop

Buds anymore, because I'll just stay up for days again and stop eating or going to class, and I'll be horny as shit, but without it, I'm like, filled with all this horrible…sadness…and the only thing that makes it go away is letting him…fuck me. What am I supposed to do?"

I didn't have an answer for her. But I understood now what Chris had seen—what he had seen happening to the girl he loved. And I understood why it had made him crazy.

But all I said was, "What the hell is this stuff?"

"I don't know," she said. "He called it Rosebud. It's these tiny little red pills."

Rosebud. Of course. Only a professor would name some new happy-drug "Rosebud." The pretentious, self-important shit.

"And it was Arlo? Who gave it to you."

She shrugged. "It doesn't matter. It's not like you can get it anymore."

"You can't?"

She laughed—a smallish, harsh kind of laugh. "The way they clamped down after Chris died, you're lucky if you can get an aspirin."

She was quiet for a moment. Then she leaned down again, with her head in her hands.

"Do you want another beer?" I asked.

"No," she said. "I'm pretty…dizzy."

"What can I do?" I asked. "How can I help you?"

She shrugged. "The show's just so hard," she said, talking into her hands, her voice muffled. "And midterms are coming and I'm totally unprepared. It's all ganging up on me. And if I fuck up my grades again, I'm out." She groaned. "I just wish he was still here, so he could tell me what to do."

I reached out and pushed her long hair out of her face, and let my hand rest on her cheek. "Listen," I said. "I'm not Chris, but if you need a friend, I can be a friend. Don't go through this alone."

She nodded, looked up at me, and then reached both arms out, like a child. I hugged her, and she started to cry.

"It's okay," I said. "It's going to be okay."

"Tell me what I should do."

I pulled away so that she could see my face. "You want my advice?"

She nodded.

"All right. First, you tell Arlo you're done."

She groaned.

"You've got to do it, Maddy. And if he gives you any trouble, I mean in rehearsal or anywhere, you tell him you're going to file a complaint against him."

"Oh, God…"

"You've got to protect yourself. You don't have to turn him in, but you've got to let him know you *can*. You've got to show him you're strong."

"But I'm not," she said quietly.

"Well, you're an actress," I said. "Pretend."

She nodded, and buried her head in my shoulder again. I stroked her hair and listened to her heartbeat and her breath. And while we sat there together, there was just one word rolling around in my head, repeating itself over and over again, just like in the movie where the name came from.

Rosebud.

We sat there for at least five minutes, Maddy in the chair and me on the floor, her arms wrapped tight around me, until my legs cramped up so badly that I couldn't keep crouching anymore. But when I tried to pull away, I realized she had fallen fast asleep. I pulled away as best I could, walked around to get the blood flowing again, and then did my best to half-carry, half-walk her into Pete's spare bedroom. I laid her down on the futon, pulled off her shoes, and covered her up with a blanket. When I walked back into the living room, Pete was there.

"It got quiet," he said. "I was worried."

"She passed out," I said, pointing toward the room.

"Great. So now what?"

"Now…I don't know. We let her sleep."

"Yeah," he said, "but what happens in the morning?"

"I don't know. She takes some aspirin and she goes home."

Pete stared at me like I was a moron, which apparently I was.

"I mean," he said, "what happens when she wakes up and you're not here? What am I supposed to tell her? You're supposed to live here, right?"

Right. Damn.

"I don't know," I said. "Tell her I had an early class or something."

"Yeah, which is fine if she wakes up at ten. But what happens if she wakes up at six? Or an hour from now? Come on, man, help me out. I don't know how this stuff works."

"All right, all right," I said, looking at my watch and wondering how I was ever going to explain this to Susannah. "I'll sleep on the floor or something, and I'll…take her back to campus in the morning."

I started to move toward the bathroom, but he grabbed my arm.

"She's a train wreck," he said.

"Yeah," I said, looking into the room at her. "Probably."

"And she knows where you live," he said. "Or where she thinks you live. Where *I* live."

"So?" I said, suddenly very tired.

"So, what if she comes back, looking for you? Like, every night?"

"She's not going to do that," I said, wearily.

"You're sure?"

"Yes, I'm sure, Pete."

"Okay," he said. He looked at me for a second. "You *do* know what you're doing here, right? I mean, you've got a plan and everything?"

"Of course," I said. "Don't I always?"

He looked in at the sleeping girl lying on his spare futon, and then turned back to me. He didn't seem convinced.

He wasn't the only one.

24

"Are you for real, man?" Oticha said, pulling his horn from his lips and scowling at me.

"Is that a rhetorical question?" I asked.

"I'm telling you, she's over there, like, constantly," Pete said, continuing the process of throwing me under the bus.

"You know, you can be replaced," I said.

"No, I can't," he said. "We're already short a drummer."

I looked back at our trumpeter, who was clearly expecting some kind of answer from me.

"I'm not *doing* anything to her," I said. "She's a messed-up kid, and she doesn't have any friends. I'm just trying to help her."

"Uh-huh."

"*And* it's my job to find out who she bought drugs from, so the more she talks to me, the better. What's the big deal? She gets what she needs, I get what I need."

"Yeah," Oticha said. "I'm sure Child Protective Services would see it just that way."

"She's nineteen years old," I said. "CPS has got nothing to do with it."

"Well, your little wifey doesn't see it that way," said Lydia, nonchalantly.

That pretty much stopped the conversation cold. We all turned to look at her.

"And how would you know that?" I asked.

She shrugged.

"Seriously, Lydia. What, are you two hanging out now?"

Another shrug.

"Jesus," I said. "That's all I need."

"Me, I just want my apartment back," said Pete. And having said his piece, he started in on the next song we were supposed to be practicing.

He was right, though—I had pretty much taken over his apartment and his life in the week since Maddy had come for her visit. I had moved some clothes and instruments into his spare bedroom. I had brought Blair and Scott over for after-rehearsal drinks. I had even spent a couple of nights on the futon. For all intents and purposes, I had moved in with Pete without ever asking him if I could. It had gone from a one-night emergency to a running gig.

And he was right that Maddy had been over a lot. I would argue with "constantly," but for someone unused to houseguests of the female persuasion, it was probably more than he was comfortable with. She had come over once to get some help with her Gregorian chant paper, then she had come over again a few days later to study for a test. She had said it was less distracting than the library or the dorms, which was probably a half-truth at best, but I didn't care. Having her around was tricky, but it let me keep a close eye on her while rehearsals got more intense and midterms loomed on the horizon. If something was going to turn ugly, I wanted to be there to catch it. Or her.

"I hope you know what you're doing," Susannah said, sitting on the edge of our bed and watching me pack a few more clothes for my fake bedroom.

"You want the answer I gave Pete?" I asked.

"Not really," she said. "It was probably bullshit."

"I'm sorry," I said, stopping and sitting next to her. "But this is the only shot I have. Either there's something here or there's nothing. Either it was a stupid accident or Chris stuck his nose where it didn't belong and he got killed."

"And you think this girl knows something?"

"I know she does," I said. "She's sitting on all kinds of ugly shit, and she's just barely keeping a lid on it. The only question is whether I'm in earshot when the lid comes off."

She nodded.

"Look," I said. "It's the only lead I've got, and if I miss it, this thing could drag on all year. You don't want that, do you?"

"Doesn't mean I want you hanging out with crazy, nineteen-year-old actresses, either."

"I've got to go all-in to make this thing work," I said. "I didn't ask for it to play out this way, but, you know, here it is. It kind of just landed in my lap." The imagery was probably not the best, but I hoped it didn't register. "Besides, Pete's there all the time. I make sure he's there, any time she's around."

She nodded, but she didn't say anything. I got up and finished packing, impatient with the little drama we were acting. I didn't know what else I could do. I had given her all the guarantees and promises I could, and I had tried to set things up to be as safe as possible. In the end, either I did the job or I didn't, and if she wanted me to not do the job, she had to say so. And she wasn't saying so.

"It's just like a stakeout," I said. "It's a place where I can snoop like I always snoop. It's just...closer."

"And longer."

"Yeah, and longer. Hopefully not too much longer." I closed my bag and looked around for any personal items that might help sell the idea I was living over at Pete's. "It's an act. It's make-believe."

"If you're not here in bed with me, it's not make-believe," she said softly.

"I'll be here," I said. "I promise."

"Not every night," she said.

I sighed. "No, not every night. *Mostly* every night. I'm only going to stay over if I have to. And Pete's there. You trust Pete, don't you?"

"I trust Pete," she said, a little wearily. "I trust you. That's not the point. It just sucks, that's all. Can't it suck? Can't I have that?"

I sat down again. "Yeah, of course you can have that. I'm sorry."

But I wasn't as sorry as she was, and she knew it.

I'm not sure why I wasn't as sorry. I should have been. If I cared anything about her, and of course I did, I should have been paying attention to the warning signs. But I wasn't. The game was on. My pulse was racing. It was hard to sit still.

So I didn't. I grabbed my bag and threw it in the trunk, and I headed back to the dark little melodrama I was creating, never worrying about what might happen when the lights came on at the end.

Part Three

1

"Look in her eyes," Arlo Alden said as he drifted around the rehearsal room. "*Feel* her looking at you. This is all about connection. I don't want your standard-issue mirror exercise, like you've all done since grade school. I don't care if you never move a muscle. *Connect!*"

All around the room, kids were sitting or standing in pairs, eyes locked on each other, deep in some kind of funky actor-trance. A couple of the pair s had jumped right in as soon as Arlo had partnered them. They had been moving and gesturing like they were shaving or brushing their teeth, trying to match each other's movements. Now they were sitting motionless, red with embarrassment.

"Don't do what I *tell* you to do. Do what you feel!" he bellowed at them. As usual, I had no idea what was going on. Blair and Scott were no help. Sitting behind the director's table, they were ignoring the action and texting their friends.

The room was silent. The earnest little actors kept staring at each other. From outside, it looked intensely boring and pointless...and as a rule, I hate being trapped in other people's boredom. So I walked up to Arlo and asked him, in a whisper, if it would help to have me lay down a quiet bass line. He grinned and gave me a thumbs-up. So I grabbed an electric bass, which I had been keeping in the rehearsal room, and I found a place to sit. I don't use an electric much, but it's a little more portable than my big monster, and I decided Josh Green could be less of a stickler than me.

I sat down at the edge of the room and started noodling around, moving up and down a few simple chords in search of a melody I could play with—something slow and moody and repetitive to help with the trance. After a minute or two, I hit on something I liked and leaned back to let the music take over.

When I'm playing like that, kind of tunelessly, I can let my mind wander. I don't latch on to stupid things like bills, or taxes, or whether I'm wasting my life on music. Having a tune in my head helps lift me out of the everyday crap and think more creatively. I was hoping it might do the same for the actors. I knew if I had been one of them, I would have had a lot of trouble "connecting," whatever that meant. I would have had a lot of trouble thinking anything except, "this is bullshit." But I guess that's why I'm not an actor.

Maddy glanced up at me when I started playing, but I gave her a dirty look and pointed my head back to her partner. She rolled her eyes and went back to the exercise.

I was sitting where I could keep an eye on her, like I always did during rehearsals. The play was hard on her—when

Arlo bothered to spend time on the actual play. She didn't have a lot of time on stage, but her character had this crazy list of prophecies she had to spit out at everyone, which was important to the plot. The axe Arlo had hurled across the room was always hanging over her—literally dangling above her head in the hands of one of the chorus girls—to make sure she always remembered how doomed and fucked her character was. So she had some challenges. And if that wasn't bad enough, Arlo kept making her do her long speeches in this horrible, high-pitched wail, and then yelled at her for being "emotionally detached." If it had been me, I think I would have emotionally detached his nose from his face. More reason why I wasn't cut out for this kind of work.

Thinking back over the last few days, knowing Maddy had been trying to keep her distance from the director in the after-rehearsal hours, I wondered whether today's weirdness had been dreamed up just for her benefit—some kind of special torture for his special friend. I wondered if the whole cast was thinking the same thing. Were they all being punished for Maddy's "detachment" from Arlo?

I kept playing and the actors kept staring at each other. Little by little, the energy in the room started feeling more intense and electric. Early on, there had been some giggling, but now people seemed to be locked into each other. Some of the pairs were moving their hands with each other, but some of the others were just sitting still and staring. Maddy was motionless.

I figured Arlo would move into something like an actual rehearsal after ten or fifteen minutes, but he didn't. The weirdness went on. Twenty minutes. Thirty minutes. My fingers started to get sore from the repetition, but Arlo just kept walking around, watching the kids watch each other, getting off on…whatever he was seeing. I looked back at Blair and Scott, but they just shrugged. Forty-five minutes. This thing was insane. I couldn't believe the kids hadn't given up, gotten up, and stormed out of the room in protest. I sure as hell would have.

Finally, after almost an hour, Arlo called it. At the sound of his voice, the kids snapped out of their trances. Some of them shook their heads and rubbed their eyes. Some of them fell back on the floor and collapsed. Maddy leaned down, head in her hands, and closed her eyes.

"That was fucking *intense*," one of the kids said.

"Seriously," another one said. "It's like I could hear you inside my head."

"That's what we're looking for," said Arlo. "Primal connection. Beyond thought. Beyond logic. This is deep stuff we're dealing with. Murder. War. Sex. Vengeance. We've got to be able to plug into that." He nodded a few times, very satisfied with himself, and then clapped his hands and said, "All right. Let's set up for Hecuba's entrance. *Be strong, Hecuba. Fate wraps her cold arms around you!*" He strode back to the director's table, preening and happy, while actors got up off the floor at different speeds and got themselves ready for the scene. Maddy stayed put, down on the floor, head in her hands like she had a splitting headache. Arlo sat down, arranged his papers, and then looked up and barked, "Maddy. Places."

Maddy buried her head more deeply into her hands and her lap. A couple of kids started calling her name. One or two tried to nudge her with their feet. She wouldn't get up.

"Let's go! Let's move!" Arlo yelled, clapping his hands. The actors trotted around the room, getting ready for their scene. Maddy got up unsteadily and looked around. Everyone was in place, staring at her.

"Are we ready, Princess?" Arlo asked. "Or do we need to sit around and talk about our feelings first?"

Maddy walked over to where her coat was piled on the floor, grabbed it, and ran out of the room.

Arlo sighed, looked up to the heavens, raised his arms, and said, "*Sákandros*! Save me from divas." Then he dropped his arms and said, "Skip Cassandra. Hecuba, enter."

The actors started their scene. I looked back at Blair and Scott, and said, "Isn't anybody going to go check on her?"

"Better not," said Blair.

I must have looked confused, because Scott chimed in to explain. "He's doing it on purpose," he said. "Singling her out, making her feel like shit. He does it whenever he can, now that he's rehearsing her separately."

"Why?"

"It's just...you know, help her feel what it's like. To be Cassandra. It's like the thing he does with the axe over her head."

"Think about it," said Blair. "I mean, you got this ancient story, she's a princess, a prophet, war booty, sex slave— it's a shitload of weird for some kid from the suburbs to wrap her head around."

"So he figures insulting her in front of her friends is the way to go?" I said.

"You do what you've got to do," said Blair with a shrug. "Every actor needs something different."

I got up, stuffed my script in my bag, grabbed my coat and said, "You...and you: assholes."

What do you want? I'm a musician. Sometimes, words fail me.

I found her right away. She hadn't gotten far. She was sitting on the stairs just outside the building, wrapped up in her coat, hands stuffed into her pockets, her face tucked down for warmth. I zipped up my own coat and sat next to her.

"You okay?" I asked. It was a stupid question.

She didn't say anything. But she leaned over, still cocooned, and touched her head to mine.

"What happened in there?" I asked.

She shook her head.

"You want to go somewhere and not talk about it?" I asked.

She nodded.

I stood up and reached for her hand.

2

The Majestic Diner was its usual, loud self, but at my little table, silence prevailed. I sat there watching Maddy work on her burger, head down, blocking out everything except her plate. Every once in a while, she'd look up at me, checking to make sure I was still there, her bright, blue eyes shining out from under her dark hair. I'd smile at her, and she'd go back to her food.

Finally, I got fed up with the silence and said, "So tell me something. What do you get out of all of this?"

"What?"

"The whole theatre thing. I've never understood it. I mean, is it just 'I'm gonna be a movie star,' or is there something else going on?"

She shrugged.

"Seriously," I said. "I'm curious. What makes it worth putting up with endless rehearsals and asshats like Arlo Alden?"

She sighed. "He's not so bad. We've had worse. Crazier. At least he knows what he's talking about."

"He's an abusive jerk," I said.

She shrugged again. "*Qua* Arlo," she said, and went back to her hamburger. She thought of something and started to speak, but stopped when she realized she had a mouth full of food. She rolled her eyes with dramatic exasperation as she chewed, then took a sip of water and said, "Don't you ever have to deal with assholes when you're doing music?"

"Not so much anymore," I said, stealing a fry off her plate. "I just play with my buddies, now."

"And do you think you're gonna be a rock star or something?"

I laughed and said, "Not anymore."

"So why do *you* do it?"

I took another fry and thought about it for a moment. "I like the way I feel when I'm doing it. Kind of outside myself, outside my life."

"Oooh," she said. "Very zen."

"I guess so. It's like everything else goes away. All the day-to-day bullshit."

She nodded. "Exactly," she said. "You have to be totally there, in the moment."

"Open, listening, ready to respond. You can't be trapped in your head."

She nodded vigorously. "Totally totally totally. That's what it feels like for me."

"Yeah?"

"No matter how much you rehearse, you've got to be plugged in to the moment when you're up there, because anything can happen. You've got to respond to what the other guy says, not what you *think* he's going to say or what he's supposed to say."

"That's right. That's jazz."

"And when you get in that groove with the other person, it's a total high. You're, like, flying."

"Mm-hm."

"And, plus, you get to be this whole other person in this whole other life, which is nice."

"Huh. That one, I don't get. What's wrong with being you?"

"Pff. Don't get me started."

"Seriously."

She rolled her eyes in that way she had. "It's not a big deal. It's just nice to disappear once in a while. Be somebody else."

"Ah," I said. "Got it." I waited for a second, pretending another question was just coming to me. "So what happened last semester? You were doing a cool show with your friends. Why wasn't that enough? Why'd you need that shit you were telling me about? That Rosebud stuff?"

I was worried that maybe I was crossing a line, being too obvious, but she just shrugged and said, "I don't know." But then she thought about it for a moment. "I guess it was the same kind of feeling. At first. The same kind of disappearing. Except you disappear into yourself, but in a good way—going back to being a little kid."

"Is that what it feels like?"

"Totally. You get these intense memories from God-knows-where, things you haven't thought about in forever—things you didn't even think were *in* there anymore—and then you're just *there* again—in the moment. Not remembering, but totally reliving it. For a while."

"And then, what? Bad comedown?"

"Kind of. Nothing gross or anything. It just…you know. It's like waking up from a good dream and thinking, 'Oh, I'm just *here*.' But it got fucked-up for me after a while. It didn't even feel good when I was popping. Plus it made me horny as shit. I told you that. That's how I got all tangled up with…"

"Asshat."

"Yeah."

"And that's why Chris was worried about you?"

She stopped eating and looked out the window for a minute. "Yeah. I guess."

"What did he say about it?"

She kept looking out the window, as if he was standing in the parking lot, waiting for her. "He just started asking all these questions, like what Rosebud was like, why I was doing it, where I was getting it. He just kept pestering me, that way he had. Kind of like you're doing right now."

She smiled—the first in a long time. I smiled back.

"Anyway, I pushed him away. Again. I didn't realize he was dealing with his own shit. I guess he was trying to find some kind of answer or something. But I didn't hear him. He came to me for help, and I let him down. I shut him out. And now...you know. There it is. I'm a shitty friend." She turned back to me and smiled a sad, tired smile. "I'm a shitty friend, Green. You should stay the fuck away from me."

"Yeah, probably," I said, waving for the waitress and the check. "But you're so cute when you're eating giant hamburgers, I can't resist."

She smiled a sunnier smile at that, and leaned out across the table toward me. "Does that mean I can stay over tonight?"

I didn't say anything, so she pouted and said, "Pretty please? I'm still freaked out by that rehearsal, and I don't want to be alone. Let me hang out with you and Pete. I'll be good."

"You don't want to be good," I said, wagging my finger at her and hoping I sounded parental.

"No," she said. "But I will be."

So we headed home, or fake-home, Maddy in her car and me in mine. I called Pete to warn him, but he didn't pick up. And when we got to his apartment, it was empty. Which was good and bad. Good because I didn't have to explain or apologize, and bad because I wasn't comfortable being alone with her. Or maybe I *was* comfortable, which was even worse.

Either way, I had my own key, now, so I let us in. Maddy dropped her coat, sat down on the floor by the couch and said, in her deliberately dramatic way, "God, I feel like shit." She bent over her crossed legs in a quasi-yoga pose and groaned.

I sat on the couch and thumped her on the back. "Sit up," I said. "I'll rub your back if you tell me what happened at rehearsal."

She sat up and pulled her hair forward over her shoulders, giving me access to her neck and her back. I dug my thumbs in and tried to knead out the rock-like tension I felt there.

"So?" I said.

"I thought we weren't going to talk about it."

"I said we could go somewhere and not talk about it, which we did. Now we're somewhere else. New location, new rules."

"Whatever," she said. "Just don't stop doing that."

I didn't.

"I had no idea what you guys were doing," I said, "but it felt like the whole thing went on way too long."

"Crazy long," she agreed.

"But why did it freak you out? Why wasn't it just boring?"

"It *was* boring," she said. "I've done that exercise a million times. There's nothing weird about it. But I've never done it that long. It just kept dragging on and on. And at some point, it went past boring into something weird. Like the more I was plugged in to Sean's energy, trying to match his movements and stuff, the more I was plugged in to *him*, like…"

"What?"

"Like…I could hear his voice in my head. Inside my head, like he was *in* there."

"Yeah, I heard some of the others say the same thing."

"It was creepy. This guy in your head, uninvited. Rattling around wherever he wanted to go. It felt the way you feel when you find out someone's been reading your diary."

"Violated?"

"Yeah, violated. Invaded. Fucking A. And Sean's kind of an asshole, so I wouldn't want him inside any part of me, you know? But there he was, and I couldn't push him out, and…" She trailed off, looking out into nowhere.

"And so?"

She shrugged. "And so I freaked."

"Hmm," I said, noncommittally.

"Hmm?" she said. "That's all you've got to say?"

"Just processing."

She looked back at me and said, "If you're working on some comment about how I let assholes in all the time, e.g., Arlo, just keep it to yourself."

"I wasn't going to."

"Good."

I massaged the top of her head. "But it sure seems like you've got some shit trapped in here that's not doing you a whole lot of good."

"Hmm," she said.

"Hmm?"

"Yes, hmm. As in Not Responding."

"All right. Can I ask you something else that's been bugging me, if it's not you-related?"

"Fire away."

"Where did this Rosebud shit come from? I've never even heard of it."

She shrugged and said, "You're old."

I put both hands on her shoulders and gave her a shove. She fell over, sideways, and lay on Pete's carpet, motionless. "Unfair," she whined.

"Seriously. Am I really that old and out of it? Or are you part of some super-secret avant-garde, testing new, cool, designer drugs for the masses?"

"Somebody brought it to a party last fall. Some after-rehearsal thing at somebody's house. I don't remember when."

Then she sat up. "No—yes, I do. It was Tommy Einhorn's house, because we were up on his roof, and some people were dancing—doing a routine from the show. So it must have been, like, early October."

"And?"

"And he started talking about this thing called Rosebud, and how it was like the perfect Method-acting drug, because it totally put you in the moment, in a different place in your life, and made you feel like you were right there—gave you access to everything you were feeling at the time. So we tried it, and it was amazing."

"A lot of people were using it?"

"A lot? I don't know. There were four or five of us that night, but after that, I have no idea. Nobody ever talked about it. I think I'm the only one who fucked it up."

"I think it fucked you up, not the other way around."

"Whatever."

I started working on her shoulders again. Whatever tension I had kneaded out of them was already back. But I couldn't shut up. She was so open, so willing to talk, I couldn't let myself lose the chance to learn more.

"So Chris saw the whole crew taking it, and got worried?"

She turned around and looked straight at me. I had gone too far. "Why are you so interested in Chris, all of a sudden?"

"I'm not," I said, hoping I didn't look like a deer caught in the headlights. "I'm interested in you. I worry about you."

"And you think I'll feel better if I think Chris was trying to mom *everybody*, not just me?"

"Exactly." I tried to keep my sigh of relief contained.

"Nice try. But it was all me, all the time. I'm the only one who started missing rehearsals and failing classes and shit. I was the problem child."

"Okay."

She turned back around and I went back to her shoulders. But again, I couldn't resist. "Can I ask you one more thing?"

She gave one of her dramatic sighs and lay back down on the carpet, flat on her back, arms extended sacrificially. "Go ahead," she said.

"Was it Arlo who brought Rosebud to the party?"

She brought her hands up to her face, squeezed them on the top of her head, and screamed.

"Hey!" I said. "Keep it down."

"Could we please, for fuck's sake, stop talking about *Arlo*?" She sat bolt upright and stared at me again. "What is *wrong* with you?"

"What?"

She made a face. "What? What?" she said, trying to imitate my voice. "You rescue me from a nightmare rehearsal, we have this nice time together, I'm in your apartment, you're rubbing my back, and suddenly it's Chris and Arlo, Chris and Arlo. What the *fuck*?"

"I told you, I'm just worried about you."

"Well, *don't* be."

"All right, all right."

"I mean, Jesus. What are we doing here?"

"What do you mean? We're just—"

"We're just what? What do you want from me?"

"I'm just trying to be a friend."

"Yeah, right."

"Seriously, Maddy—"

"Don't talk to me like I'm a fucking child! Everybody wants something."

"There's no such thing as just being friends?"

"Jesus. I don't want to get into a philosophical argument about it."

"Friendship *qua* friendship?"

"Fuck you." She stood up and walked toward the door.

"What about Chris?" I asked, hoping it would stop her. "Wasn't he your friend?"

It did stop her. But she didn't turn around to look at me. "Chris wanted to fuck me," she said. "Like everyone else."

"You don't believe that."

"I was there."

"He wrote you love poems, Maddy."

She snorted. "What do you think love poems are *for*?"

I stood up and walked toward her. "Okay, fine. So what do *you* want? Why are you here?"

She tensed up, her hands tight little fists. "You're such a…"

"What?"

She shook her head, then opened her hands and shook them out. "Nothing. Never mind. Forget about it."

"I'm serious, Maddy. What do you want from me?"

"Nothing," she said. "I don't want anything from you. I'm an idiot."

And without looking back, she left. The door slammed and I was left there, feeling weird and alone. Weird, alone, and in someone else's apartment.

I paced around for a few minutes, trying to make sense of what had happened, but it was way too raw, and I was too conflicted. Jordan Greenblatt was trying to process all the new information, and he was feeling good about his evening's work. But Josh Green? Josh Green was thinking about those eyes, and those lips, and he was saying, "I can't believe I blew it!" As though the smiles and the backrubs and the promise of something more had been the whole point, like Maddy had thought—like Maddy had wanted. Like maybe Josh had wanted. Except there *was* no Josh—only Jordan. Jordan wanted something more, and that was *me*, and it was wrong. Except all I could see in my mind was Maddy, looking up at me, needing me—Maddy, that first time, at the party, when Arlo had his arm draped over her shoulder like he owned her, fingers dangling inches away from her tits, brushing them when he thought nobody was looking…

Fuck. This was bad. You can't keep stuff separate when you're playing a game like this. Not unless you're a great actor, which I'm not. I don't have those skills. I don't know how to spend hours and hours with a girl like Maddy and not feel things I shouldn't be feeling—things that can get in the way and wreck your life if you don't watch out.

I needed to talk to someone. I wanted to talk to Susannah. I wanted to be home, in my own home, with my own wife, in my own bed, being…just me. But instead, I was caught in this weird little drama in this shitty apartment, feeling all knotted up, and I couldn't bring myself to call her. Not about this. And I hated that fact, and it made me feel even guiltier than I was already feeling. But I needed a familiar voice—any familiar voice—so I called Oticha, and I spooled out the whole story for him.

"So what do you need me to tell you?" he asked, practical as always.

"I don't know," I said. "Nothing. I can't do anything about it. I don't *want* to do anything. I'm just worried where this is all going."

"Ain't going nowhere unless you take it there."

"I don't know, man...you weren't here."

"Yeah, but...who's the grown-up in the room? Right?"

I sighed. "Right, yeah. It's just hard. She's so...she's such an unhappy kid."

"Kid being the operative word."

"No, unhappy—that's the word. It bleeds off her all the time, and I feel so bad for her. I want to do something, and it's like she's reaching out, begging for just some...affection, you know? Some kindness."

"So be kind."

"I'm trying. But it crosses over so fast. And she acts like she needs it, so badly."

"Wants. Not needs."

"Maybe. I don't know."

"Jordy. I'm telling you. Girl like that doesn't know what she needs. I taught kids just a couple years younger. I don't even got to meet her, I know her. She's all raw nerve endings and hormones and shit—just a little girl in big-girl clothes. She doesn't know what she needs. Only what she wants. That's what screws her up. You want to help her, *you* got to know the difference."

"Yeah."

"She doesn't need someone else to fuck her. She needs a friend."

"I'm trying. Believe me."

"I do believe you. I know you."

I stood there, holding the phone, not sure what else to say. I felt miles away from him—him, Pete, Susannah—all of them.

"Thanks," I said, hopelessly.

"Be cool, man," he said. "Remember who you are. And go home."

I nodded, as though he could see me.

"And check out the song I sent you, too," he added. "Lydia wants to work it up for the festival."

I hung up and stood there for a moment, feeling useless. He was right; I should have gone home. But I couldn't do it. I didn't want to bring Josh's feelings into Jordan's house.

I checked my phone to see what Oticha had sent me. It was the charts and lyrics for an old torch song from the '30s—a classic 12-bar, minor-key blues, a perfect number for Lydia. I downloaded the Benny Goodman recording, got my bass out of my room, or Pete's guest room, or whatever it was, and I played along for a while, listening to Peggy Lee and imagining what our little group might do with the number:

You had plenty money, 1922
You let other women make a fool of you
Why don't you do right, like some other men do?
Get out of here and get me some money too

You're sittin' there and wonderin' what it's all about
You ain't got no money, they will put you out
Why don't you do right, like some other men do?
Get out of here and get me some money too

It didn't help.

The song ended, and I was left with the refrain hanging in the air, asking me why *I* wasn't doing right. I was trying, wasn't I?

Maybe yes, maybe no. Maybe I didn't know what "right" even was.

3

I didn't see Maddy again for a couple of days. Arlo was rehearsing with the leads in one room while I worked through some music with the chorus in another. I was grateful for the breathing room, and happy to get some snooping time with the chorus members. I did see her from a distance in her Intro to Music class, but she didn't make any move to say hello. Which was fine, because I was busy dealing with the day's guest lecturer, one Professor Alden from the Classics department.

"The music of ancient Greece was everywhere," he boomed, clearly enjoying the sound of his own voice in the big lecture hall. "It filled the air. There was music at weddings, music at religious services, music at the theatre, music in the home. They built statues to honor their greatest composers and performers. I daresay Justin Bieber would have felt right at home." The students laughed dutifully, and he beamed. "Let me show you how we know what we know." He pointed a clicker at the screen above him and launched a PowerPoint show. He was off and running.

I tuned out and looked around the room. Blair and Scott were standing up by the rear door, so I walked over to kibitz with them while Arlo did his thing.

"You two really have to follow the big man around, wherever he goes?" I asked.

"It's so much worse than that," Scott said. "We're actually here to hand out flyers for the show."

"That's sad," I agreed.

"We've all got to pay our dues," he said.

"I don't mind paying dues," said Blair, "but someday, years from now, when I'm paying my monthly installment on my student loans…"

"Oh, God," groaned Scott.

"I'm gonna look back on days like this and wonder what the hell I was thinking, signing up for a Ph.D in theatre."

"Dude," said Scott, "at least that's all you'll be paying. I've still got shit left over from college."

Blair nodded sadly and put his hand on his friend's shoulder. "Well, I may be an idiot, but you're a fucking moron," he said.

"I know, I know…"

We turned our attention to the front of the room, where Arlo had segued into a discussion of Dionysus and the rituals of ancient theatre, which seemed to include some borderline-inappropriate talk about orgies.

"Do you think he plans this shit, or does he make it up as he goes?" asked Scott.

"The man is a role model," said Blair. "I want to be just like him when I grow up."

"Rhythmic drumming!" yelled the professor. "Trancelike dancing. On and on into the night. Possibly the ingestion of mind-altering herbs. Freedom—liberation—the unshackling of all restraints in the pursuit of vision and truth. You think Chuck Berry invented rock and roll? You think Jim Morrison discovered the seductive, phallic power of music? This is one of our most ancient inheritances!"

"God bless tenure," said Blair.

"The wonderful thing about the ancients," said Arlo, bringing his voice down to something approaching conversational, "is that we find so many parallels, so many correlatives everywhere. So much about them was different, yes, alien, yes, but so much was shockingly familiar. Whenever you think you've invented something new, beware. Odysseus traveled to the land of the lotus-eaters long before Candler students discovered Rosebud."

I tried to catch the look on students' faces, but unfortunately, I was still up at the back of the room. But there were a few audible gasps and some shifting in seats.

Arlo looked triumphant. "Yes, we're not supposed to talk about such things, are we? But we know what goes on. And

I'm not here to chastise or lecture. Well, not about *that*." There was some laughter of relief. "All I'm saying is that, as Ecclesiastes tells us, there is nothing new under the sun. The mariner eats of the lotus, and 'deep-asleep he seem'd, yet all awake/ And music in his ears his beating heart did make,' as Tennyson puts it. And believe me, I have seen some of you stumble into classrooms, deep asleep, yet all awake!" Arlo paused for a moment and looked around the room. "*Sauton*, the oracle tells us: know thyself."

I had drifted to the side of the room by this point so that I could see more faces in the crowd. Some of the students seemed fascinated, others just looked confused. One or two looked uncomfortable, as though they had been caught, somehow—pinned like insects to a display board. Maddy Taylor was one of those.

"And so we have music and narcotics as implements of vision and transcendence when harnessed to religious or theatrical ritual, and we have music and narcotics as casual playthings, leading users to dark death or dreamful ease. I would argue that we, in our time, have far too much of the latter and far too little of the former." The professor paused and scanned the room. Then he smiled. "This does *not* mean that we will be handing out drugs during *The Trojan Women*." He signaled to Blair and Scott, who started walking down the aisles, passing out their flyers. "But I *can* promise some transcendent sounds from our friends in the music department." And he nodded toward me, as though he had been planning this as his big finish, the whole time.

I caught up with Blair after class, but Scott was already gone. "Cafeteria," he said, by way of explanation. "He's working the sandwich line now, Wednesdays and Thursdays. Work-study."

"On top of being a TA?"

Blair shrugged his bony shoulders. "Man's got bills," he said. "You heard him. Plus, I think his wife is pregs again."

I grabbed his arm and stopped him. "Wife? Pregnant? Again? These are three totally new pieces of information."

"Yeah? Yeah. Our Scotty is a certified grown-up," said Blair. "Wife, kid. He said something about another kid last week and I wasn't sure if it was actual news or just something he was afraid of."

"Man," I said. "And he looks younger than me."

"Well, I don't know what *you* are, but he's definitely younger than me," Blair said. "Won't look like it for long, though, I bet."

He started walking again—that long, noodle-legged lope I had trouble keeping up with. But I did my best, wanting to make sure I didn't lose the chance to talk about Arlo's weird lecture.

"What did you make of all that drug stuff?"

Blair shrugged. "Typical Arlo," he said. "God forbid anyone thinks he's passé. Ten bucks says he had to look up Justin Bieber on Wikipedia."

I laughed. "Yeah, but Rosebud? I don't think he found that online."

"Well, you weren't here last semester. It was all the talk around the department before people got spooked."

"Why spooked?"

"You know that old joke that ends with 'It seemed like a good idea at the time'?"

I thought for a moment, then said, "No."

"Yeah, me neither. I just remember the punch line. But it was kind of like that. Shit was supposed to be some kind of heroin-lite. Feels great at first, but then you wake up and find out you flunked all your classes."

"Huh," I said. "I never even heard of it before coming here."

"Well, you know how it is. Shit comes and goes. People are always looking for something new, prove they've found something no one ever thought about before. That's why I kind of dig what Arlo does, crazy as he is. Reaching back to the ancient to find something new."

"But it's not your gig?" I asked. "Heroin-lite?"

"Nah. I'm an old-fashioned, blunt-and-beer kind of guy." He stopped outside the Humanities building and looked at me. "Where you going?" he asked.

The truth was, I wasn't going anywhere—I was just tagging along with him to get as much information as I could. Which would not have been a good answer.

"I'm avoiding my Schoenberg seminar," I lied. "Twelve-tone composition is too much for my simple, Dixieland soul."

"*Sauton!*" Blair yelled, raising his fist in the air.

I laughed and returned the salute. "*Sauton,* brother. See you tonight."

And we went our separate ways.

4

"Heroin-lite," I said. "That's what he called it."

"Personal experience?"

"No, but I think he saw it plenty."

I could hear a pen scratching on the other end of the phone, so I waited until I heard my friend say, "Uh-huh. Go on."

"I also heard the professor compare it to something from Greek mythology. Sleepy. Dreamy. Losing your motivation."

"All right. What else?" Carter said.

I got up and started pacing around Pete's living room, trying to remember what I had wanted to capture for my friend. "Something about nostalgia, or childhood, or happy memories. Memories from long ago, stuff you didn't think you remembered. The girl talked about that more than once."

"Huh. That's a new one."

"I think it's got to be a real effect, or they wouldn't call it Rosebud, right?"

Silence.

"Like, from *Citizen Kane*? The sled?"

"What now?"

"It's a movie. *Citizen Kane*. Greatest film of all time, et cetera, et cetera. You're telling me you've never heard of it?"

"Whatever, man. What else you got?"

"Well, this isn't exactly objective, but the girl said she was the only one who had trouble handling it."

"Meaning what?"

"I'm not sure. I guess she thinks it wasn't a big deal for anyone else. Maybe that's why nobody in administration picked up on a problem. But I know *she* missed rehearsals, failed a couple of classes, almost got kicked out of school. I don't know how much of that's the drug and how much is this fucked-up relationship she's having with the professor."

I could hear pages flicking around as Carter looked back at his notes.

"This is Madeleine Taylor?" he asked.

"Yeah. Maddy."

"Uh-huh. All right. And she's the girlfriend?"

"What?"

"Of the vic?"

"Right. No. We thought she was, but it turns out they were just friends."

"Uh-huh."

"He wanted a relationship, she didn't. He sent her flowers, wrote her poetry. She rejected him, embarrassed him, the whole thing."

"All righty. Thanks for cracking *that* mystery, Donnie Brasco."

I resisted the urge to snark back at him. "Listen," I said. "She was the whole reason Chris came to see me, so whatever she was going through, it must have been serious. She says this Rosebud shit did a number on her, so I'm taking her word for it."

"Got it."

I started pacing again. "Now, *she* says the stuff kept her awake for days. I don't know how that fits with the dreamy, heroin angle. It sounded more like a stimulant when she talked about it. And there's something aphrodisiac or...I don't know...sexual about it. She said it a couple of times. How horny it made her feel, and how it got her into trouble."

"Huh. Now you lost me."

"You don't understand horny?"

"I understand it fine. I just don't see it nowhere."

"Nowhere where? Now you're losing me."

"I'm cross-referencing a bunch of reports while you're talking—stuff from around the region, even out west. Everything you're telling me is right here. Different name, but the same basic shit. So it's definitely a real deal you're onto. Only I don't see a sex angle."

"Well, maybe this version's cut with ecstasy or something."

"Or maybe it's just your girl."

"Be nice."

"I don't mean nothing by it. I just seen enough meth- and crackheads to know there's a whole lot of ways to be slave to the shit. Everybody's wired different. Maybe she's wired weird."

"Okay."

"See if you can get somebody else to say what she said. Maybe it *is* a whole different strain. Might help us figure out where it's coming from."

"I'll try. But I don't know if it's even around anymore. Nobody's talking about it in the present tense."

"But you still like this professor for dealing it? This Alden guy?"

I stopped my pacing and thought for a minute. Did I? "I don't know," I said. "Maybe not. He came right out and talked about it in front of a classroom of kids. I don't think a dealer would do that—even an egomaniac like him."

"I got you."

"But I don't have another candidate."

"All right. Well, keep at it. Least we got *something* now. You ain't chasing ghosts."

That was good to know.

"Oh, and by the way, I got the tox report on your boy," Carter said. "I was finally able to finagle a copy."

"And?"

"Xanax and alcohol. Classic combo."

Something about the news made me need to sit down. Maybe it was the clinical reality of it. I don't know.

"Fill me in. I don't even know what Xanax is, exactly."

"It's your basic sleeping pill. Anti-anxiety meds. It's all over the place."

"And Chris had a prescription for it?"

"Now *that*, we don't know. Nor am I authorized by the Baby Cops to ask the parents. I do know they didn't find a bottle in his room."

I sat with that for a few seconds.

"Course, he could have borrowed a fistful from a friend if he was feeling low. That only happens every goddamn day."

"But we don't know."

"High-school kids, too. Hell—middle-school kids. You have no idea."

"But we don't know for sure about Chris."

"We don't know. All we know is, he had a badass combo of Xanax and Stoli in his system."

"A kid who never drank or did drugs…"

"According to you. Anyway, officially, it's still an accident. Or a suicide. Whatever it is, it ain't nothing people are interested in."

"*You're* interested," I said—more a statement than a question.

"Well," he said, drawing out the syllable in his best, South Georgia way. "You know me, Jordy. I'm a curious son of a bitch. That's why I'm still taking your calls."

I laughed. It was nice to have someone on my side.

"Take care of yourself, Bulldog," he said. "You're swimming in some interesting shit out there."

5

If I was swimming in shit, I wasn't the only one. At lunch the next day, Blair's gang was looking pretty glum. Word had just come down from the Theatre department that scholarship and aid money were being cut back. Pretty drastically, from the sound of it. By the time I sat down with my food, they were already deep in the Gloom. Except for Blair, who tried to get someone—anyone—to laugh about it. "Seven years of college down the drain," he said. He looked around the table for a response. "*Animal House?* Anybody?"

"Shut up, Blair," said Gates, looking more severe than usual.

"It's not funny," said Scott. "I'm going to be making guacamole the rest of my life."

"Jesus," I said. "I haven't heard anything from *my* department yet, but you guys are making me nervous."

"At least when you're done, you'll have a marketable skill," said Blair.

"Doing what?" I asked. "Teaching music to elementary school students?"

"Teaching music to *anyone*, dude," he said. "Kids in school. Kids at home. Kids at band camp. Grown-ups. Whatever. Everybody wants to learn music. You know what I get to do with my Ph.D? Teach the next goddamn generation of *me*. That's all I'm good for. It's a hermetically sealed environment."

"There's too many of us. That's the problem," said Gates. "How many theatre scholars does the world really need?"

"Don't answer that," said Scott, to no one in particular.

"They gave us an overgrown, inflamed tit, and we've all been sucking on it, and it's more than the market can bear. The milk's running dry, and if some of the babies don't die, we're all gonna die."

"Holy shit, Gates," said Blair. "Maybe you should have gone into writing."

"Pfff," she said. "Their aid got cut, too."

There was a pause. My old friends would have yelled, "Lull!" and laughed about it, but that didn't seem like a good move here. "So what are you going to do?" I asked.

"I'm considering selling sperm," Blair said. "Mine, I mean. Obviously."

The table just stared at him.

Scott picked up his sandwich, looked at it for a moment, then threw it down on the plate in disgust. He shoved his chair back with a squeak, got up, and walked away.

"Nice job," said Gates, glaring at Blair.

"What?"

"You know what," she said. "This is serious shit for him."

"Yeah," Blair said quietly.

"He's gonna go Bev on us if we're not careful."

There were solemn nods around the table. I was lost.

"Go Bev?" I asked.

"As in Chimsky," Gates said.

"Chensky," said one of the students I didn't know very well.

"Whatever," Gates said, angrily. "She was a freshman a couple of years ago. Decent actress, but way too high-strung. Like inbred-poodle high-strung."

"Yeah," said Blair. "And just before Thanksgiving, she snapped. Climbed on top of the Physics building with a guitar and just sat there, singing sad little folk songs for like eight hours. Till they came and took her away."

"Why the Physics building?" I asked.

Everyone stared at me. "Really?" said Gates. "That's the interesting part, to you?"

"I get freshman girls going nuts. I don't get the Physics building."

"I think it has easy roof access," someone else said.

"Who cares?" yelled Gates. "The point of the story is she snapped, okay? And then, the next semester, she came back, all fresh-faced and happy and right with the world. Until just before spring break, when the whole thing happened again."

"Seriously?" I asked. "Right down to the guitar?"

"Yes: guitar, roof, *Circle Game*, the whole nine yards. And everyone was talking about it all day. 'Bev's on the roof again.' Until they came and took her away."

"Wow. And then?"

"And then, that was the end of Bev. Unless she went someplace else. Hopefully without her guitar."

I let the story sink in for a minute, and then said, "And you're worried Scott's heading there?"

"Well," she said, and then stopped. She seemed to be thinking about what to say next, but then she gave up and just shrugged.

"He's probably closer than the rest of us," said Blair. "What with, and all."

"Wife…kid…"

"Exactly."

"Well," I said, grabbing my tray and standing, "I'm available for piano lessons, if any of you want to learn a marketable skill." I didn't know what else to say.

"Thanks," said Blair glumly. Gates just stared at me.

I headed over to the Music department to put in some practice time, not wanting to fail exams and put the dean in a difficult position. I plinked away at a couple of pieces and thought about what I had just heard. I had wondered why Chris wasn't weighing heavily on anyone's mind when I first got here. But maybe he was just the latest version of Bev on the Roof. A good story to talk about over sandwiches and frozen yogurt. Another in a long line of freaky anecdotes. Maybe once the person is gone and the suffering is out of sight, all you're left with is the story.

I wondered: was Scotty going to be the next anecdote? Or was it going to be Maddy? Maddy was more visible—more obvious. But maybe Scotty was the one who was in real trouble. Maybe he merited some looking after. Nobody ever paid much attention to Scott. He was Silent Sam. He was the scholar. The writer. If the Theatre department had been a rock band, Scott would have been the bass player—the quiet guy in the background, giving support, shining his light on other people, keeping his own counsel. He was a deflector. I knew the type.

So that night, I decided to keep an eye on Scotty Flynn. I started noticing the tension in his face: the way the corners of his mouth pinched a little too tightly; the way his eyes moved around the room, even when his head was down in his script; the way he kept checking his watch. His body was with us, but his head was elsewhere. You wouldn't have seen it unless you were looking.

We were in the big theatre that night. Arlo wanted to see how some of his "stage pictures" were going to work in the big, open space where the play was going to be performed. And "space" was the right word. There was no stage anywhere—just a round pit marked by masking tape, where two tons of sand was going to get dumped. A few seats were set up around the circle, but most sat in stacks up against a wall, to make room for a huge, rolling scaffold that students were using to hang lights from big pipes that crisscrossed the ceiling. It was total chaos, impossible to hear anyone. But Arlo seemed to be getting what he wanted.

Arlo always got what he wanted. I could tell from the looks and mutterings from the lighting crew that they hadn't been planning on having him and the actors underfoot, and they were annoyed by the distraction. But he was the boss, so they tried to make room for him.

I was walking around the periphery of the circle, watching the action and wishing there was something useful for me to do. Arlo decided to pace next to me and share his theories about theatre.

"What I'm trying to do here, Josh, is create an enveloping kind of environment—destroy the artificial barrier between audience and action. You see how that's going to work?"

"I guess so," I said.

"I want our soundscape to envelop the audience in exactly the same way. Music coming at them from back there, from over here, maybe even from under the seating platforms."

Before I could say anything in response, something metallic clanged high above me and somebody yelled. I don't think it was a warning, exactly—more like a string of curses—but it got my attention, and just in time. I looked up and saw a flashing piece of metal heading my way. I jumped to the side and let it clatter to the floor. It was a large wrench. It could have killed me or Arlo, or at least sent us to the hospital.

"What the fuck?" yelled someone standing right behind me.

"Sorry!" a voice yelled back from the ceiling. "Something's blocking the pipe. I didn't see it."

"Do you *mind*?" said Arlo. "I'm trying to work here."

"Well, what is it?" yelled the guy behind me, ignoring Arlo.

"I don't know," the voice from above called back. "There's some lumpy-assed shit up here, taped to the ceiling. Duct tape or something. I couldn't budge it. I lost my grip."

"Could we talk about this elsewhere, please," said Arlo. "Or another time. Or perhaps never?"

The guy behind me, probably the lighting crew chief, sighed, continuing to ignore Arlo, who was standing right next to him. "You all right?" he called back up to his guy.

"Yeah, yeah, I'm fine. So what do you want? You want me to pry this shit off, or what?" scaffold guy yelled.

"COULD WE HAVE SOME QUIET, FOR THE LOVE OF CHRIST?" bellowed Arlo.

Everything stopped for a moment. Then the crew chief whisper-shouted, "Leave it. I don't know what the fuck it is. Just slide the Fresnel over a foot or two. No one's going to know the difference. Finish up and let's get out of here."

Arlo gave up, called for a break, and actors moved across the big floor in every direction simultaneously. Arlo didn't stick around either. I looked for Scotty and noticed him making a beeline for the door, and there was something about the way he was moving that seemed a lot less casual than everyone else. So I waited a couple of seconds and then followed him out into the hallway, where I found him pacing and talking on his cell phone. I stayed back a bit, pretending to check messages on my own phone. And I listened.

It wasn't hard to eavesdrop. He was talking in that hopeless phone-voice where you try to have some privacy and keep things quiet, but if you speak too softly, the person on the other end can't hear you.

"I know," he said, over and over, hitting the "know" as if whoever he was talking to didn't believe him.

"Well, what do you want me to do about it?.....When?.....Seriously, when? I'm taking a full load. You know that......Yeah, yeah. And *I'm* in rehearsals all night. And at the cafeteria, so…No, I'm not saying you should…..Fine……No, *fine.* I'll look around. I don't know. What do you want from me?"

He pulled the phone from his head and leaned against the wall with his eyes closed. Wife. Kid. Another on the way. It wasn't hard to put the pieces together.

He opened his eyes and saw me lurking. "Sorry about that," he said.

"No worries," I said.

"You're not married, are you?" he asked.

"No," I said, trying to remember my Josh Green bio. "Came close, once."

"You're lucky."

"Yeah." I moved in closer—he seemed like he wanted to talk. "Must be hard to balance everything."

"Balance," he said, laughing at the word. "I've heard of that." He twisted his head around, like he was trying to loosen a sore neck muscle. "I never should have started this shit—that's the problem. Once you're a couple of years in, you don't want to quit and lose everything. But man…If I had known we were going to have kids so soon…"

"Took you by surprise?"

"Totally." He leaned back against the wall and closed his eyes.

"And Blair said you're expecting another?"

"Yeah," he said. "Another fabulous surprise. I just found out a week ago."

"Congratulations."

"…they said, as they hammered the last nail in his coffin…"

I wasn't sure what to say, so I said nothing. He banged the back of his head lightly against the wall and shook his head. "We were so stupid. We should have paid shit off. We shouldn't have bought a house. Now, it's just…the whole thing is just a money pit."

"The house?"

"The house, the school, the life." He banged his head again. "My whole fucking life. I keep thinking I'm out of the trap, and then the next thing happens, and I'm right back where I started."

"Are you going to have to quit the program?"

"No," he said sharply. "No way. Not after the shit I've done to stay here…the things I've had to do…you have no idea."

"Selling your sperm? Or was it Blair's?"

He smiled at me and shook his head. "If only it were that easy," he said.

We were quiet for a moment. I realized this was the most I had heard Scott speak since I had met him. And the most emotion I had ever seen from him.

"Whatever," he said with a sigh. "It's not your problem. Let's get back to weeping Hecuba."

I wanted to say something, but then *my* phone started ringing—or, actually, playing the snatch of "Potatohead Blues" that I used as a ringtone.

Scotty laughed and said, "At least yours will be better than mine." Then he headed back into the theatre. But he was mistaken. My call was the same call as his. It was Susannah, and she needed to see me at home—right away.

6

Home. I didn't realize how long I'd been away until I walked in and noticed how strange the place felt—like when you come back after a vacation. I'd only been gone a couple of days, but the place felt not-mine, somehow. Maybe it was just having Susannah's stuff flung around the living room in ways she doesn't do when I'm at home. Maybe it was just the fact that we don't usually spend time apart. Kissing her felt weird. Like I had to get used to her lips again.

"Hey, stranger," she said, touching her forehead to mine.

"Hey, yourself," I said. "What's wrong?"

She straightened up, looked me in the eye, and said, "Rot."

"Rot?"

She nodded. "The wood, the grout, everything. Serious water damage in the walls."

"Where?"

"Come see," she said. She grabbed my arm and pulled me toward our one bathroom. I could see from the doorway that she was right. Something had been leaking, and there was damage all along the wall by the shower. The paint was bulgy and buckled, and you could tell whatever lay behind it was soft.

"When did that happen?" I whined.

"Go on, touch it," she said. "You know you want to."

"I don't, really," I said. But I did it anyway. I crouched down, pushed in where the paint was buckling, and felt my hand sink right through the sheetrock and into the soft, pulpy wood.

"Great," I said. "That should only cost a fortune. How far does it go?"

"I don't know," she said. "But the tile's all fucked in the shower, too."

I sat back and leaned against a non-rotten wall.

"When are they gonna pay you for this thing you're doing at Candler?" she asked.

"When I finish it," I said. "I didn't ask for a per diem."

"Swell."

"You know the gig," I said. "I'm getting paid under the table."

She nodded. "You want a beer?"

"Sure." I pushed myself up and followed her to the kitchen. "Is that really what you called me about?"

She opened the refrigerator and leaned into it to grab a beer. "Well, normally I'd just turn to you on the couch and say,

'What do you want to do about the bathroom?' But you barely live here anymore."

She handed me the bottle, and as I reached for it, I noticed something strange on her arm. I hadn't seen it before, or maybe I just hadn't processed it. It looked like she was wearing a bracelet, which she never does, but when she moved her arm, the colors didn't move. I bypassed the beer bottle and grabbed her wrist.

"You got ink?" I said, turning her wrist a little to get a better look at it.

"I did."

"When did *that* happen?"

"A few days ago. I was out with Melanie and a couple of her friends. Margaritas were involved."

I leaned in and looked a little closer. It did look like a bracelet, with crisscrossing vines or stems circling her wrist, in two or three shades of green. On the underside, right where the veins were visible, a word was woven into the vines, in a deep, rich red. The word was, "Jordan."

"What do you think?" she asked.

"It's pretty," I said, turning her wrist around again. "Really delicate."

"I figured you'd be happy I didn't go with the tramp stamp."

"You figured right," I said, turning her hand over again and looking at my name resting right over her veins. "That must have hurt."

"Like a motherfucker," she agreed. "But the guy was amazing. I asked him if he could do the vines first and then weave the name into it, so I could add more names down the road, and he had zero problems with it."

"More names?" I said, dumbly.

"Yeah, you know…" she said, "for the future babies. It's not going to be just you and me forever, right? So…I left room for them. Whenever."

I nodded. Obviously. Of course. Kids.

"Can I have my hand back now?" she asked.

I let her go and took my beer. She cocked her head and narrowed her eyes at me.

"You all right?"

"Totally."

"You think my mother's going to freak when she sees it?"

"Totally."

She grinned and said, "Win-win!" And she went back into the living room and flopped down on the couch.

I just stood there—immobile in the kitchen. I wasn't sure why.

"You're weirded out, aren't you?" she yelled. "What's the matter?"

I turned around and leaned against the wall in a place where she could see me from the couch. "I don't know," I said. "It's just weird."

"We know lots of people with ink," she said.

"Yeah, but not each other."

"You don't like it?"

"No, I like it. I like it. It's just strange seeing my name. You know. Carved into you like that. It's so…permanent."

"That's the point," she said. "You're my man, aren't you?"

"Of course."

"You're the most important person in my life. So there you are, right where the blood flows. Where they take my pulse."

"Very poetic. You come up with that yourself, drunk on margaritas?"

"No, the tattoo guy said it, but I liked it, so I'm owning it."

I nodded.

"Are you okay with it? Because if you're not okay with it—"

"I'm fine with it," I said. "It's just going to take some getting used to."

"All right, well…drink up, Bubba, and start getting used to it. 'Cause it's not going anywhere, and neither am I."

Before I could figure out what to say in return, my phone started Louis Armstronging at me.

"Don't you dare," Susannah said.

I looked at the phone and saw it was Pete calling. Which meant something was going on at the apartment. Something with Maddy, probably.

"Seriously, Jordan," she said. "Stay with me tonight."

I put the phone down and let the call go to voice mail. "I'll stay," I said.

And I did. But not long enough.

7

"Where the hell have you been?" Pete rasped at me, trying to sound angry without raising his voice. He turned away and walked back into his apartment, not waiting for an answer. Inside, I saw Lydia Sinclair sitting on his ratty, old sofa, with Maddy curled up in a fetal position next to her.

"What's going on?" I said.

Pete turned back to me and wordlessly gestured to the scene around him. The room was a mess—books shoved off bookshelves, keyboard knocked off its stand, plates on the floor, with halos of food flung in circles on the carpet.

"How long has she been here?" I asked.

"I don't know. Two hours, maybe," he said. "She was in the bathroom, most of the time, upchucking. After the initial shit storm you see here."

"Is she asleep now?" I asked.

Lydia looked up at me and gave me a "so-so" gesture.

"I'm really sorry, guys," I said. "I was home with Susannah, and there was…you know. It wasn't a good time to leave."

"Well, *do* something with her," Pete said. His voice was unusually hard. "I can't have her hanging out here all the time, falling apart like this. I have a life, you know."

"You do?"

"Yeah, Jordan, I do. And your shit is getting tangled up in it."

I looked over at the couch and suddenly it registered. He had been here with Lydia when Maddy had barged in. He had been here with Lydia. But…for what? I saw her clarinet sitting near his spilled keyboard, so maybe they had been rehearsing. But why just them, without the rest of us?

He must have read all of that in my face, because he rolled his eyes, gave me a dirty look, and said, "Yeah. Whatever. It's none of your business. Just…do something with her, will you?"

I walked over to the couch and knelt by the lump of clothes and hair that was Maddy. I reached out, touched her shoulder, and called her name, but she didn't respond.

"What do you think she's on?" I asked Lydia.

"No clue," she said. "She was talking like she was drunk. Kind of slurry and confused. But she was jittery and amped like she was on coke. She was worked up about *something*."

"What?"

"I don't know," she said. "She was all over the map. But mostly it was about men. You, some guy called Arlo, some other guy called Richard."

"Richard? That's a new one."

"Well, I don't think it's a club you want to be a member of."

"No?"

"No."

I shook Maddy again, gently, and called her name. This time, she opened her eyes and looked at me. She smiled a weak, little smile, and said, "Hey, you."

"Hey, yourself," I said. "What are you doing here?"

"Looking for you."

Lydia took the hint and stood up, joining Pete in the kitchen. I watched them through the open archway, standing close to each other and talking quietly, conspiratorially. I noticed how easy they were with each other, physically—how comfortable they were. And I realized—late to the game—that they were together. A couple. There was something kind of perfect about it, and it made me smile. But it also made me sad, because it was one more thing that was going on without me noticing. Another reminder that my world was turning and changing while I was off playing Joe College. I wondered if it would still be my world when I got back to it.

As if on cue, Maddy reached out and grabbed my arm. "I was looking for you, and you weren't here. Where were you?" she said.

"Just driving around," I said. "Thinking about stuff."

She nodded, and closed her eyes again. "I used to do that."

"Not anymore?"

"Not-thinking is better."

"You think so?"

"I know so. Tell Mr. Brain to shut up."

"Why? What does Mr. Brain say to you?"

"Bad shit. You know…"

"I don't."

She sighed and shook her head.

"I want to help you, Maddy, but I don't know what's going on."

She opened her eyes and looked at me. "You shouldn't help me. I'm bad news."

"Says you."

"Says everyone."

"Arlo?"

"Arlo. Richard. All of them."

"Who's Richard?"

She scrunched up her eyes and turned her head away.

"Why do they say you're bad news, Maddy?"

She shrugged a Lydia Sinclair shrug, and I wondered if she had picked up the mannerism just in the evening they had spent together.

"Why?" I pressed.

"Because I fuck everything up," she said. "I'm selfish. Mean. A selfish little cunt. Didn't you know that?"

"Maddy—"

"Isn't that what they say?"

"No."

"It is, though. *You're a little whore, aren't you?*" she said nastily. "*You know exactly what you're doing.*" She was mimicking...somebody. "*I can't control myself when I'm around you. Look what you do to me.*"

"That's bullshit, Maddy. Who says that? Arlo?"

She squeezed her eyes shut again and shook her head.

"Richard?"

I felt horrible and manipulative, sitting there and pressing her with questions, but there was no other way to break this thing open.

"Is Richard the one who gave you Rosebud?"

She just snorted—almost a laugh.

"Was it Arlo?"

"Arlo, Arlo, Arlo. What's with you and fucking Arlo? Fuck Arlo." Then she giggled a little. "Everyone does, you know that? His wife caught him in the greenroom with Cindy Lakshmi. Now *there's* a total cunt for you…"

"Is that what got you so upset?"

"Please. I could give a shit about Arlo Alden and his wifey wife. All you fucking men and your wifey-wifes. Men *qua* men *qua* men *qua* men…"

She started drifting again, so I shook her shoulders and tried to keep her awake.

"You're not a whore or…anything like that, Maddy. He's an asshole, you know that."

She shook her head, her eyes still closed. Then she whispered, *"You think you can walk away from me? You think you can just say Stop? We're tied together, you and me."*

"Who says that?"

She squeezed her eyes even tighter, as though merely having them closed wasn't enough, and she said, "I can't do it anymore." She turned away from me, her face buried in the sofa cushions, and she cried. I put my hand on her shoulder and just left it there, for whatever little comfort it might give her. After a minute or two, I could hear her breath coming slower and more even. She was asleep.

I looked up and saw Pete and Lydia watching me from the kitchen archway. Their faces were like stone. I stood up and joined them.

"I wish I knew what the hell that was about," I said.

Lydia looked at me strangely, then checked Pete's face for a reaction, then looked back at me.

"You're supposed to be a detective, right?"

"Investigator."

"You ever investigate this?" She held up Maddy's backpack.

"No."

"You should. She knocked it over in the kitchen. Half the shit fell out. I was just trying to put it all back. And…yeah, okay, maybe I was snooping a little."

"So what did you find?"

She pulled out a small piece of paper which had been crumpled up and then smoothed over. She handed it to me. It was a check for a thousand dollars, written to Maddy. The memo line said, "Allowance."

"Look who it's from," Lydia said.

I looked. It was a trust fund check, from the estate of someone named Richard Taylor.

"Estate means someone's dead, right?" she asked.

I nodded.

"And Taylor's her last name?"

"Yeah."

Nobody said anything.

"So…father? Grandfather?" I offered. "I don't know."

I could feel Lydia staring at me. There was something I was missing.

"Richard," she said, trying to connect the dots for me. "The Richard she was talking about…the club you don't want to belong to…"

There was a bad feeling in the pit of my stomach. My gut understood what was going on a split second before my brain figured it out.

"No," I said. I looked up at Lydia. She just shrugged her shrug.

We looked over at sleeping Maddy for a minute, unsure what to say. Finally, Lydia broke the silence and said, "Fuck. I'd be on drugs, too."

Pete said, "What do you want to do?"

"I don't know," I said. "I'll sit with her till she wakes up. Make sure she gets home okay."

"And then what?" Pete asked.

"I don't know," I said.

"All right," he said. "Well. I'm going to bed." He said it without thinking, and then blushed, realizing the statement had new meaning with Lydia standing by his side.

"Come on," she said, taking his hand and leading him to the bedroom. Their bedroom.

The door clicked closed and I was left in the silence of the living room, trying to make sense of what was going on in this sleeping girl's head and heart. Trying to connect the dots for real and figure out what to do next. This was all so much more than I had bargained for.

I sat down and looked at her pretty face, calm and serene in sleep. I thought about the first time I had seen her, at that party with Arlo's arm draped over her shoulder. The whole thing felt obscene now—even worse than it had on that night. I thought about Blair's comment that she always slept with her directors, and *that* felt horrible, too. So did my own feelings, mixed-up as they were. I wished I knew how to help her without messing her up even worse.

The next thing I knew, it was morning. Pete was sitting at his little dining table, drinking coffee and reading the paper, while Lydia puttered around the kitchen, wearing a T-shirt and sweatpants that were obviously Pete's. I watched them through half-closed eyes for a few minutes, not wanting to let on that I was awake. They looked adorably domestic and happy in a low-key, normal way. I was amazed they had gotten to that place so quickly—that place where you can be totally silent with another person and it doesn't feel uncomfortable—where you can just *be* with someone, without thinking about…anything. And I thought: Good for you, Pete. I felt very proprietary and happy for both of them.

The scent of coffee finally overwhelmed me, so I stood up and padded into the kitchen to get myself a cup. Lydia nodded to me but said nothing. I filled up and sat down across the table from Pete. He looked up and caught me smiling at him, and he said, "Shut up."

"I'm not saying anything," I said.

"Good."

"But if I'm not your best man, there's going to be trouble."

"Seriously. Shut up," he said. But there was a smile hiding behind his mouth.

Back on the couch, I could hear Maddy stirring. Pete and I shared a meaningful look, and I took my coffee and went back to sit with her. Maddy was sitting up and rubbing her eyes.

"She's alive," I said.

Maddy took her hands from her face and peeked at me. "Where'd you come from?" she asked.

"Long Island," I said.

Maddy looked around, getting her bearings. The room was still pretty trashed.

"You kind of freaked out Pete and Lydia last night," I said quietly.

"Sorry," she said.

"You remember this?"

She looked around and said, "Kind of." She looked over at Pete and Lydia and apologized again. They waved if off, graciously.

"I was in a bad place," she said to me. "I didn't know where to go."

"I'm sorry I wasn't here for you."

"It's not your fault," she said. "I shouldn't have assumed. You don't owe me anything."

"Even so."

"No, you don't owe me shit. I shouldn't keep coming over here with all my..."

"Shit?"

"Exactly. All my shit. My so-called life. Is there any more of that?" she said, pointing to my coffee. I nodded. She groaned herself to a standing position and shuffled over to the kitchen. She met Lydia coming out, and the two of them stood awkwardly, face to face. Then, out of the blue, Lydia wrapped her arms around her and gave her a long hug. Maddy looked over at me, a little panicked, but then gave in and hugged her back. Then the moment ended, and Lydia walked past her and sat at the table.

"Dude," she said to Pete. "Where's the Sports?"

"Seriously?" he asked.

"Sports. Don't be judgy."

He pushed the section across the table, and I got up and followed Maddy into the kitchen, to make sure she was all right. She was standing in front of the refrigerator, door open, staring inside. I whistled to her and she shook her head, snapping out of whatever reverie she had been in. She grabbed a bottle of milk and shut the door.

"Listen," I said. "Can I be the friend who says stuff you don't want to hear? Just for a minute?"

"Isn't that who you always are?" she asked, pouring herself a cup of coffee.

"Fine," I said. "Here it is. Whatever you were on last night, it's not helping."

"Says you."

"I was there, Maddy. I mean, I wasn't there for the screaming and the throwing-up, but I was around for the after-party, and it wasn't pretty."

"I said I was sorry. What do you want? It gets me through."

"I don't think it's getting you through anything," I said. "Whatever it is, you're up to your eyeballs in it."

She shrugged and sipped her coffee.

"Look," I said. "I had my own shit to deal with in college. I'm no saint, believe me. You've just got to tough it out."

"What are you, my gym teacher? I should just walk it off?"

"I'm just saying."

"Maybe I'm not tough enough to tough it out. You ever think of that? Maybe some of us need a little help."

"We *all* need a little help."

"So fine."

"So fine. Get some help."

"I did."

"Maddy."

"Josh."

This was getting really frustrating, and I didn't know how to deal with it.

"This shit you're taking, whatever it is, it isn't solving anything. And whoever's giving it to you isn't your friend."

"He is, though."

"Not from where I'm standing."

"Well, who am I supposed to go to? The girlie-girls in the dorm? They fucking hate me. Arlo Alden? You?"

"Yeah, me. Why not me?"

She shrugged. "I don't know. Maybe I shouldn't trust you."

"Why not?"

"Can't tell. There's something suspicious about you."

"What? You mean how I'm the only guy in your life who's not trying to have sex with you?"

"Yeah. That must be it," she said, giving me a little kick in the shins.

Outside the kitchen, we heard Pete's keyboard starting to tinkle out some old, jazzy music. As we stepped out into the bigger room, Lydia started to sing the song Oticha had sent me.

You had plenty money, 1922
You let other women make a fool of you
Why don't you do right, like some other men do?
Get out of here and get me some money too

Pete was nodding along as she sang, adding a few frills and trills in support. His eyes weren't on the keyboard, though. They were 100 percent on Lydia. She looked like a teenager in Pete's old sweats, but her voice was old and wise.

You're sittin' there and wonderin' what it's all about
You ain't got no money, they will put you out
Why don't you do right, like some other men do?
Get out of here and get me some money too

She turned to Pete and smiled, and I could feel the spark between them. The connection. It charged the whole song for me, and it sent my mind bouncing all over the place. I could see Susannah singing it—Susannah with her tattoo, her wrist branded with my name, room for children we didn't even have yet—waiting for some kind of reaction from me and getting nothing.

Why don't you do right, like some other men do?

What did she want from me? A tattoo on *my* wrist? Some promise beyond all the promises I had already made? Kids? What would that even look like—us with kids? Would she give up her job and stay at home? No, why would she do that? She's the one with a real job. It's me who'd have to give up my...whatever. Quit goofing around with the guys till all hours, slacking off and doing the bare minimum, lazing around on a Sunday, barely getting out of bed. Why was I even living like that? I wasn't a rock star. I wasn't an artist. Why didn't I just grow up, get a decent job, and raise a family? I could see them all yelling at me—my wife, my father, my friends—just like that guy in that song, that guy who couldn't do right.

And suddenly, it wasn't just *me* I was imagining; it was Scotty Flynn, too. All the things I had heard him say, all those things I had overheard. And that look in his eyes when he thought no one was watching. That weight of the world, and all that Silent Sam sadness. It was all filtering through the song and into my brain, and mixing with me. Me, being him—trapped.

If you had prepared twenty years ago
You wouldn't be a-wanderin' from door to door
Why don't you do right, like some other men do?
Get out of here and get me some money too

I tried to tune out the panic and listen to the music, but it was all twirling together, and Lydia was singing to *me*, now—to every guy like me, and Scotty, and even Pete, someday.

> *I fell for your jivin' and I took you in*
> *Now all you got to offer me's a drink of gin*
> *Why don't you do right, like some other men do?*
> *Get out of here and get me some money too*

I remembered Scotty on the phone, pacing like a trapped animal but getting nowhere. He was trying to fight back, but he was losing ground. He was slipping. But how had he managed it this long? How was he staying in school, with all the walls closing in on him? I was ready to quit right now, just at the thought of kids, but he was still going, with one at home and one on the way.

Something was tickling at my brain, scratching at it, and I couldn't quite reach it. He had said something to me. What was it? "The things I've had to do. You have no idea…" That was it. But what did it mean? What had he been doing, that he thought I wouldn't believe?

> *Why don't you do right, like some other men do?*
> *Get out of here and get me some money too*

Of course. Of course. It was so obvious. I was an idiot. It was Scotty. All this time. Quiet little Scotty Flynn, making his guacamole, writing down his rehearsal notes, biding his time. It was Scotty up on the roof with Maddy that night—Scotty who first gave her Rosebud, Scotty who supplied it to her—and everybody else. Hell, he was probably the one who came up with the name. Scott Flynn was my snake in the garden—watching and learning and figuring out who needed a little bit of something to get them through the night. My friend Scotty. Right in front of me, this whole time.

But could I prove it? God knows he had motive, and opportunity was a piece of cake. But what about means? Where did he get it? How did he sell it? Who was he working for? I didn't know any of that. And that was the smoking gun I was going to have to find.

But had he pulled the trigger with Chris? Our little Scotty? I couldn't even imagine it. It had to be someone else— someone behind Scotty, calling the shots. But whatever had happened that night, Scotty knew. He knew what and he knew why. He'd been carrying the secret around for months, keeping it hidden, keeping it safe—and now I was going to have to dig it out of him. Rip it out, bloody and raw, and put it up on display for the police and the dean. He was going to have to go down for this. And then I could pack my bags and go home.

Except there was Maddy, standing next to me—Maddy with the axe over her head. What would happen to *her* when all of this was over? What would happen when she lost her bad friend, Scott, and her false friend, Rosebud—and her even falser friend, Josh? What was going to happen to all the pain she was trying so hard to keep bottled up?

So many secrets. Chris's secrets. Scotty's secrets. Maddy's secrets. So much toxic shit buried out there. I could picture all of them, all over campus, piling dirt on top of dirt to keep the poison down. Thousands of kids and thousands of secrets, pushed deeper and deeper but never going away—always seeping up, oozing up, ready to explode. How was I supposed to stop any of that? How was I supposed to help them?

Maddy leaned her head on my shoulder, looked up at me with her teal blue eyes, and said, "Can I join the band? I could play the tambourine."

How could I help any of them when I could barely help myself?

8

"Here's an idea. You could do your job," said Carter Wiggins, more annoyed than I thought he had a right to sound.

"I'm *doing* it," I said. "You know, sometimes, my job involves coming to you for help."

Carter just grunted.

"Come on. Would you rather have me do some crazy shit, totally unadvised, or seek the counsel of a sworn officer of the law?"

"You do crazy shit, no matter what I tell you," he said.

"I know. That's our whole thing. It's beautiful."

He shook his head and sighed theatrically. Another drama queen. I was surrounded by them.

"Look," he said. "You got evidence against this new guy, I can bring him in. Other than that, as usual, I don't know what the hell you want from me."

"Pressure," I said. "That's what I need."

"Pressure?" He laughed. "What am I, Tony Soprano? You want me to *lean* on the guy?"

"Yeah. Kind of," I said. "As long as he can think straight and stay calm, this thing's going to drag on forever. If we can rattle the guy, he might do something stupid."

"Rattle him."

"Yeah," I said. "Rattle him. Spook him. If he thinks you're on to him, he'll start to sweat. *I* can't do it—I'm in too close. It's got to come from somewhere else."

"What do you think a little sweat is gonna get you? A signed confession?"

"I don't know. I'm just trying to play all the angles."

"How sweaty you think this guy needs to get before he starts dealing again?" he asked. "'Cause that's the only goddamn thing that matters here."

"I don't know. Right now, as far as I can tell, he's not selling."

"But the guy's in debt, baby's on the way, et cetera, et cetera."

"I know, I know. Look, maybe he's dealing some weed to friends. I don't know."

"Weed ain't gonna cut it. You want to nail this guy, you're gonna have to get him back in the game. The big, bad game. *You're* gonna have to."

I stared at him, processing what he was saying. He just shrugged.

"I mean, listen, I can spook him a little, if that's what you want," he said. "But I don't see how that gets your fish in the net. Might even push him farther away. You want to catch him, you gotta bait the hook and get him to bite. See what I'm saying?"

"Yeah. You need to catch him selling."

"I need to catch him selling Rosebud. That particular shit. That, or worse."

"Fine. So I'll get him to sell me some. I can figure that out. Somehow."

He shook his head. "Can't be you."

My head was starting to hurt. "You just said I had to be the one—"

"You can't push him to sell to you. That'd be entrapment."

"How? I'm not law enforcement."

"You're close enough. He gets himself a good lawyer, he'll be out in a day and the whole game'll go underground again."

I sat down across from him, exasperated. "All right, fine. What do you want from me? What do you want me to do?"

"You know what it's got to be, J."

"You want him selling to a kid. A student."

He nodded.

"Preferably a minor."

"Fuckin' A, Bubba. You get me that, with a witness, I'll put him away for a *long*-ass time."

"But nobody's even using it anymore. Nobody's even asking for it."

He looked evenly at me, like he was waiting for me.

"Seriously," I said.

"Nobody?" he asked. "Come on, now, ain't there *one* little hungry worm you can think of—one little tasty tidbit you can dangle from the hook?"

I stared at him for a moment, putting the pieces together. Then I said, "Jesus, Carter. What kind of an asshole do you think I am?"

He shrugged again. "You tell me, son. You want this fish, or don't you?"

He picked up an apple that was sitting on his desk and took a big bite out of it. He chewed for a few seconds, wiped the juice off his chin, and looked up at me, a little surprised to see me still sitting there.

"Was there something else you wanted to talk about?" he asked.

9

Time was running out. In two weeks, the show was going to open; in three weeks, it was going to close. And after that, the pressure would ease up, the cast would disperse, and everyone would drift back into their little lives. If Carter was willing to put some pressure on Scotty, I had to put pressure on Maddy and tighten the noose around the two of them.

The noose—listen to me. But that's what it amounted to. I had to push Maddy into Scotty's arms and then hope like hell we could nail him before there was any real damage.

It didn't look like it was going to take much of a push, to be honest. Rehearsals were more intense every day, and every rehearsal of Maddy's scenes was torture. Every time she had to work on a speech, it was like the rest of the world disappeared for Arlo. All his powers of nastiness focused on her like a laser. And he always had an audience. The rest of the cast was always there to watch, sitting on the sidelines with their yoga pants and their water bottles, stretching their calf muscles and watching the lamb perform for the wolf.

                              MADDY

Wrap my head with laurels, Mother
Dress me like a bride
If I give you any trouble
If I hold back
If I scream
Then drag me to the altar
By my hair

                              ARLO

All right, hold it.

                              MADDY

Okay.

                              ARLO

What the fuck was that supposed to be?

                              MADDY

Um…I thought that's how you wanted it?

                              ARLO

Really? You thought I wanted Cassandra to sound like a valley girl at
the mall? I don't remember asking for that. Scotty—check my notes.
Did I ask for the Princess of Troy, prophetess of Apollo, to sound like
a whiny, teenage bitch?

                              MADDY

You—

                              ARLO

Yes? What?

                              MADDY

You said you wanted the speech to start out innocently. Almost

happy, so we'd be surprised later when she does the prophecy.

>   (ARLO scrunches up his face,
>   like he's trying to remember.
>   Then he sighs dramatically, like
>   it's all just too much for him, and
>   he waves the thought away)

                              ARLO

Again.

                              MADDY

Wrap my head with laurels, Mother
Dress me like a bride
If I give you any trouble
If I hold back
If I scream
Then drag me to the altar
By my hair

Go on?

                              ARLO

Yes, yes, go on.

MADDY

If I tell you that my wedding
Is to be my funeral pyre
Then drag me like a rag doll
And strap me to my chair
Because it's true
Dear mother
All too true
This wedding must go on

ARLO

Hold, please.

> (ARLO grabs a script off the
> director's table and walks, oh, so
> patiently, over to MADDY)

ARLO

Madeleine. You're an allegedly literate young woman. Look at the
verbs here. Look!

> (He shoves the script in her face)

ARLO

Drag me…*strap* me… *scream.* Do you hear the violence in the
language? Are you aware that there are actual words coming out of
your mouth, words carefully selected by an author, and that these
particular words matter?

> (MADDY nods)

ARLO

Again.

On and on like that it went, with everyone watching, stretching, and sucking down water like it was some great spectator sport. And asshole that I was, I watched it too, and said nothing, silently telling Arlo, "Push her harder. Push her to the edge."

The worse it got in rehearsal, the more she hung out at Pete's place—my place—the one place she said she felt safe. She had no idea how unsafe it was.

"Fuck!" she yelled, slamming a textbook shut. It was the fourth or fifth time she had yelled like that. She was lying on her stomach on the floor of the living room, studying for midterms. It didn't seem to be working.

I was studying, too, sitting on the couch with my head plugged in to my iPod, listening to versions of "Why Don't You Do Right?" for our nameless little band, from Lil Green's original to Sinead O'Connor's cover and even Jessica Rabbit's version. Green had the right tone, slow and mournful as hell, but it was all piano and guitar. Sinead was a little peppy, but she had some good brass in the arrangement. Peggy Lee had a great bass line, but she was also a little too shiny-happy-people for Lydia's voice. I was trying to figure out how to synthesize all these versions into something for our little group. I was also trying not to stare at Maddy's ass.

"This is crap," she announced.

"That's an improvement," I said. "You said the last one was bullshit."

She sighed and said, "Nothing to be done," in a philosophical tone that suggested she was quoting someone. She shoved the textbook away and grabbed her script, looked up at me, and smiled. "Want to run lines with me?"

"Sure," I said, pulling off my earbuds. When Maddy was in the room, the room was all about Maddy. She wasn't bitchy about it; some people are just like that. You can fight it all you want, but it's going to be a losing battle. Some people just have gravity, and small things are pulled into their orbit.

She tossed me her script and told me where she wanted to start. I said Go and she started reciting—not acting, just trying to remember the lines.

> *When next you see me*
> *I shall be a corpse*
> *Tossed about by winter waves*
> *As they go crashing violently*
> *Around my husband's grave.*
> *A naked corpse for wild beasts to feed on*

"This sure is a fun play you kids are doing," I said. "I bet your friends will be banging down the doors to see it."

"Never mind that. Did I get it right?" she asked.

"Spot on," I said.

"Yay," she said, totally without enthusiasm.

"Getting the lines right is the easy part," I said.

"I know, I know. Arlo isn't going to be satisfied until there's an actual lion eating my actual dead body on stage," she said.

"Sure, blow it all on opening night. What are we supposed to do for the Sunday matinee?"

"Thanks," she said.

"And now, maybe you should start giving a shit about midterms."

"Papa, don't preach."

"I ain't your papa."

She laughed and said, "All right, all right. Back to work," and dragged her textbook back over to where she was lying. She propped herself up on her elbows and went back to studying.

That was daylight Maddy. Daylight Maddy was funny, smart, and tough. Daylight Maddy would have been any boy's dream date. But Daylight Maddy wasn't the only girl in the room. Nighttime Maddy was there, too, just waiting to come out and play, and that was good, because Nighttime Maddy was the Maddy I needed. In rehearsal, she alternated between storming out of the room in a screaming rage and hiding in a corner on the verge of tears. Arlo couldn't have been happier. This is exactly what he wanted his Cassandra to be. Blair seemed to think he was some kind of directorial genius. I thought he was a prick. And because I was a prick, too, I silently thanked him for doing my dirty work for me.

Nighttime Maddy went home after rehearsal, got drunk, and called me, lonely and scared—worried she was going to do something worse than drinking. She reached out to me for help, and I gave her nothing. I held myself back. I let her walk into the fire.

"I want it so *bad*," she would say, sounding lost and scared over the phone. "Why?"

"I don't know," I would say. "We all need a little help sometimes."

"You're saying I should do it?"

"Could you get some?"

"Probably. But…I don't know."

"Whatever gets you through the night," I would say, more than once, biting my lip as soon as the words came out of my mouth and hating myself for saying it.

"What the fuck do you know?" she'd yell. "You never did anything stronger than weed—you told me that yourself. Clean-cut goody-two-shoes fuckhead, pretending to be some kind of artist, some kind of *musician*—"

"Yeah, but we're talking about you,"

I'd bait the hook and she'd circling it, eyeing the bait hungrily but never biting. "I'm sorry," she'd say quietly. "I'm just clawing at the furniture, Josh. I can't stand it. I don't want to be here."

"Where?"

"Anywhere. My life. My stupid body. I need a break. Just a little…break. It was so perfect. You don't understand. It was like it washed all the dirt out of life—just…washed it away. It was the awesomest feeling. Like it sent you back to the…the purest time you can remember—clean and happy. Like you're right there, *in* it. Like none of what happened after was real."

"Sounds amazing."

"It was. But then it always got twisted up. I've got to remember that."

"Was it really that bad?"

"It was. It was like this nasty…stain would start creeping into my head and infecting everything. Blotting it out. Making it dirty. And then I was inside the dirt, underwater in it, like something was holding my head down, and I couldn't break out till it wore off. Hours and hours until it all wore off. I've got to remember that."

"Yep."

"Yep. Yep. Yessiree, all righty. Ah-*yup*. I mean, what the fuck, Josh? Is that all you can say?"

"I'm not saying anything, Maddy. I'm just trying to listen."

"Oh, you want to *listen*. What are you, my goddamned shrink? What are you, jacking off while I tell you my shit? More! More! Details!"

"Maddy—"

"I don't care. Go ahead. Whip it out. I'd fucking do it *for* you if you had any Rosebud. I was a whore for that shit. I'm serious. I'd do anything for it. Any*one*. You should have seen me."

"Maddy…"

"You think I'm kidding?"

"I don't know, Maddy. What do you want me to think?"

Then quiet again. A moment while she readjusted.

"I wasn't really. Not the first time."

"Up on the roof?"

"But later, when I didn't have any money. *Can't help you this time, Mads. We need some quid for the quo, you know what I mean?*"

She'd let some clue slip out like that, and it would sit in the pit of my stomach like acid. She'd play out these scenes, doing all the voices, and I'd obsess over them, asking myself, who is that? Whose voice is she doing? Is that Scotty? Did Scotty do that to her?

And then, in the end, she'd say, "You know what? I think I'm good now, Josh. I barely feel drunk anymore. I think I'm okay."

"Are you sure?"

"Yeah. Totally. You talked me down. Thank you."

And she'd hang up.

And I'd sit there in the darkness of Pete's apartment, holding the dead phone in my hand, wondering if I had succeeded or failed, wondering what the hell I was doing. If I cared about her, I should have been helping her, or getting help for her—real help. Instead, I was standing by and watching her fall apart, hoping it would go faster so that I could nail Scotty and...win. For what? For Chris? For some dead boy I barely knew? Some kid I left out in the cold when he needed me? How was putting Scott in jail going to help *Chris*? I was mucking around in the life he left behind, flattering myself I was some kind of avenging angel or something. Pretending to be a Great Detective. Pretending to be on the verge of breaking some kind of drug ring. Pretending to be a friend or a big brother to Maddy, when really I just wanted to grab her and kiss those soft lips of hers, and forget about being good, or polite, or useful, or *anything*.

Jesus Christ. This was insane. Insane. I had to get out of there. Drop the whole stupid thing and let it go—let it all go. Just give up and get the fuck out.

And I tried. More than once. I'd hang up with Maddy, grab my suitcase, and start packing to get out, once and for all. Close it up—rip up my Josh Green ID card and disappear back into my life. She'd manage. They'd all manage. Carter was right—there was always a snake in the grass. Always had been, always would be. They'd get through it, just like we did. Or they wouldn't.

But every time I started, I'd end up taking my clothes out of the bag and putting them back on the shelf. Every time. I couldn't let it go. Idiot bulldog that I was, I couldn't let it go. I couldn't know what I knew and just walk away. It was too late. I had to see this through.

I knew what that was going to mean. And it wasn't going to be pretty.

10

"Look at him, man. He looks like he hasn't slept in a week."

That was Blair, whispering at me during rehearsal while Scotty worked through a difficult verse passage with members of the chorus. I nodded back to him. I'd been keeping a close eye on my new target to see if anything was changing. Was he rattled? Was he spooked? It was hard to tell. He looked wiped out, but it could have just been his home pressures. God knows, he had enough of those. What does your face look like when the police have been hassling you? *Had* they been hassling him? I hadn't been in touch with Carter in a few days. I had no idea what was going on.

"I told him he was coming to Manny's with us after rehearsal. I enlisted you. Hope you don't mind."

"That's fine," I said. "I've got nothing going on."

Taking Scott out for a drink was a great idea. I'd have a chance to hear what was going on with him, and having Blair as cover would take some of the heat off me when asking questions. But Manny's worried me as a location.

"Manny's" was Manuel's Tavern, where I had enjoyed that long, beer-filled lunch with Porkchop after Kenny Bansky's trial. Manuel's was the Platonic ideal of the dive bar, and it sat just outside my home turf. It was a favorite haunt of local politicians, lawyers, and artists—one of the few places you could find a truly diverse crowd. It had been one of my favorite places for a long time, and that was precisely what worried me. It was one of those worlds-colliding moments I had been trying so hard to avoid. I was going to be there as Josh, in a place where people might recognize me as Jordan. But I couldn't worry about that now. It would have been too weird to suggest an alternate location. Manny's was the obvious place, so that's where we went.

I let Blair take the lead on the third degree, and he didn't disappoint. As soon as we sat down, he leaned across the table and said, "Dude," with a fatherly, disappointed kind of tone. Blair was one of those people who could wrestle twenty different meanings out of that word.

"I know," said Scott.

"Are you pussy-whipped, baby-whipped, or just Arlo-whipped?"

"It's the whole combo."

"When's the baby due?" I asked.

"July," he said. "Doesn't matter. We wouldn't be ready, even if it was Christmas."

"What's going on?" Blair asked.

Scott shrugged. "You know it all, already. Aid's cut to ribbons. Summer work doesn't exist. And we should be doing, like, a million things to get the place ready. If we could afford it. The house is just too small."

Blair was about to say something, but the waiter came by with our beers, so he pulled back and waited. The waiter, a big, biker-looking guy, slammed our beers down, sloshing foam all over the table, and then walked away—classic Manuel's behavior. I wiped the foam away while Blair reached out with his long, spaghetti arm and whacked Scotty on the arm.

"What about your, you know…" he looked around, conspiratorially, and then looked back at Scott. "Your extracurricular activities?"

"Yeah. Great idea. When's the last time *you* bought weed?"

"I'm broke," Blair said.

"We're all broke. The whole department's broke."

"So why don't you try the business school?" Blair said, waggling his eyebrows.

Scotty just stared at him.

"What? I'm trying to be a creative problem-solver, here."

"I think it's called aiding and abetting. Also, you're upsetting Josh—look at him."

"Me?" I said. "I'm fine. I love learning new things about my friends."

If I was upset, it was only because I felt like an idiot for not realizing how easy this conversation could have been, any time in the past few weeks. I had been treating the whole drug thing like it was some kind of James Bond movie, and it totally wasn't. God knows, I smoked the occasional joint back in college, and it wasn't always just handed to me. People always knew who had the stuff and who you could buy it from. No one ever worried about saying it out loud.

"Don't listen to him," said Scott. "It's nothing. I brought some stuff to a party once—"

"Once!" Blair laughed.

"A few times. It's not like it's a career choice."

Blair shrugged and sipped his beer.

"Anyway, I can't do that, anymore. It's too risky."

"Still?"

He nodded. "There's actually a guy snooping around campus now, asking questions."

"Dude. That's crazy."

I stayed still, hoping no one could hear my heart beating.

"I know," said Scotty. "Some detective or something. I thought I was being paranoid, but I asked around, and it's true."

"What do you mean, paranoid?" I asked. "What's going on?"

"All right," he said. "You're going to think I'm crazy, but I keep seeing this one car, wherever I go."

"You're being followed?"

"I don't know. Maybe. Maybe it's the whole department, after what happened.."

"But that was forever ago," said Blair.

"That's not all," Scott said. He paused for a minute and looked around. Even the dramaturg was a drama queen. "Sometimes, at home, I swear the mail looks like someone's been messing with it."

"Oh, come on!" Blair laughed. "Now I do think you're losing it."

"I thought so, too. That's why I asked."

"Asked who?" I said.

"Someone who should know," Scott said. "All I'm saying is, it's probably a good thing everyone's been broke. They're watching everything we do."

"Seriously?" I said. I was trying to stay involved and seem reasonably skeptical, but my mind was racing. I kept running the tape of what he had just said. *I asked around...Someone who should know.* That couldn't have been Carter. That had to be somebody else—somebody Scott knew personally. But why would that someone think an ominous-looking car meant private investigator?

"I think our little show is getting to your head," said Blair. "All that misery."

"Believe what you like," said Scott. "Just keep an eye out for the men in black."

I steered the conversation away to safer subjects, and the rest of the night burbled on harmlessly.

The next day, I called Carter and said, "Whatever you've been doing, it's working."

"I just put Lewis in a black car in front of your theatre building, that's all," said Carter. "It's about all I *can* do."

"So you're not reading his mail?"

I could hear him snort on the other end of the line. "You crazy? I can't do shit like that."

So Scotty was imagining things. Which was great. Let him imagine the worst. Let him stew in his juices till he boiled.

With Scotty keeping his eye on the black car, I felt a little freer to snoop around without having to worry about getting caught. I knew where he was every night: with us at rehearsal. But what did his days look like? I decided to find out. Maybe if I could catch him someplace he shouldn't be, doing something he shouldn't be doing, I could spare using Maddy as bait.

For three days, the boredom nearly killed me. Day 1: home to campus, then to the library. Library to home. Day 2: home to campus, then to the lecture hall. Lecture hall to cafeteria. Back to the lecture hall. Lecture hall to home. Day 3:

repeat Day 1. I was getting to know the back of his car really well.

I was staring at his car after he had gone into his house, the night of Day 3, when I had an idea to help turn up the heat a little. I found a nearby Staples, bought some markers and paper, and made a little sign to leave on Scotty's windshield. It's an old trick, but it usually pays off. It wasn't a complicated sign—just a few easy words: "Chris knew. Now we know."

Simple is your friend.

Day 4 turned out to be interesting, though not at first. I watched from a distance, to see his reaction when he came out of his house. He picked up the sign, looked around after reading it, and then threw it into his car. He drove off, faster than usual, but for the rest of the morning, it was Day 1 all over again. Snoozeville. But after lunch, trailing him in my car as he was walking back to the lecture hall, I saw him stop on the street and take a phone call. He nodded. He paced. He gesticulated with his free hand. He grabbed his head with his free hand. Then he paced again. When the call was over, he looked around for a moment (looking for his ghost car?), and then started walking quickly away from the lecture hall. He called somebody else *en route* to his car, then jumped in and drove off. I pulled out behind him and followed at a discreet distance.

He had never noticed my car before, fixated as he was on Officer Lewis's vehicle, but today turned out to be different.

Within a few blocks, he figured out that someone was following him, and he started speeding up. Most people never notice when you follow them; it would never even occur to them to check. But I guess Scott was paranoid enough to check and keep checking, and when he did, he saw the same old Volkswagen in his rear-view mirror. So he gunned the engine and took off, and I took off after him.

There aren't a whole lot of things more dangerous than being led on a chase through suburban streets by a nervous, distracted, amateur driver. Especially if you happen to be a nervous, distracted, amateur driver, too. I know it looks cool in the movies, but trust me, when it's you behind the wheel, it's no fun.

We were okay pushing a little above the speed limit on Briarcliff; it's a wide-open street. But then Scotty decided to try some evasive maneuvers. At least, I'm guessing that's what he was doing, because the sharp rights and lefts that weaved us across the little residential streets and into Virginia Highlands didn't make any navigational sense. It only made sense if he was trying to prove himself right. And he did. By the time we hit Highland Avenue, there was no way to ignore that someone was following him.

Scott turned left onto Highland, putting us back onto our original trajectory toward Ponce de Leon Avenue. As soon as he turned, Scott picked up speed—fast enough, now, that he had to start weaving from lane to lane to get ahead of traffic. Fifty, sixty miles an hour—at one point he pushed seventy—all on surface streets. I weaved and swerved with him, my little car yanking back and forth and thumping over every bump in the road. Every time I hit a flaw in the asphalt, I felt the car shimmy to the side, and I had to pull it back in line. Every time I lurched around a commuter, cars honked at me and my stomach rose in my throat. I stayed on his tail as best I could, but the voice in my head kept saying, "too fast, too fast." My mouth was dry and scratchy and my breath was heavy and sour. I had no idea what Scott was thinking, but he had to be panicking just as much. We were both locked in: he couldn't get away from me and I couldn't give him up. Wherever he was going, he didn't want me along for the ride—and wherever he was going, I knew it was my only chance to catch him in the act.

But the whole thing was idiotic. He could have changed his mind and gone somewhere else—nothing was stopping him. He could have just gone shopping, or to the movies, and left me totally bewildered. I could have given up, too. After all, once he knew someone was following him, what were the odds he'd actually follow through with whatever he was planning? If I stayed on his tail, and he knew I was there, was he going to lead me straight to something illegal? Of course not. It was ridiculous. Once the secret was blown, the whole enterprise was pointless. And yet, neither of us could let it go.

We zoomed past Ponce into Little Five Points, where the streets got narrower and more crowded. Scott turned his car hard right on Blue Ridge and then left on Linwood, and then we were on North Avenue, heading straight into downtown. And that's where I lost him. Sometime before we hit Boulevard, he just vanished into traffic, and I wasn't able to weave my way past enough cars to keep sight of him. And that was the end of that.

Once I was sure he was gone for good, I pulled over and waited for my saliva glands to start working again and my pulse to get back to normal. I was lucky I hadn't killed somebody, or myself. I was lucky I hadn't gotten myself arrested. And that was about the extent of my luck. Whatever that phone call had been about—whatever had made Scott abandon his class and tear off for downtown—I wasn't going to find out about it today.

Once my hands stopped shaking, I pulled my car back out into traffic and took myself home. I wasn't going to be good for anything else—not for a while. I felt absolutely stripped, adrenaline bleeding out of my system at such a rate that I worried I might pass out behind the wheel. I was close to home, and looking forward to being in my own house, in my own bed, pulling the covers over my head and staying hidden for the rest of the day.

Unfortunately, when I got to the house, I saw a bunch of cars out front, and I could see people through the front window. When I opened the door, there was pretty much everybody I knew. Oticha and Pete, Kitty and Kate, Patty and Porkchop—all milling around, beers in hand, talking and laughing and having a great time. All my friends—the whole life I'd been hiding from. And there was Susannah, standing by the kitchen door with Lydia. As soon as she saw me, the room got quiet, and I could feel eyes moving back and forth between us.

"I told you!" she said, with some angry triumph in her voice. "Did I not predict this? Exactly this? Nobody listens to me." She turned to me and put her hands on her hips. "You forgot, didn't you?"

The best I could manage was, "What?"

"What? What?" she said, mimicking me. "Our anniversary, Homer Simpson. Ring a bell?"

"I know when our anniversary is."

"Do you?"

"It's not till tomorrow—the fifteenth."

I caught people looking at their shoes, or studying the paint job on the wall.

"Today's the fifteenth?"

"Good job," she said, raising her beer bottle in a toast. Then she turned around and walked into the kitchen, leaving me standing there, looking like a complete jackass.

Porkchop brought me a beer, clapped me on the shoulder, and said, "You're my hero in all things."

"Just…don't even…" I said. I took a swig of the beer and walked into the kitchen. Susannah was staring out the window, her back to me.

"I lost track of days," I said. "I'm sorry."

"That's not all you're losing track of," she said.

"I know."

She turned to face me. "You know, Lydia told me about the girl. Over at Pete's place."

I took a breath and said, "It's not what you think."

"What is this, some Lifetime movie?" she said. "Don't talk lame shit to me, Jordan. And don't pretend you know what I think."

"All right."

"I don't know whether you're fucking up our marriage or just *this-close* to fucking up our marriage. I don't know *what* you're doing. As usual."

"I'm just trying to do my job," I said. "I really am."

"By regressing back to college?"

"No. I'm…I'm just trying to help this girl. That's all I'm doing."

"Yeah," she said. "You're a real knight in shining armor. Look at you."

"I know," I said. "It's been a bad day."

She nodded for a moment, and sipped her beer.

"The police came by for a visit, by the way," she said. "That was fun."

"Carter?"

"No, the Candler police."

"Here? Today?"

"Yeah."

"What did they want?"

"It was just one guy. He didn't say. Didn't leave a name, either, Just said he'd come back another time."

I nodded, trying to push the fog away and make sense of things.

"Jordan."

I looked up at her. There were tears in her eyes, but she looked away quickly, to keep them from me.

"I don't know who this girl is, but...please don't fuck us up," she whispered. "I'm begging you."

I went over to her and wrapped my arms around her. "I promise."

I felt her shudder, trying to keep the tears at bay. "*I'm* supposed to be the girl. You know?"

"I know."

"Aren't I your girl?"

"Of course you are," I said. "You are, Susie. I swear to God."

We stood there for a long time. But I could tell we were standing still.

11

After the explosion: quiet. Everyone went home, and the house got quiet. We cleaned up the mess, allowing the silence to settle down around us. I turned off my phone and didn't look at my email. Not for the rest of the night, and not for the next day. I knew I'd have to pick up the thread I'd lost, but what did it matter whether I did it now or later? It would be there—hard to find and hard to follow, but out there somewhere. Right now, I didn't want to know. I didn't want to know if Maddy was showing up at Pete's place angry or needy or drunk or whatever. He'd be pissed at me if I didn't pick up the phone, but I didn't care. I needed to be home.

Which is why Carter Wiggins showed up at my door in person the next day.

It was around 2 p.m. I was working on the bass line for "Why Don't You Do Right?" and Susannah was curled up on the couch, reading. She had taken the day off, too, so we could be together and just…be together. And we were doing a pretty good job of it, until Sergeant Wiggins showed up and banged on the door.

"You dead in there or what?" he yelled. I opened the door and he came in, punching my arm and nodding at Susannah.

"I figured you had to be holed up here when I couldn't find you nowhere else," he said.

"You figured right."

"Well, turn your goddamned phone on, boy, 'cause there's all kinds of shit going down you need to deal with."

I caught Susannah's eye. She stared at me for a second, but then rolled her eyes, shook her head, and went back to her book.

"What's going on?" I asked.

"Your little girlfriend had a break-in," he said.

"Jesus, Carter."

"I'm kidding," he said—loudly, for Susannah's benefit. Then: "Not about the break-in. She called the Baby Cops about an hour ago. My buddy over there let me know."

"What do you mean, break-in?"

"Somebody got into her dorm room, took a bunch of stuff."

"And?"

"And my buddy said they trashed the place. Not like some kid stealing eye shadow or whatever. This was somebody sending a message."

"He said that?"

"I said."

"Huh."

"Listen, you wanted to spook your boy, I think he's spooked."

"What makes you think it's him, though?"

"Just a hunch. Timing's a little too perfect."

I thought about the note I had left on Scott's windshield. Yes, too perfect by half. But why go after Maddy?

He saw the question forming and cut me off. "All's I know is, you'd better get your ass back in the game and find out what's going on."

"Right. Got it."

He thumped me on the arm again and turned to go.

"Oh, hey, Carter…"

He stopped and turned back. "Yeah?"

"You didn't tell anyone to let my guy know there was a PI on the case, did you?"

He cocked his head and looked confused. "Why would I do that?"

"I don't know. Part of putting pressure on him, maybe."

"I didn't tell nobody to say nothing to your boy directly, and I sure as hell didn't tell anyone you were over there playing Kindergarten Cop."

"Okay."

"All right, then. Let's go, Bulldog. Phone on. Back in the game. Keep me posted."

I headed to campus, parked, and walked over to the Heywood dorm. I stood outside and looked up at the building. Then I remembered the last time I had stood there, loitering, and I went inside. I didn't need another encounter with the Baby Cops right now.

I found Maddy in her room, past a shattered door, sitting on a pile of garbage. Carter had been right—this was definitely not a casual break-in. Every drawer had been pulled out and emptied, every shelf had been cleared, books and papers had been pushed to the floor. It didn't look like Maddy had made much progress in putting things back together. In fact, it didn't look like she had moved from the spot she was in.

I sat down next to her, and she leaned her head onto my shoulder. We sat there like that, silently, for a couple of minutes.

"Who told you?" she asked.

"I have my sources," I said. "How's the cleanup going?"

She looked around at the mess, and said, "What's the point in cleaning up?"

"Well, you live here."

"Sort of."

"Yeah, sort of. And it's only March. Months yet, before you go home."

She laughed grimly. "The only place I go after finals is a summer-school dorm. Back and forth. Forth and back. Home *qua* home *qua* home." She picked up some papers from the floor and then dropped them again. "I should burn it all. Travel light, like a ninja."

"You have any idea who would want to do this to you?"

"Oh, it's probably one of Arlo's minions, trying to get me in the mood for rehearsal." She closed her eyes and fell back into the paper pile.

"You're taking this really well," I said.

"It's my new thing," she said. "Radical acceptance. I learned it from a girl down the hall. Just let the waves wash over you and leave you untouched. Don't move, don't fight. It's very Zen."

"Does it work for her?"

"Sure. That and Zoloft."

"Very funny. So, did they take anything valuable?"

She snorted. "What do you think I have in here, the crown jewels?"

"I don't know. Papers, letters, things you want to remember."

"The only things I want to remember are my lines for the stupid play. The rest of it can burn."

Was she hiding the truth, avoiding it, or just not thinking about it? As usual, I had to be the guy who pushed—the guy who picked at the scab. "Even the stuff you got from Chris?"

She froze. I could feel the tension in her body, keeping her rigid—like a rabbit sensing a predator in the tall grass. She was waiting. So was I. I had no idea what she owned that anyone else would want, but someone must have thought she had *something*. Maybe she knew what it was, maybe she didn't—but I needed to hear it from her.

"Look," I said (pushing...pushing...), "I know there's more to this whole Chris story than you're letting on, so you might as well stop pretending. It's obvious he meant something to you, and it's obvious you feel guilty about him. You told me so, yourself, in case you can't remember. You were drunk at the time. So if you're telling me you didn't keep his love letters, I don't buy it."

She sat up, carefully, and looked at me. Glared at me, more like. Then she stood up, walked over to her desk, and pulled out one of the few drawers that was closed. There were still some papers and file folders in there, and she looked through them for a moment. Then she pushed the drawer closed, and stared at the wall in front of her.

"Gone?" I asked.

She nodded.

Very clever of them, I thought, to trash the room but make the one drawer that mattered look untouched. "What was it?" I asked. "What did they take?"

"Exactly what you said. Letters, poems, everything he ever gave me."

"I'm sorry."

She was quiet for a moment. Then: "Why would someone take *that*?"

"I don't know," I said. "Was there anything important in there?"

She shrugged. "No, it was just…love notes and stuff. Unless it really *was* Arlo, trying to embarrass me."

"I don't think so, Maddy."

"Then what?"

"You tell me. Were they *all* love notes?"

She turned around in her desk chair and looked at me. "No," she said. She was looking at me strangely. Dangerously. "What makes you think there was something more?"

I was on thin ice, but I had to keep skating. "The look on your face," I said. "What aren't you telling me?"

She shook her head, biting her lip nervously.

"Maddy, I can't help you if you don't tell me what's going on."

She closed her eyes and laughed quietly. She put her hands up to her eyes, sat there for a moment, and then started punching herself in the head. I jumped up and grabbed her wrists.

"Maddy, please. Tell me what's got you freaked out. I need to know."

"Why?"

"Because I care about you and I'm worried about you."

"Bullshit." She tried to wrestle out of my grip, but I held on tight. "Josh...stop..." she said, a little bit of fear creeping into her voice. "You're hurting me."

"Tell me."

"Why? What do you...why is it so important to you?"

"What is it they took?"

"Stop it!"

I let go of her wrists and grabbed her arms up by her shoulders, to make her look at me. "Maddy, I think you're in danger—actual danger—and I need to know what's going on. What did they take from your room?"

"It was a letter," she said. "A letter he slipped under my door, just before he died."

"Okay. Good. Why is that important? What did it say?"

She didn't say anything.

"Listen, Maddy...look at me."

She turned away.

"No, look at me. It's all right. I have to tell you something."

She looked up at me. I took a deep breath, not sure if this was the right move, but not sure what else to do.

"Listen. You said you were a bad friend to Chris. Well...you weren't the only one. I knew him, too. And I was a bad friend, just like you. Maybe worse. I let him down a lot worse than you did."

She stared at me, confused.

"I know—I said I didn't know who he was or what happened to him. But I did. He came to me for help last fall, and I...didn't help him. That's why I'm here. I'm trying to do right by him now, even if...you know. Even if it's too late. Do you understand any of this?"

She shook her head.

"Maddy, I'm not a grad student. I'm...this is complicated."

"You're not...what are you talking about?"

"I'm not really a student here. I'm a guy people hire to investigate bad stuff that other people do. That's why I'm here. This is my job. The rest of it is just...a lie."

She looked at me like I was an alien, stepping off a flying saucer. I waited for her, but all she could manage was, "What...the fuck?"

"I know. I'm sorry. I didn't...I didn't know how else to do this."

"Do *what*?"

"Chris was worried about what Rosebud was doing to you—all of you—and he was worried about you, especially. He wanted me to find out who was selling it, so the police could stop it."

If anything, Maddy looked even more confused. "He did...he *hired* you? I don't..."

"He was trying to protect you, Maddy. He was scared you were in trouble."

She closed her eyes and stayed very quiet.

"Now, I'm guessing some of this isn't news to you. Is it? You knew he was asking around. You knew what he found out."

She nodded again.

"And that's what's in this letter they took."

"Yes."

"Okay. Good. So what did he say, exactly? What's in there that somebody would want to get their hands on?"

"I don't know."

"Did he name Scott? Did he name him as the dealer? It's okay, Maddy; I already know."

She nodded.

"Good. And anybody else?"

"I don't think so. I don't remember anyone else."

It was starting to make sense. If there was a letter that named Scott as the dealer, I could see why he'd want to get his hands on it. Even if the whole theatre department knew about him, having it on paper was still dangerous.

"There's something else," Maddy said. "I remember something else in the letter."

"What?"

"He said there were pictures. He had pictures on his phone."

"Pictures."

"Of Scott. I don't remember exactly what he said. But it's in there."

I felt a sharp pain right between my eyes—that kind of pain you get when you finally figure out something that's been nagging at you for a long time.

"The phone," I said. "The goddamned phone. I *knew* it meant something."

"What?"

"It's the only thing that was missing when the cops found his body. *That's* why."

Maddy turned pale and looked like she was going to be sick. "You mean Chris was...oh, my God...he was..."

"When did he give you the letter?"

"No, no. That can't...he was just depressed. They said. They said he was depressed..."

"Maddy, stay with me. When did he give you the letter?"

"The night he died. I think. He slipped it under the door. I didn't see it right away. But I was the only one who ever saw it. How would anyone else even know about it?"

"Well…someone did."

Maddy was crying.

"I'm sorry to dump all this on you. I really am. But we don't have a lot of time."

"I don't understand…any of this…"

I took her hand and tried to get her to look at me. "He wasn't depressed, Maddy. He didn't do this to himself. He was killed."

Now she looked at me.

"Probably because of those pictures. And that means you're not safe, either."

"Me? Why? I don't know anything."

"You knew Scott was dealing."

"Everyone knew that!" she yelled.

"You know something more than everyone else," I said. "Or, at least, they think you do. Otherwise, why'd they break down your door just to take one letter? Why not do it secretly, so you wouldn't know? Why did they want to scare you?"

She looked at me with real fear in her eyes, and, very quietly, said, "I have no idea."

"Well, neither do I, and unless we can get our hands on what they took, we may not figure it out until it's too late."

"Too late?"

I got up to check the door. The lock looked like cottage cheese. No finesse. Someone had just bashed at it until he got in. Was that a message for Maddy or just an act of rage, or panic?

"Nobody heard them kick this in?" I asked. "Seriously?"

"No one's ever here in the afternoon."

I checked what was left of the lock mechanism. They'd have to replace the whole door, and it wouldn't be any safer than the old one. But the cottage cheese was interesting. That meant it was an amateur job—and a rush job. Probably Scott, trying to cover his tracks in a hurry. Which meant this was my fault. Something in the note I had left on his car spooked him. A *lot*.

It also meant the letter might still be with him. If I remembered right from the days I was tailing him, Scotty had a late afternoon class and a meeting with his advisor right up until rehearsal. He was stuck on campus, and the letter was probably on him or in his car.

"Listen," I said. "I'm going to try and get the letter back before anyone else sees it, but you're going to have to play it cool at rehearsal. I mean, super cool. He can't know you've figured *any* of this out."

"You think Scotty *killed* him?"

"I don't know. Probably not. Probably he just said, 'Hey, there's some kid snooping around,' and someone else did the dirty work. But it's still on him, as far as I'm concerned, and he's still going to have to answer for it."

"Not Scotty. I mean, he's a normal...he's a nice guy..."

"Yeah, he's a prince. Quiet scholar, married man, great friend. And on the side, he sells drugs to teenagers and makes them fuck him if they can't pay. Right?"

She looked at me, wide-eyed.

"Sorry. Losing focus. First we get your stuff back. Then we deal with him."

12

I needed to be in two places at the same time. I needed to get into Scotty's car while he was safely in rehearsal, but I also needed to be in rehearsal with him, to keep an eye on him and make sure Maddy stayed safe. Nobody else could sub for me at rehearsal, so that meant I needed someone to jack Scott's car— someone with special talents. Who did I know?

As soon as I left Maddy, I called my attorney. "How's your friend, Kenny Bansky, these days?" I asked.

"Walking with Jesus, I hope," Porkchop said. "But I wouldn't swear to it."

"Would it violate your professional ethics if I asked you for his phone number?"

"Depends what you want it for."

"I need someone with his particular skill-set."

"Ho, I see. Well, yes, in that case, it would definitely violate my professional ethics. It would butt-rape my professional ethics with a goddamned broom handle. Are you kidding me?"

"Listen…"

"No, seriously. Are you actually asking me to help you hire a reformed felon to commit another crime?"

"Come on. He's probably not all *that* reformed."

There was a pause on the line.

"All right, I'll give you that. He's probably not. But still."

"It's for a noble cause. I'm trying to recover some stolen evidence from a person of interest. He'd be helping the good guys, this time. Come on…"

"Grr," he said. "Hulk not happy."

"I know, big guy. Just think about it. But quickly, because I need him tonight."

I have no idea what happened at rehearsal that night. I was busy watching Scott's every move, to see if he revealed anything important. Scott didn't seem to notice me; he was too busy watching Maddy, trying to catch some reaction to the break-in. Maddy didn't seem to notice him; she was too busy watching *me*. I could feel her eyes on me, constantly. What was Scott making of that?

Off in the distance, somewhere, Arlo was yapping about the walls and parapets the set crew was building for the final scene. Blair was closer by, getting frustrated that no one was listening to his jokes. They were all a million miles away, but I did have to focus on rehearsal-reality at one point, when Arlo shoved me out in front of the group and asked me to give notes to the chorus. It was a challenge, since I hadn't been listening to anything they were doing. I babbled some words that I thought would please the boss and then sat back down.

Arlo called a break, and Maddy walked oh-so-casually past the directors' table and dropped a note in front of me. When I opened it, I saw a bad sketch of me holding something that looked like an Academy Award, with "Best Actor" scrawled on the bottom. I couldn't tell if she meant it pleasantly or not.

More importantly, while everyone was milling around during the break, I managed to sneak over to the chair where Scotty had left his jacket, and quickly checked the pockets. No letter. Of course not. That would have been too easy.

Rehearsal dragged on. I kept checking my phone to see if Porkchop or Bansky had texted me, but there was nothing. Rehearsal ended, and still there was nothing. The cast walked out of the building and began to disperse, taking different pathways to different dorms, when all of a sudden, we heard someone yell, "No!" On the quiet campus, it roared and echoed. Everyone looked around to figure out where the noise had come from. Then some people started running. I grabbed Maddy's hand, wanting to keep her close, and pulled her along with me. She was not happy about it.

Around the corner, a small crowd was gathering around Scotty, who was standing—swaying—looking like he was about to fall down—in front of his car, which had been stripped, smashed, and effectively left for dead.

"What the FUCK?" he yelled, looking around for some kind of answer. "What is this?"

I could feel Maddy looking at me, and I tried, as hard as I could, to send her a psychic message to keep her mouth shut. Whatever was going to happen next, I didn't think either of us should be there for it, so I pulled her back with me, and we quietly made our way to my car and away from campus.

"Why did you do that?" she whispered, once we were under way.

"I didn't," I said. "I told a guy to find your letters. That's it."

She was quiet for a moment.

"What's he supposed to do now?" she asked. "They've only got one car. Him and his wife."

"Yeah?" I said. "How do you know so much about his home life?"

"We're friends," she said.

"Right, of course," I said, feeling anger creep into my voice. "Did he talk to you about his marriage while you were in bed together? Was it after, or during? He gets sex and marriage counseling, you get drugs? Was that the deal?"

She didn't say anything—not that there was anything useful to say. She just turned away and looked out the window.

Finally, she said, "So where are the letters?"

"I don't know," I said. "I'll call the guy when we get home. I mean, to Pete's place. You can't stay in your dorm tonight."

She nodded, still looking out the window.

"I'm sorry about…what I said. I sounded like a complete asshole."

"Maybe you *are* an asshole," she said. "In real life. How would I know?"

We drove the rest of the way in silence. It was probably better that way.

We parked at Pete's building, still in silence, and walked up to his apartment. The lights were off and no one seemed to be around. When we walked in, we both spotted a bundle of letters sitting on the floor in the middle of the room. Maddy ran to them. I turned back to the door and tried to remember if it had been locked. I was pretty sure it had been. I winced, thinking about the risk I had taken, inviting a convicted felon to my friend's apartment, but…where else was I going to stage this scene? My house? No.

Maddy thumbed through the packet, nodding. Then she looked at me and said,
"I think they're all here."

"Glad to hear it," said a male voice from the darkness. Maddy and I both jumped like cartoon characters. Sitting in a corner of the room, waiting for us to come home, was Kenny Bansky.

"Holy shit," I said, trying to calm my racing heart. Maddy just stared at me, wide-eyed.

Bansky unfolded himself from his chair and walked over to me. "I hope I got you what you needed," he said. "I did his car for you, extra."

"I saw that," I said.

"No charge for that," he said. "I don't hold with drug dealers."

"Right," I said.

He just stood there, watching me, waiting.

"So…if you're satisfied with the job I done…"

"Oh. Right, right," I said. I pulled out my wallet and paid him the amount we had agreed to on the phone.

Bansky counted the money and smiled. Then he turned to Maddy, nodded, and said, "Ma'am," like some weird, redneck cowboy. Maddy nodded back to him, completely confused, and he slipped out the door without another word.

The apartment was quiet for a moment, and then Maddy said, "What the fuck was *that*?"

"Friend of a friend," I said. "Professional acquaintance."

"Seriously?"

"I'm in a strange line of work," I said. "Did you get everything back?"

She nodded and then handed one of the letters to me. "This is the one—the one he put under my door."

I took it and sat down at Pete's dining room table.

"Hey?" Maddy said, in a small voice. I turned around. She was still standing in the middle of the room, clutching the rest of the notes and letters.

"Yeah?"

"Thank you."

I nodded and turned back to the letter she had given me. It was handwritten on a sheet of notebook paper, with a small piece of black duct tape stuck to the bottom. It said:

> *Maddy: I know I've been weird. I'm sorry. Sorry about all the stupid poems and stuff, too. Sorry it took me too long to figure it out. But I need you to know something. I've been watching Scott, and it's worse than I thought. I know you don't want to hear it, but when you see the pictures I took, you're going to know I was right. It goes way beyond Scott, and I got it all. I can't take it to the campus cops, but there's a guy I know who can help me. Can't say anything till I talk to him, but then I'll show you. Maybe you'll hate me for it. I don't know. But no one's going to stop me. This is too important. I even hid some copies, just in case something goes wrong. Okay, I'm paranoid. I don't care. You don't know what I know. But just wait. You'll see.*

After the text, there was a scrawly arrow pointing down to the little rectangle of duct tape. The corner of the tape had been pulled back and folded down over itself, to make an easily lift-able tab. I pulled it gently. Under the tape, he had written, "*Deus Ex Machina.*"

"Jesus Christ," I muttered. "Everyone's a drama queen."

I could feel Maddy standing behind me now, reading over my shoulder. I looked up at her.

"So what's this dues machine thing?" I asked.

"*Deus ex machina.* It's from Greek theatre."

"And it means?"

"God in the machine, I think. It was this thing where a god would appear at the end of the play to explain everything or save the day."

I put the tape back and laid the letter down on the table.

"I guess that was supposed to be me," I said. "He was going to send me the pictures, and I was going to ride in and save the day."

"Would you have?" she asked.

I picked up the letter again and looked at it. "I don't know," I said. "Pictures of Scott selling drugs? It's exactly what I said I needed. I guess I would have done something. Shared them with one of the deans, maybe. Or a friend of mine who's a cop. I *hope* I would have."

"He said he couldn't call the cops."

"Not the Baby Cops. Atlanta police." I put the letter back down. "Anyway, it doesn't matter. I wasn't there for him when it mattered. I laughed him out of my office and he went off and got himself killed. And now we'll never know what he found."

Maddy sat down next to me. "He said he made copies."

"Yeah? Where? How come nobody's found them?"

"I don't know. He must have hid them really well. I remember he said something about it in an email."

"What email?"

"I don't know. It must have been right after he slid the note under my door. It was something about, like, sorry for speaking in code and being weird, but—"

"Hold on," I said, feeling that tickling sensation on the back of my neck—that warning that there was something I needed to pay attention to. "He gave you this note, then he went back to his room and sent you an email?"

"I guess. Sometime that night."

"And the email talked about this note? Specifically this note?"

"Yes. The pictures and the note."

I sat with the information for a minute. It was a long minute. Maddy knew, somehow, not to say anything. I could feel it coming together, and I knew not to rush it.

"Then that's it," I said. "That's how they knew."

"What do you mean?"

"They knew you had a note and they knew it said something important, because Chris wrote it in an email. Which means they read his email."

"How?"

"I don't know," I said. "A good hacker, maybe. Or they know his password. Or…no. They have his phone, right? So there you go. Unless he had a password on it."

"But why now?" she said. "Why are they coming after me *now*?"

"Because I fucked up," I said. "I got him worried—him and his friends—and I guess they went back and looked at everything again. I'm the one who put you in danger." I rubbed my eyes, suddenly tired.

Maddy reached out and touched my arm. I looked up at her. "I'm sorry," I said. "I thought maybe we figured something out, but it's just another brick wall."

"We know why they wanted the letters. That's something."

"But we don't know who they are. And if we don't know that, how can I keep you safe?"

She rubbed my arm a little and smiled. "You don't have to keep me safe."

"Yeah, I do," I said. "I made a promise, remember? Too little, too late, but whatever."

She nodded, and looked down at the notes in her hand.

"Those are the notes he left in your mailbox?"

"Yes."

"Why'd you keep them, if they were so embarrassing?"

She shrugged. "I don't know." She looked at one or two of them. "No one ever wrote stuff like that to me before."

"Can I see one?"

She scrunched up her face and then handed one to me. It was handwritten in very careful lettering:

> *She walks the silent space*
>
> *That separates my heartbeats*
>
> *Never trips or falters*
>
> *Into something sound*
>
> *She keeps her love in shadows*
>
> *Where it's never yes or no*
>
> *Her touch is warm and orange*
>
> *But it never lingers long*
>
> *Just a brush across the cheek*
>
> *And as I raise my hand to hold it*
>
> *She pulls away again*
>
> *I close my hand on air and orange*
>
> *Leaning into warmth already cooling*
>
> *Barely remembering the feel of it*

I wait in silence to feel it one more time

I handed it back to her. It was a strange feeling, reading a dead boy's love poem—a dead boy's poem about love being out of reach. It was worse than reading a diary. "So," I said, to break the silence, "no love poems in high school? Is that not a thing anymore?"

"Not in *my* life."

I thought back to some of her drunken outbursts and the crumpled check from Richard. "For what it's worth," I said, "you deserve some. Someone should be writing you love poems every day."

"You wouldn't," she said quietly. "You won't even touch me."

"Oh, Maddy," I said, sighing. "You don't...you don't know anything about me."

She looked up at me, her eyes shining with tears. "I know you came here to protect me. I know you care about me."

"You don't even know my name," I said.

"So what's your name?"

"It's Jordan," I said.

She nodded. "Hi, Jordan," she said. And she leaned in before I knew what was happening, and she kissed me, her hand behind my head to keep me from escaping. Those soft lips I'd been trying not to think about for weeks, touching mine, opening slightly, taking me in. That soft skin, so close to mine. I inhaled her scent and leaned forward—leaned into her—unable to resist. She felt me opening up and she responded, wrapping her arms around me and pushing hungrily against my mouth. I wanted her so badly. I could have disappeared inside her and never come out again. It would have been so easy. As easy as falling down.

And I *wanted* to fall down. I'm not going to lie to you. In that moment, I wanted her as badly as I'd ever wanted anything. But I couldn't stop the voice in my head—the voice saying, "Then what? You fall down, and then what? What are you? This isn't what you came here for. This isn't what she needs you for." And yes, of course, there was another voice, too, saying, "It's what she wants. It's what she's wanted for weeks. She wants it, you want it, it's not real life, it's not real time, it doesn't have to matter, it doesn't have to count…"

And that was all I needed. Not the rational voice, but that second voice in my head, that whiny, hungry, "I want" voice. I knew exactly who it was. It was high-school Jordan—angry, self-justifying Jordan. It was the voice that had ruined me, the voice I had worked so hard to put behind me. Maddy and I were in this incredible moment together, but what both of us wanted wasn't what either of us needed. Someone had to be the grown-up and say, "This is a bad idea."

So I did it. I pulled back from her, and I put my hand on her lovely cheek, and I said, "We can't do this, Maddy."

"We could," she said, trying to kiss me again.

I pushed back, just a little, and I said, "I know we could. But we're not going to. I'm not going to. I'm sorry."

I sat up, gathered the letters that had gotten strewn across the table, and I handed them to her. She looked hurt, and I didn't blame her.

"Listen," I said. "There are some differences between Josh and Jordan, and one of them is that Jordan is married."

"Oh," she said.

"Yeah," I said. "Oh."

"I'm sorry," she said.

"You've got nothing to be sorry about," I said. "Look, I came here to do a job, and when the job is over, I have to go back to my life. I *want* to go back to my life."

She nodded.

"All this shit you're dealing with here...I've been through it already. Years ago. I can't stay here with you and go backwards. I just...can't."

She looked crushed, but I kept going. "I know it all seems shitty and awful right now, but it gets better. I swear to God, it does. You've just got to get through this. One step at a time."

She nodded again.

"And anyway," I said, "you know...I don't want to be one of the guys on the list."

"What list?" she said, sounding a little suspicious.

"You know. Arlo, Scotty. Whoever came before them. Your stepfather."

She stared at me, stunned. Horrified. I pushed on, trying to make it better. "I heard you say some things. A few nights ago, when you were drunk. I'm sorry."

She covered her mouth, stifling a horrible, pained kind of cry. Then she jumped up and ran away from the table.

"I'm sorry," I called after her.

She stopped in the middle of the room, her back to me. "You think I *chose* them?" she yelled. "You think I chose *any* of them? Jesus Christ…"

"No. Of course not."

"Oh, my God. How do you even know that? What did I tell you?"

"Nothing. Really. Nothing. Just the name, and some…it doesn't matter."

She put her hands up over her head and sank down into the sofa. I started to say something, but she put one hand up, as if to block the words from reaching her. I kept my distance and waited for her. After a few minutes, she looked up at me, stone-faced.

"So you think you're just…next on the list? Is that it? Done with Arlo, on to Josh? Jordan? Whatever?"

"That's not what I meant. At all. I just don't want to be something you'll regret."

"Regret!"

"I don't want you to feel ashamed of anything or regret anything when it comes to us, and *I* don't want to, either. I told you before, I did things when I was younger... I don't want to be that guy again."

"So it's *my* fault?"

"No, no..."

"Oh, of course it is. As usual. *Maddy, I can't resist you, I can't help myself, you have to help me, I'm going to explode.* The same shit, every time."

"I never said that. You know I didn't."

"What am I supposed to do? Fight them? Kick them in the balls? They're, like, my professors, my directors, even my...even *him*. I have to *live* with them, don't you understand that? I have to deal with them—every day."

"But if you don't fight back—I mean, if you just let it all happen, how does it ever end?"

"It doesn't end!" she yelled. "Don't you get it? There *is* no end. It ends when they get sick of me and throw me away, until the next one comes sniffing around. Over and over again."

"Maddy..."

"Maybe if I killed myself, huh? Like Chris? You think that would make it stop?"

"Chris didn't kill himself," I said. "You know that. He was fighting. For you."

She calmed down and was quiet for a moment. Then she said, "Well, he shouldn't have. He shouldn't have bothered." She stood up, smoothed her clothes, ran a hand through her hair, and said, "I wasn't worth it."

She walked past me into the bedroom she had long ago claimed as her own. She didn't say anything else, or even look at me. She just walked in and closed the door.

There was so much more I wanted to say to her, explain to her, apologize for. I didn't dare open the door and go in there, but I wanted to. Not that it would have made a difference, but I wanted to try one more time—try to make it make sense. Try to make it all better.

But I couldn't. I couldn't say another word to her. Not right then, anyway.

Maybe tomorrow, you say to yourself. You can always try again tomorrow.

How can you know that you've missed your last chance?

13

I woke up on Pete's couch—achy, annoyed, and alone. Pete had never come home, and Maddy was gone. She must have called for a cab at some point in the night or early in the morning, not wanting a repeat performance. I was sorry, but also, I wasn't; I had no idea how to face her or what to say. I wasn't even sure how I should feel. No, that's not true. I knew exactly how I *should* feel. It was just taking some time to get my heart and my guts to line up with my head. But it didn't matter how I felt; she was alone on campus, and I had no idea what anyone's next move was going to be.

I wanted to check in with Carter, but I knew he'd be hard to catch until later in the day, so I headed over to campus to see if I could find Maddy, and pick up the gossip about Scott and his car along the way. Blair would know what everyone was saying, which meant putting in an appearance in Dr. Villareal's class.

The minute I walked in, I could tell he was ready to burst, but we behaved ourselves and sat quietly through the lecture. As soon as class was over, he grabbed me and started talking. Mostly, he just recounted what I had seen for myself—Scott coming upon his wrecked car and screaming into the night.

"So, what's he going to do?" I asked.

"Well, he biked in today. That's got to be close to ten miles. But his wife's stranded at home with a little kid and, you know, what happens if she's got to go shopping, or take the kid to the doctor, or whatever?"

"I know. I get it. That's why I said, what's he going to do?"

"I don't know, man. What *can* he do? He's probably going to have to take a semester off and get a job. More than a semester, maybe. It totally sucks."

We were closing in on the cafeteria, where I assumed we'd meet up with Scotty, so I raced to get my last question in. "What about his...you know. What did you call it? His extracurricular activity? Couldn't that help?"

"Dude. Do you have any idea how much undergraduate weed you'd have to sell to make a car down payment?"

"I do not."

"Neither do I. But it's got to be a lot, right?"

"So, not weed, then. Something pricier."

"Come on, man. I was only joking, the other day. He scored some stuff for parties, from some friend of his or whatever. It's not like he's been working a street corner down in Kirkwood. He's just Scotty, right?"

"Yeah, of course," I said, right when Just Scotty and the usual lunch crew came into view. As usual, Gates was deep in some argument with one of the floppy-haired actors, whose name I could never remember. Scotty was sitting silently, watching and listening. He looked like absolute hell—like he hadn't slept in days. We sat down just as Gates and Floppy got up to go inside and get some food.

"What are they arguing about today?" asked Blair. Scotty looked up at him with a blank, dead stare. "Never mind," said Blair. "Not important."

Scott looked at me and said, "Did you see what they did to my car?"

"I did," I said. "Craziness."

He leaned forward, earnestly. "You see? You see what I was telling you? They're fucking with me."

"Who?"

"I told you—this PI."

"PI?" I asked. "What's that?"

"Dude," said Blair. "Seriously? Private investigator."

"There's a guy named Greenblatt or Greenbaum or something. He's been snooping around campus for months. I have it on good authority."

"From who?" I asked, trying not to throw up. How could he know that?

"Never mind. It's the real deal. The guy nearly ran me off the road, the other day. I'm so fucked."

"Why is he after *you*?" said Blair, looking genuinely concerned. It wasn't a look I had ever seen before. "What's his deal?"

Scott stood up and started pacing. "I don't know. I don't know. I'm…I got myself into some shit. I thought I was clear of it, but it just gets worse and worse. I don't know what to do. I can't…move."

"Maybe you should talk to somebody," I said.

"I think it might be too late for that."

"Dude, stop," said Blair. "You're freaking me out, for real."

Scott stopped pacing and looked at his friend. "You're right," he said. "You're both right. I do need to talk to someone. I'll…I'll make it right. I have to." And with that, he took off.

Neither of us spoke for a minute. There was no way I could run after Scott, so I just sta there. Then Blair said, "Are you still hungry?"

I shook my head.

"Yeah," he said. "Me neither."

Blair and I left the cafeteria and wandered around, pointlessly and wordlessly, until he had to go to class. I could tell he was imagining his best friend standing on a dangerous street corner, peddling drugs. He didn't know what to do with the pictures in his head. Welcome to the club.

I checked my watch and found a semi-private spot behind a tree to call Carter. I played the whole tune for him in three-part harmony—the stolen phone, the missing letter, the recovered letter, the trashed car, the scene with Scott. He filled in the pauses with an occasional "Uh-huh," but refrained from commenting until I was done. And then, when I was done, he continued to say nothing.

"So?" I said. "What do you think it points to?"

"Well," he said, "There's pictures of your boy and he wants them back. That's plain and simple."

"Right, but why now? Why didn't he do anything before?"

"Didn't know about 'em? Thought he already had 'em?"

"He knew about them. That's why he took the phone."

"Uh-huh."

"So he already had them. And either he didn't care about the copies or he didn't pay attention to the fact that there *were* copies somewhere. So what changed?"

"What changed?" I could hear him tapping his teeth with a pen while he thought. "Let's run it down. When did shit start to move on this?"

"You put Lewis on him, then I followed him, then I left him a nasty note…"

"Hold on there, Hoss. What note?"

Hadn't I told him about the note? It was hard to remember. "I left a note on his windshield: Chris knew about him, now we knew about him. Vague but threatening."

"We who?"

"Whoever."

"Uh-huh. Go on." Back he went to tapping his teeth.

"Then I see him get a phone call the next day which freaks him out, and I kind of chase him for awhile, till I lose him."

"Which is how he knows it's you."

"No. He didn't see me in the car, and he doesn't know my car. I don't think. Anyway, if he had seen me, he'd think Josh Green was the PI, not Jordan Greenblatt. Where'd he get my name?"

"Uh-huh." Tap, tap.

"And why does he suddenly care about Chris's letter after all this time? He takes the phone to get the pictures, he thinks he's safe, and now suddenly, he knows he's not. Why?"

"'Cause you been snooping around, looking for something. Gets him nervous."

"But how does he know there's something to look for? *I* didn't."

"'Cause he read the kid's email and found out. You said so. Him or whoever he's working for."

"But they've had that stuff since he died. They have the phone, they have the email, they have my name. Suddenly it all matters to them. Why? And who the fuck *are* they, by the way? I understand the phone; how did they get the rest of it?"

I heard his chair creak—he was either leaning back or sitting up straight. I heard him take a deep breath.

"Who knows you're out there, working this—I mean, you as in Jordan Greenblatt? I know it. Your dean knows. Your wife. Your pa. Who else?"

"A few friends. Old friends. Nobody close to any of this."

"Who else?"

I thought about it for a minute. "Nobody," I said.

"Nobody? You sure? Nobody's stumbled on you since you been there, said, 'Oh, my God, Jordan Greenblatt, what the fuck are you doing on campus?'"

I don't know why it hit me, right then. Maybe it was because I had been standing outside the dorm, the day before. Maybe it was just hearing a southern accent say my name a couple of times. But suddenly it all came back to me.

"There was a cop," I said. "A campus cop. Right outside Chris's dorm. He checked my ID, saw my PI license, and told me to get lost. He knew my name and he knew what I was."

"Well, when the fuck were you going to tell me *that* little piece of news?" he yelled at me.

"I forgot," I said. "It happened before I even started the job. It was months ago."

"God *damn* it," he spat. "What is it with you and law enforcement, anyway?"

"Hold on. Shit. A campus cop stopped by my house, too, looking for me. Just a couple of days ago."

"Son of a bitch."

"You think that's Scott's dealer? One of the Baby Cops?"

"Maybe him, maybe someone a layer up, I don't know. But it sure sounds too good to be true, doesn't it? The whole crew over there knows I been asking questions about the case. They got the kid's computer, they got access to his email. Anyone over there can open up anything and take a look around—no one's gonna think twice. And the only person you can think of who saw you on campus and can ID you by your real name is a cop. Don't all them pieces fall together a little too nice for you?"

"They do, kind of."

"And listen here. If you wanted to move shit on campus, could you think of a safer way to move it than with a goddamn police escort?"

My head was starting to hurt. "So Scotty goes to them— him—whoever it is—and he says there's a guy following me, there's somebody snooping around, and the guy puts that together with my name."

"And he digs back into the email. What's this fucker looking for? What did I miss? And he sees that last email, and he knows the girl's got a letter saying *something* he ain't gonna like but maybe now he better find out about it."

"The question is, did Scotty read the letter before I took it back? Does he realize now that there's another set of pictures somewhere?"

"And where the fuck is somewhere?" Carter said.

"Yeah, where."

"'Cause if he finds them before you do, we end up with a handful of shit. But if *you* find them, we might actually have ourselves a case."

"Right."

Now my head was pounding. And Carter was laughing.

"God damn! You know what this is, boy?" he said, barely able to contain himself. "This is a for-real, no-fooling treasure hunt. And that girl of yours has got the map right in her hands."

14

I hung up the phone and closed my eyes. All right, it's a treasure hunt. And if everyone's searching, no one's going to be in a hurry to go back to my house, looking for Jordan. Which means Susannah should be safe. For now. The photos are here, somewhere. The players are here, somewhere. Everything that matters is right here, on campus.

I looked around the quad. The weather was still too cold for sunbathers and Frisbee players, but there were a few brave souls hunkered down on benches, trying to read. Even in late winter, the quad was buzzing with activity. The whole campus was like that—always humming, all day long.

If I were a set of incriminating photos, where would I hide?

What an idiotic question. It was a huge campus, and I had no idea which buildings Chris liked to spend time in, aside from the theatre department and the theatre itself, both of which were crawling with people, even late at night. And his dorm, but there was no chance he would have hidden anything there. Even if he had, Scott *and* the cops would have gone over every inch of his room. No, it was somewhere else. Somewhere out here.

Deus ex Machina. Come to the rescue, Jordan. Figure it out and save the day.

Fat fucking chance.

All right. The theatre department. Might as well start there. All I could hope was that our bad guys hadn't figured out what they should be looking for. As soon as I turned the corner toward the building, though, I knew I was too late. There was a crowd of people standing around the entrance, making distressed-crowd noises. Something had happened, and recently.

"What's going on?" I said, as soon as I got close enough.

"I don't know. Somebody got arrested, I think," a student yelled over his shoulder. Then he called out to a friend. "Right? Arrested?"

"I think so. Cop came by and hauled them right off."

I started looking around for a familiar face, but I couldn't find one.

"Who was it?" I asked. "Guy or girl?"

"Girl, I think. Dark-haired girl. I don't know her name. Hey!" over his shoulder again. "Did you see who it was?"

But I didn't need to hear the name. I knew who it was. Because down on the ground, blowing around at my feet, were Chris's love notes, scattering in the wind or getting stepped on by undergraduate feet. She'd been hauled off in a hurry.

I gathered up the letters and then looked around, left, right—wildly looking for a sign or a clue or even just an idea of what to do or where to go. But it was all just noise and chaos. *Resolve!* I yelled at my brain. Resolve the fucking chord. And there it was. A hundred yards out—away from the crowd. Running away from the building. Scotty.

I tore after him as fast as I could. I had no idea what he was running toward, or from, but he had no idea what was coming up behind him. I gained on him quickly and threw myself at him, crashing him down across the grass and onto a walkway, his glasses skittering off his face. He screamed, "Let me go!" before he even knew who was on top of him. But I didn't let him go. I turned him over and crouched down hard on his chest. His chin was scraped and his cheek was bleeding, and he looked like a trapped animal. Which he was.

"Where is she?" I yelled. "Who took her?"

"I can't—" he said, trying to squirm away from me.

I kneed him harder in the chest, and he cried out.

"You can't what? Tell the truth? Here, I'll go first. Pay attention." I leaned in on him again, and he yelped. "My name is Jordan Greenblatt. I'm a private investigator working for the school."

He groaned.

"Yeah. That's right. I'm the guy. I know all about you. I know you sold drugs last semester. I know you're a slimy piece of shit who thinks he's a great family man, but who turns girls into whores if they can't pay him. Quid pro quo, right? And I know you killed Chris Tremaine."

"I didn't!" he screamed. "I didn't kill him."

"Where's Maddy?" I said, grinding my knee into his chest mercilessly. "Where the fuck is Maddy?"

"Stop it! Stop!" He screamed, wildly in pain. I let up, and he rolled over, pulling up his legs and hedgehogging into a safe position. "I don't know where he took her. I tried to get to her first, but I was too late. He just...he just wants the pictures. He's not going to hurt her. He just can't have those pictures...out there."

"He's not going to hurt her? You swear to God?"

"He just wants the pictures."

"And then? What happens? What happens when she's just a witness?"

He didn't have an answer for that one. I pulled him up to a sitting position. "Who is this guy?" I asked. "Campus police, yes?"

"Yes."

"And he's your supplier?"

"He was."

"And he took her? Just...*took* her, in broad daylight?"

"He's in uniform. Who's going to stop him?"

"Not you, obviously," I said, standing up. I handed him my phone and said, "His name. Type it. Right now." Step one— get the name to Carter.

I looked around, unsure what to do next. The clock was ticking. Have a name was great, but I couldn't do anything until I knew where he took her. His office? Unlikely. Some dark alley? There weren't any. So *where?*

"I tried to warn her," he said, miserably. "I ran over there and I tried to tell her. But then he showed up, and…it was too late."

"All right, all right. So he has the letter now, yeah?"

"Yeah. She had it in her backpack."

"So he knows what she knows. Which is basically nothing."

"The letter didn't say?"

"No, dipshit, the letter doesn't say. It's in code, or something. Chris gave her a little hint, but she couldn't figure it out. I guess he didn't think he'd be *dead* when he needed to get his pictures back."

He covered his face with his hands. "Why couldn't he just leave it alone?" he said. "I begged him to leave it alone."

"Don't fucking cry on me. Please."

"I didn't kill him," he said.

"Fine."

"They told me to give him a Xanax and knock him out so I could take his phone and get the pictures. That's all."

"Just a little Xanax and some vodka, right?"

"One drink! One drink, and it took forever to convince him."

"Why would he want to have a drink with *you*? He already knew you were selling Rosebud and messing with Maddy's head."

"Yes, he knew," Scott said, nodding. He was starting to calm down. "He knew what I was doing. But he didn't know I'd been sleeping with her." He reached over and picked up his glasses. "He drank after I told him that."

I stared at him for a moment. "You're a real piece of shit," I said. "It's not bad enough, what you did to him? You had to break his heart, too?"

"I didn't want any of this," he said, miserably. "I just wanted to make a little extra money. For my family."

"And your family trumps Chris's life?"

"I wasn't trying to hurt him. One Xanax, that's all I gave him. He should have been fine."

"It wasn't one, and it wasn't one drink, either. What'd you do, leave the bottle?"

He hung his head and nodded. "It wouldn't have mattered, though. They upped the dosage. I had no idea what I was giving him. Not till later. I told them I could reason with him, get him to stop making trouble, but…they didn't trust me."

"Christ," I said. "This is hopeless." I sat down on the pavement next to him. "Look at us. Maddy's dragged off and we just *sit* here, talking about a kid who's already dead. Some fucking *deus* I turned out to be."

Scott looked at me strangely.

"*Deus ex machina*," I said. "That was Chris's brilliant clue, framed in duct tape."

"In the letter?"

"Yes, in the letter. He was trying to let her know someone was coming to the rescue. Me, in theory."

"No…" Scott said carefully. "No, that's not it. Hold on…"

I watched him trying to think it through.

"We talked about it. I remember. He was asking me….it's not the *deus* he cared about; it was the *machina*. The machine," he said. "The thing that held the actor. It came *down*…from above. Some kind of winch or something. Down from the heavens. He was fascinated by the…"

"The machine? That was his clue?"

"It's high up in something. In the theatre. It's in the theatre." He got up and started to move.

"Where?" I said, following him. "On the ceiling? The roof?"

"The ceiling, the grid—in the lights, maybe."

The lights.

"Holy fuck," I said, grabbing his arm and pulling him to move faster. "Black duct tape. I've seen it."

We raced toward the theatre, which was across campus in the student center. Kids were getting out of early-afternoon classes, and the quad and the walkways were starting to fill up with lazy, meandering souls in no hurry to get to their next destinations. "Move!" I yelled, at whoever might be listening. It didn't seem to make a difference. Scott and I weaved dangerously through the crowd, trying not to knock down anyone in our path. But both of us were just barely in control of what we were doing.

Had Maddy figured it out? Had our cop twisted it out of her already? I didn't want to waste any time. Maddy might be useful to these people for a while, but once they found what they were looking for, she'd become an instant liability. Just like Chris.

We ran up the stairs into the theatre lobby, and I knew something was wrong. A bunch of the crew was standing around, covered in paint and plaster, looking confused.

"What happened?" I asked.

"This cop chased us out—said it was an active crime scene, or something."

"He's in there now?"

"Yeah. With Maddy. What the fuck's going on? We've got walls and shit to build."

"Nothing," I said. "Don't worry about it. You guys can...go take a break, or whatever."

They looked at each other, and one of them said, "What are you, the director now?"

"Go!" I yelled.

They muttered and rolled their eyes, but they shuffled off and left Scotty and me alone in the lobby. I cracked the door open and stuck my head in to look around. The houselights were on and the place looked empty, except for some metal folding chairs set up in a semicircle and a half-plastered, metal framework for the walls of Troy. I opened the door a crack more, so I could find that place on the ceiling where I had seen the lump of duct tape. "There," I whispered, pointing.

Scott leaned his head in and looked. "How did you ever see that?" he whispered back.

"They were hanging lights and it got in their way. I heard them bitching about it."

The rolling scaffold that the crew used for hanging lights was still in the middle of the room, close to the lump of tape, but it wasn't right underneath anymore. It was probably four or five feet away—a stretch, but not an easy one...*if* I could get up there without being noticed.

"Shut that door!" someone yelled. We both looked up at where the sound was coming from and saw a man up on the catwalk that ran beneath a portion of the lighting grid. He was on the opposite side of the theatre from the scaffold. Six feet tall, maybe. Older. He was definitely the cop who had hassled me outside the dorm. And he had Maddy with him.

What to do? Push the door open and confront him? Tell him the cops were on their way? No—one word like that and Maddy would be a hostage. And even Baby Cops have guns.

"I said shut it!" he yelled.

I looked around the room, trying to find the light switch. It wasn't close by. I could run for it, but then he'd see me—and he knew exactly who I was. Do that, and there's a gun to Maddy's head. Everything I could think of ended the same way—with a gun to her head. So I backed my head out and let the door swing shut.

"At least he's looking in the wrong place," Scotty said.

"For now," I said. Then I had a thought. "Is there another way to kill the lights in there?"

"Sure," he said. "From the booth."

I looked back at the door and bit my lip. He knew what I was thinking. "I can get there from outside. Up the stairs."

I nodded. "Good. Go." He started to run, but I called after him. "He's going to make a lot of noise once you put him in the dark. Keep him talking, if you can. I'm going to need cover."

He gave me a thumbs-up and ran up the stairs. I texted Carter and told him to bring the troops. Then I cracked the door open just an inch and waited. It didn't take more than a minute. The lights clicked off and I heard the man inside howl. Scotty yelled back at him, "Let her go!"

"Flynn?" the man yelled. "What the fuck are you doing?"

"Let her go. She walks out, you get your lights back."

I didn't wait to hear more. I pushed the door open as little as I could and slipped in, running for the scaffold with my hands outstretched, to keep from smacking into anything. It was dark in the big room, with only a couple of dim exit signs for light. The cop and Maddy, up by the ceiling, were in total darkness.

"She walks, you and me go to jail, you fucking moron!" the man yelled.

I reached the scaffold and grabbed hold of one of the metal uprights. I had no idea if the thing was anchored down or if it would roll as soon as I started climbing, but I had no time to experiment. I had to get up there as fast as I could.

The scaffold was a metal tower on casters—two levels up, with planks laid down to create makeshift flooring. There were bare-bones stairs going from the floor up to the second level, and from the second level to the top, but the two sets of stairs were on opposite sides of the tower. I started climbing up the first little flight, grateful that my weight wasn't shaking or moving the whole device. When I reached the second level, I stayed low and crawled across the planks toward the other set of stairs. But that's when I started making noise, because the damned planks weren't fastened down; they were just laid across the metal piping of the scaffold. The wood was thick and heavy, but it was old, splintered, and uneven. As I crawled over the planks, they jostled and rubbed and clacked against the metal. I had to go slowly to keep the noise down, but I had to go quickly to get this thing over with.

Scotty and the cop were still yelling at each other, but I couldn't hear Maddy at all. I imagined her curled up on the floor at the man's feet, trying to stay small and out of the way. I hoped that's what she was doing, because I had no idea how this was going to go down.

Last stairs. All metal. I scampered to the top, but now I had to be careful again. The top level was made of planks, like the one below, but there was very little piping here at the top—enough to get a safe grip while hanging lights, but nothing like the full height of a man. When I stood up, I'd have to grip the scaffold at waist level but then reach up into the grid with my other hand to grab the metal piping that crisscrossed the ceiling, just to keep myself stable. And it was pitch black up here. One wrong step and I could fall straight off the edge and onto the concrete floor below. That would not be pleasant.

I crawled over to the far edge of the scaffold, to get as close to the duct-taped package as I could before having to stand up. I reached up to grab the rail and slowly started to get to my feet. So far, so good. I took a step to the very edge of the scaffold, testing to make sure I knew where the edge was, and I reached up to grab a pipe in the grid. I knew the package was in front of me somewhere, a long arm's stretch away, but I couldn't tell exactly where it was. I held onto the grid with my left hand and reached as far out as I could with my right, exploring the ceiling above me, when suddenly, the plank slipped out from under my feet. I grabbed the grid with my right hand, my legs flailing in midair, with no floor to reach back to. I hung there, listening to the plank clatter against the scaffolding and crash down to the floor. It was the loudest thing I had ever heard in my life, and when the echo subsided, the silence was even worse.

There was a loud click, and a flashlight beam started swinging around toward me. Of *course* he had a flashlight. Goddamn cop uniform. I was going to have to make myself a moving target, Tarzan style. I took a deep breath and got ready. When the beam of light came near me, I let go with my right hand, swung myself left, grabbed the grid, and swung to the left again, to get myself facing front, a few feet away from where I had started. The beam followed me, so I kept moving, trying not to be predictable. That didn't stop the son of a bitch, though. I heard a shot ring out, and then another.

Suddenly, I saw lights fire up all over the grid. Two or three would come on and then suddenly go dark; then another two or three would come on. Scotty was racing through all the switches or levers, trying to disorient the man on the catwalk. The lights were so close, I could hear them hum as they started to warm up and click as they cooled down. Quickly I figured out what Scotty was up to. With me hanging at the same level as the big theatre lights, I could disappear into shadow if Scott could just figure out which levers went with which instruments. I kept swinging and gyrating, hoping for a miracle. The cop kept trying to get a clean shot at me, hoping for a miracle of his own. But I got mine first.

The instrument right at my feet started glowing and stayed on. The long can was pointing down, uselessly, but I could see it was attached to a kind of hinge. I stretched out my legs and got my feet on the back of the thing, and pushed down with my toes. The light tilted upward and beamed straight at the face of the man who was trying to kill me. I could see him perfectly now, and he couldn't see anything. The light was so strong, he threw his arms up over his face to shield his eyes. I could see Maddy, too—down on the floor like I had hoped, about ten feet away from the cop. She looked up and saw him, frozen. She knew she had a moment. It wouldn't last long. His eyes would adjust, or he'd move out of range. I had an advantage for a handful of seconds, and that was all.

I hung there, unable to move, and I watched her get up—tentatively at first. She looked around wildly, unsure what to do. She could make a run for it now. She'd probably be able to get down the stairs and out the door before he could catch her. She had to see that now.

"Run," I mouthed, hoping she could hear my thoughts. "Run!"

But she didn't run. She charged straight at the cop, arms outstretched, and she shoved him as hard as she could. The two of them went over the top of the guardrail, but Maddy caught herself before flipping over. He wasn't as lucky. He tumbled straight over the rail into darkness. He didn't even have time to scream. There was a crash of bone and metal and concrete, and then silence.

I took my foot off the light and let it swing back down. It made a pool of light on the floor, right near where the body had landed. He had fallen straight through the walls of Troy and then into the nest of folding chairs, arms and legs and neck whacking into wood and metal and concrete at different times and in different places. Everything looked twisted and broken, and he wasn't moving.

Scotty clicked the houselights on. I could see Maddy sitting on the catwalk directly across the theatre from me, staring down at the body of the cop, her hands covering her mouth.

I heard the scaffold move behind me, and I reached out with my feet until I could feel a secure plank. Scotty had raced down to save me. God knows why, after the way I had treated him. He pushed the tower over to where the duct-taped lump was, and I peeled it off and pulled it down. It was an ugly mess of black tape, some of it sticking to the pictures inside, which were just printouts on regular paper. Each sheet had two or three pictures on it, and there had to be at least ten sheets, all folded up and shoved into the little pocket of sticky tape.

By the time I got down to the floor, Carter had arrived with five or six uniformed officers. They quickly took over the crime scene…and Scotty. I watched him get cuffed and led away to a corner of the room for questioning. Maddy got bundled up and taken away, too, before I could say a word to her or even see if she was all right.

I handed my friend the pictures, and he flipped through them. He brought them over to Scott, and held them up to his face.

"This you?"

"Yes, sir."

"Uh-huh. And how about him? You know him?"

Scotty nodded.

"And this guy?"

He nodded again.

"You tell me what you know, things'll go a lot better for you. You understand what I'm saying?"

Scott nodded one more time, looking miserable but, somehow, relieved. And then they took him away.

"What now?" I asked.

"Now?" Carter said. "Now you get to go home, son."

"But—"

"Home, Bulldog. You did good. Now it's our turn. Let us do what we do."

We looked over at the body, which was being photographed and examined. Carter looked at me and picked up something unresolved in my expression.

"You think this little scene is over?" he said. "One dead loser, turn out the lights? No, sir, this ain't over by a long shot. This old boy was behind your friend, but there's three others in the pictures, and more behind them, sure as shit, and on and on. We'll be at this for months, Hoss. Years, maybe. Grass is *full* of snakes."

I nodded, and he nodded back to me.

"Go home," he said. "We got this."

He turned away from me and went to work, and I was left alone in a room full of busy people. No longer needed. If it had been a movie, it would have been a perfect time for a fade to black, end credits—or maybe a cut to some scene a month or two later, showing how everybody was happy and healthy again.

But it wasn't a movie; it was just my life. So I stood there for a while, feeling useless, until I got fed up with feeling that way and left.

I went by Pete's, packed up my bag, and left the key on the table. Then I drove back to Candler Park, to my run-down little house by the MARTA tracks, and I went inside. It was late afternoon, and the sun was getting ready to set. I walked inside, opened the fridge, and took out a beer. From the kitchen, I could see Susannah across the house in the bathroom, working on the rotting walls and tiles. I grabbed a second beer and walked toward her. She was wearing a tank top, with an old bandana tied around her hair. She was working hard, and she hadn't heard me come in the house. Now she saw me, though. She sat back, wiped the sweat from her forehead, and looked at me.

"So?" she said.

I held up my bag and dropped it with a flourish. Even I can be dramatic, sometimes.

"You catch your bad guy?"

"I did, actually."

"And now?"

"And now I'm home."

She nodded. "Good. So how about helping *me*?"

"You got it." I walked into the bathroom, gave her a beer, and squatted down in the bathtub to chisel out the old grout and make way for the new.

We sat there working until the light failed, and then we ordered Chinese food and talked through the night—the two of us in our sweaty clothes, caulk smeared on our cheeks, telling stories, laughing, crying a little. Back where I belonged.

15

April in Atlanta is a special time. The winters are mild, the fall can give you some nice colors, but Atlanta is at its best in the spring. The weather warms up and the skies move from grey to blue. The humidity is still under control. And most important, the dogwoods and azaleas are in bloom. They bloom at exactly the same time—explosions of pink and white reaching up from the ground and down from the sky simultaneously. They're a perfect match for each other—a perfect fit.

With the dogwoods and azaleas comes the beginning of festival season. Music festivals, arts and crafts festivals—really, any excuse you can come up with for bringing people together to eat funnel cakes and buy balloons. The Dogwood Festival is the main event, and it was what our little group had been planning and practicing for. It was a huge event in Piedmont Park, right in the heart of midtown, and this year they were holding a "battle of the bands" competition across multiple categories of music. The rock bands had had their moment in the sun; a few country and bluegrass bands had come and gone. Now it was our turn. An announcer called us up to the stage by the name we had invented just ten minutes earlier, "Sack the Drummer," and we got ourselves set up to play.

It was hard to believe it had been only a month since Scotty had been arrested and the Rosebud story had erupted. And man, had it erupted. I guess when someone falls to his death from a theatre catwalk, it's hard to keep things on the down-low. I called Dean Whitman a week or two after the story broke, and she seemed philosophical about the whole thing. The college got some bad press up front, but they were able to turn it around once word got out that the school had worked with an investigator to uncover the truth.

She also told me Arlo's show had been canceled.

"I guess we left the place kind of a mess," I said.

"Yes, dear. No one was particularly eager to revisit that scene, once they saw it on the news. And, of course, they lost their dramaturg and music director in rather dramatic fashion. But that's not why it was canceled. I'm surprised you didn't hear."

"Hear what?"

"Professor Alden was put on administrative leave about a week after the incident. One of his actresses quit the play and filed charges against him for sexual harassment and misconduct."

"Really?" I said, trying to suppress a smile over the phone. "Can I guess which actress that was?"

"You can guess at anything you like, Jordan," she said primly. "But obviously, I can't confirm it."

There was some small talk after that, and much gratitude from the dean, but my mind was elsewhere. It barely registered when she told me it would be "prudent" to stay away from the campus for a while. But I was fine with that. A little while or a long while; it didn't make a difference to me. I was done with school.

And now, here I was, back in my life—up on a stage again, but a slightly more appropriate one. While I waited for Pete to get his keyboard arranged, I looked out at the festival. Out past the performance area, the park was filled with tents, with hundreds of people walking around to check out the pottery, the paintings, and the decorative bottle-stoppers that were on display. Tons of college students and people in their twenties and thirties. Lots of couples in their forties and beyond, walking lazily and happily, hand in hand. And right in front of us, on the big lawn, a hundred people waiting for the music to begin.

Oticha decided we should start with a tune people might recognize, so he counted us off and we launched into "Why Don't You Do Right?" People were nodding and smiling, especially once Lydia started singing. I scanned the crowd, looking for familiar faces, and found Melanie and her kids sitting on a blanket, with Susannah close by. I saw Kitty and Kate and

Patty in different parts of the crowd. All my people—my little Atlanta tribe.

And there, in the middle of the sea of faces, was Maddy Taylor. She had one of those inscrutable looks on her face, but she nodded to me when she knew she had caught my eye, and I nodded back from behind my bass. She smiled and laughed a little, shaking her head. A rueful laugh, maybe. It was hard to tell at a distance. She stayed there, looking up at me with that little smile on her face, until two other girls came up, hands full of sloshing beers and mouths full of exciting news about something or other. They were pointing at the tents and talking a mile a minute. She grinned and laughed at them, and they grabbed her arm and turned her around, determined to show her whatever it was they had found. I watched her walking away, and in my mind I said to her: *You see? I told you. I tried to tell you.*

Oticha whistled at me to get my attention, and we launched into our second number, "Struttin' With Some Barbecue." Lydia played her clarinet and danced around Oticha and Pete in the first pass at the melody. I watched Pete stab the keyboard and smack his washboard, his face beaming whenever Lydia looked at him. And then Lydia started to belt out that old, Louis Armstrong tune—a song that always reminded me of New Orleans and the day when my heart leaped up and said "Yes," after so many years of saying nothing.

Struttin' with some barbecue,
Swingin' with the band,
Like the happy people do,
Way down in Dixieland...

The crowd was loving it. Every time Lydia sang the word "Dixieland," they roared their approval and lifted their beers in a toast—all those Yankees and Midwesterners and foreigners claiming Atlanta as their home, just like I had. And the longer she sang, the more I felt that fine, old thing wake up in me again—that feeling I get when it's just the right song, done just the right way. That little-kid feeling of uncomplicated joy. It's a thing I never expected to feel in my life. A thing I never thought I deserved. Even now, when I feel it, I wonder whether I deserve it, whether I have any right to it at all.

Maybe that's why we think it's such a childish feeling. After all the damage we've endured—or inflicted on each other—all the things we've stored up to be ashamed of and regret, maybe we don't think we deserve anything like joy. And maybe we don't. Maybe *I* don't. But for some reason, it keeps offering itself up to me, again and again, waiting for me to take it. And it seems kind of rude, kind of stupid, not to notice.

I don't know. Maybe I'm wrong. I'm not a philosopher; I'm just the bass player. But the damage and regret can't be the whole story. It just can't be. It's like how F-major to G needs to resolve itself into C, or how "shave and a haircut" just begs for "two bits" to bring it home. You can feel it in your bones when the song isn't over.

I wanted to tell Maddy, even if I was only talking to her in my head. But when I looked for her in the crowd, she was gone.

ABOUT THE AUTHOR

Andrew Ordover is a playwright, educator, and novelist. His first novel about Jordan Greenblatt, *Cool for Cats*, is available online in paperback and eBook formats at Amazon and Barnes and Noble, and in audiobook format, read by the author, at www.andrewordover.com.

ABOUT THE AUTHOR

Andrew Ordover is a playwright, educator, and novelist. His first novel about Jordan Greenblatt, *Cool for Cats*, is available online in paperback and eBook formats at Amazon and Barnes and Noble, and in audiobook format, read by the author, at www.andrewordover.com.

www.ingramcontent.com/pod-product-compliance
Lightning Source LLC
Chambersburg PA
CBHW060833280326
41934CB00007B/769